Introduction to accounting for non-specialists

Len Hand, Carolyn Isaaks and Peter Sanderson

Nottingham Business School, The Nottingham Trent University

THOMSON

Australia • Canada • Mexico • Singapore • Spain • United Kingdom • United States

THOMSON

Introduction to Accounting for Non-Specialists

Copyright © 2005 Thomson Learning

The Thomson logo is a registered trademark used herein under licence.

For more information, contact Thomson Learning, High Holborn House; 50–51 Bedford Row, London WC1R 4LR or visit us on the World Wide Web at: http://www.thomsonlearning.co.uk

British Library Cataloguing-in-Publication Data

A catalogue record for this book is available from the British Library

ISBN 1-84480-022-9

First edition published 2005 by Thomson Learning

Typeset by J&L Composition, Filey, North Yorkshire

Printed in Croatia by Zrinski d. d.

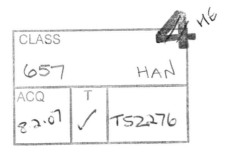

Brief contents

List of exhibits ix
Preface xi
Acknowledgements xv
Walk through tour xvi
Companion web site xviii

Chapter 1   Introducing the world of accounting   1

Chapter 2   Accounting in context: focus on the product   8

Chapter 3   Using accounting for managers' decisions   27

Chapter 4   A framework for accounting reports   46

Chapter 5   A deeper understanding of the balance sheet and profit and loss account   68

Chapter 6   The financial reporting framework: the rules of the game   90

Chapter 7   Cash-flow statements and a broader perspective on published accounts   106

Chapter 8   The interpretation of accounting statements   123

Chapter 9   Accounting for the future: planning and control through budgets   155

Chapter 10   Accounting for long-term decisions   195

Chapter 11   Corporate governance: the UK experience   227

Answer notes 241
Glossary 287
Appendix: Present value table 294
Index 297

Contents

List of exhibits	ix
Preface	xi
Acknowledgements	xv
Walk through tour	xvi
Companion web site	xviii

Introducing the world of accounting — 1

Chapter 1

Learning objectives	1
Introduction	1
But what is an accountant?	1
And what is accounting?	2
Accounting information in society	3
Plan of the book	4
Review questions	6
Numerical problem	6

Accounting in context: focus on the product — 8

Chapter 2

Learning objectives	8
Introduction	8
Product costs and cost behaviour	10
Contribution	11
Break-even points	12
Graphic analysis of product costs	12
Cost, volume and profit	15
Marginal and full cost	16
Pricing, costs and profitability	17
Final comments	19
Supplementary notes about cost behaviour	20
Summary	21
Review questions	21
Numerical problems	22

Using accounting for managers' decisions — 27

Chapter 3

Learning objectives	27
Introduction	27
Relevant cash flows	28
Opportunity costs	28
Ranking decisions	31
Product viability	34
Long-term and short-term decisions	37
Uncertainty in decision-making	38
Final comments	38

Summary 39
Review questions 39
Numerical problems 39
Case study: Countryside Dairies 42

| Chapter 4 | A framework for accounting reports | 46 |

Learning objectives 46
Introduction 46
Recording and reporting financial transactions 47
Money – the common measure 47
Pictures of an organisation 49
The financial views of a business 50
Links between decisions and financial reports 51
Reflections on profit and loss accounts and balance sheets 61
The format of accounting reports 62
Summary 65
Review questions 66
Numerical problems 66

| Chapter 5 | A deeper understanding of the balance sheet and profit and loss account | 68 |

Learning objectives 68
Introduction 68
Another look at profit 69
Revenue recognition 71
Matching expenses 72
Why are stocks and fixed assets important? 72
Cost of goods sold and stock values 73
Stock valuations 74
Expenses – accruals and prepayments 77
Depreciation 79
Final comments 85
Summary 85
Review questions 86
Numerical problems 87

| Chapter 6 | The financial reporting framework: the rules of the game | 90 |

Learning objectives 90
Introduction 90
Markets and financial information 91
What are published accounts? 91
Who uses accounting statements? 91
What is in a set of published accounts? 94
Users and accounting concepts 96
Final comments 100
Summary 100
Review questions 101
Worksheet: corporate reports 102
A supplementary note on the professional accounting bodies'
self-regulatory system 105

Chapter 7 | **Cash-flow statements and a broader perspective of published accounts** | 106
Learning objectives | 106
Introduction | 106
Why is cash important for a business? | 106
Working capital and cash flows | 107
Cash-flow statements | 109
Additional information in the financial statements | 113
Groups of companies | 116
Some drawbacks to published accounts | 117
Final comments | 117
Summary | 118
Review questions | 118
Numerical problems | 119

Chapter 8 | **The interpretation of accounting statements** | 123
Learning objectives | 123
Introduction | 123
Methods of evaluating performance | 124
Ratio analysis | 124
Profitability ratios | 125
Liquidity ratios | 130
Further liquidity ratios | 132
Gearing ratios | 135
Investment ratios | 137
A note of caution about ratio analysis | 143
Working capital management | 144
Final comments | 146
Summary | 147
Review questions | 147
Numerical problems | 147

Chapter 9 | **Accounting for the future: planning and control through budgets** | 155
Learning objectives | 155
Introduction | 155
Personal budgets | 156
Financial predictions in a business | 157
Budgeting for assets and liabilities | 162
The budget process | 163
Why produce budgets? | 171
Variances from budget | 173
Standard costing and variance analysis | 175
Final comments | 181
Summary | 182
Review questions | 182
Numerical problems | 182
Case study: Blackthorn | 187

Chapter 10 — ## Accounting for long-term decisions — 195

Learning objectives — 195
Introduction — 195
Long term and short term – a continuum — 196
Key features of long-term decisions — 198
The stages of a long-term decision — 199
Relevant cash-flow analysis for long-term decisions — 201
The time value of money — 202
Payback — 206
Internal rate of return — 207
The cost of capital – the discount rate — 209
Uncertainty in long-term decision analysis — 211
What do we know about how real companies carry out long-term
decision analysis? — 211
A broader context for long-term decision-making — 212
Goals, decisions and shareholders — 213
Long-term decisions and product costs — 214
Summary — 217
Review questions — 218
Numerical problems — 218
Case study: Zorbis Hotels — 222

Chapter 11 — ## Corporate governance; the UK experience — 227

Learning objectives — 227
Introduction — 227
Background to the emergence of corporate governance — 228
Definition of corporate governance — 229
The development of UK corporate governance — 229
The Cadbury Report — 230
The division of responsibility at the head of the company — 231
The role of non-executive directors — 231
The issue of director remuneration and the use of remuneration
committees — 232
The introduction and operation of audit committees — 236
Have the governance reports and codes made a difference? — 237
Final comments — 238
Summary — 238
Review questions — 239

Answer notes — 241
Glossary — 287
Appendix: Present value table — 294
Index — 297

List of exhibits

1.1	Accounting in the organisation	5
2.1	Vehicle fuel consumption	13
2.2	Plate revenues	14
2.3	Variable costs	14
2.4	Fixed costs	14
2.5	The general shape of a break-even chart	15
2.6	Stepped costs	20
2.7	Semi-variable costs	21
3.1	Analysis of the Jackson Hotel's revenues, costs and profits	35
4.1	Top UK companies by market value	48
4.2	Financial views of a business	50
5.1	A pictorial view of the links between the main accounting statements	69
5.2	Profit is derived from matching the revenue and expenses in a period	71
5.3	Cost of sales	73
5.4	FIFO	76
5.5	LIFO	76
5.6	Straight line depreciation	81
5.7	Straight line depreciation example	82
5.8	The reducing balance technique	83
5.9	Reducing balance example – the whole picture	83
6.1	UK standard setting and monitoring	105
7.1	The cash-flow cycle	107
7.2	Cash-flow cycle for a manufacturer	108
7.3	Cash-flow cycle for a retailer	108
7.4	Cash-flow cycle for a construction firm	108
7.5	Profits, position and cash flows	113
7.6	Marks and Spencer group auditors' report	115
9.1	Features of variable and fixed costs	158
9.2	A model of the budget process	164
9.3	Assumed relationships between costs, revenues and activity in a standard costing system	176
9.4	Monthly sales budget	188
9.5	Variable cost of sales	190
9.6	Cash budget	192

10.1 Short-term and long-term decisions   197
10.2 Stages in a long-term decision   199
10.3 Net present values and IRR   208
10.4 Net present values and internal rate of return   208
10.5 The links between project returns, the company and investor returns   209
10.6 UME – financial analysis   216

11.1 Pearson – directors renumeration, 2002   235

Preface

Welcome to the world of accounting. We hope that this book will help you to understand what is often seen as the 'mysterious language of business'. We are assuming that you know nothing about the subject, but that you want to develop an awareness of what accounting is, what it does, and where it fits into the business world.

We have tried to introduce accounting from a practical perspective through everyday examples about products, services, costs, cash and investments. We relate accounting to your everyday experiences as students, consumers, employees or managers.

Accounting is not – as it is sometimes portrayed – a distant, dry, abstract subject; accounting is rooted in real-world experiences and affects the lives of many people. It is a social mechanism for allocating money, other resources and power throughout our society.

Accounting information is used: by chief executives of companies for decisions about multi-million pound investments and plant closures; by middle managers for controlling costs including pay; by individuals in planning household expenditure and holidays. We take accounting to be a *doing* subject. While based upon certain theoretical concepts, the main value of accounting is in its application to practical problems.

This textbook has been written for two specific audiences: undergraduates, on both non-accounting and accounting degree courses, who are looking for a practical and accessible way into the study of the subject; and non-financial managers who need to have some knowledge of accounting to increase their knowledge and competence in this vital area. We have assumed that anyone starting out using this textbook will have no previous knowledge of the subject of accounting and we have deliberately tried to make the language and the examples we use as accessible as possible.

Although we will introduce you to the methods used to capture transactions and to produce accounting information, we do not want to turn you into an accountant! That said, the book does aim to provide you with insights into what accountants do when they produce financial reports, and how you can make sense of accounting information.

Why study accounting?

Accounting is a specialised field of study. However, many non-financial students and managers require an understanding of accounting because:

- You may encounter financial statements in the work that you do.

- You may have to discuss financial aspects of a business or of a particular project, and will be at a disadvantage if you do not understand this special 'language'.
- Technical activities usually have financial implications, and sometimes technical and financial considerations are in conflict. An understanding of financial aspects will, therefore, broaden your perspective on specific technical problems.
- In the UK there is a larger concentration of accountants than in any other country in the world! In the UK accountants are often the people who play a large part in the running of big business. So if you want to have some influence within business, one way is to become an accountant!

There is an old fable which runs . . .

The accountant wanted to be captain of the team. The others would not even let him play. Instead they gave him the job of scorer. So, by way of revenge, the accountant developed a system of scoring which no-one else could understand!

. . . and that is one of the problems this text sets out to solve. By increasing your understanding of the work that accountants do, and the language they use to talk about it, you will ensure that you are never (well, hardly ever!) fooled by the language and techniques used by accountants.

A note for anyone with some prior study of accounting

Perhaps you have studied accounting before? You may find that the approach that we take is slightly different from some other texts you have used – particularly the user perspective and our attempts to blend (rather than keep in separate compartments) management and financial accounting. We believe that this approach not only provides you with the basic knowledge of accounting to be expected from any introductory text (the 'what accounting is' part), but also should deepen your appreciation of 'why' the numbers are as they are and the assumptions upon which the numbers are based.

Features in the text

This book has been written and presented specifically to take you through the understanding of accounting step by step. There are certain features in the book to aid your learning and you will find a walk-through tour at the end of this preface to help you become familiar with these. In particular, we would like to highlight the following:

Tasks set throughout each chapter complement the text and allow you to explore ideas that have been introduced. Ideally tasks should be worked as you read the text, and answer notes are provided in a separate section at the back of the book.

Review questions that provide end-of-chapter discussion points. Some review questions may be answered from reading the text, while others deliberately challenge you to make new connections and to think more widely than the chapter content.

Numerical problems also appear at the end of each chapter, and provide an opportunity for you to 'play' with the numbers which characterise the study of accounting. Wherever possible we encourage you to consider the meaning and significance of the numbers as well as being concerned with the calculations. To support your private study, answer notes to some of the end-of-chapter questions are given at the end of the book, while others appear on the website that accompanies the book.

Case studies that are longer and more detailed than other problems and questions appear in some of the chapters. The case studies allow for a deeper engagement with issues and questions posed within the field of accounting in organisations. Answer notes for the cases are provided on the website that accompanies this text.

Glossary terms are highlighted in blue in their first instance in the text. This indicates to you that there is a glossary definition in the back of the book. The glossary will give you a more detailed explanation of the meaning of some common accounting terminology.

Web references are used throughout the book to introduce practical examples of accounting in the real world. By the end of the book you will be able to understand and utilise financial data and these web references are provided to give you access to real company accounts. We have provided hyperlinks to these sites on the companion website to the book (in addition, major companies cited in the text also appear as hyperlinks organised by chapter). Please visit www.thomsonlearning.co.uk/accountingandfinance/hand and go into the weblinks section. Click on the links to be taken directly to the relevant pages of various company websites.

Acknowledgements

We would like to thank our colleagues and students within Nottingham Business School who have used and commented upon various parts of the book during its evolution. Thanks also to the reviewers, Mary Bishop (Bristol Business School, UWE) and Malcolm Anderson (Cardiff Business School), for their helpful comments in revising the textbook, and to our publishing partners at Thomson Learning who have kept us on track when deadlines approached (and were passed!).

Walk through tour

Learning objectives
are given at the start of each chapter so
that you have an idea of what will be
covered.

Introductory paragraphs
put the topics covered in the chapter
into a practical context.

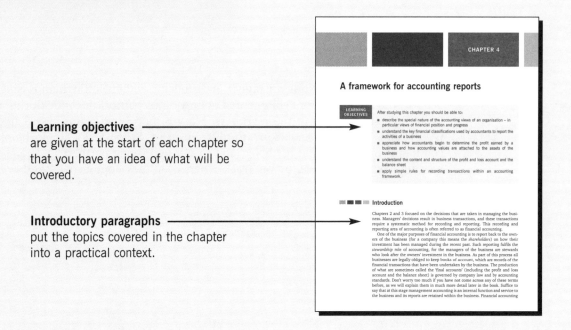

Case studies
Some chapters have selected case studies that provide an in depth look at an
area or topic. These cases are based on real or realistic organisations and their
accounting problems.

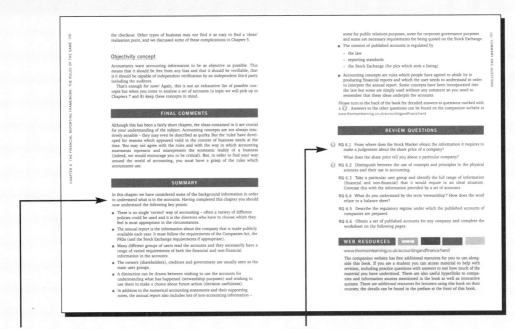

Chapter summary

The end of each chapter has a summary of the main points covered.

Review questions

appear at the end of each chapter. These are discursive questions that give you an opportunity to think more deeply about issues covered.

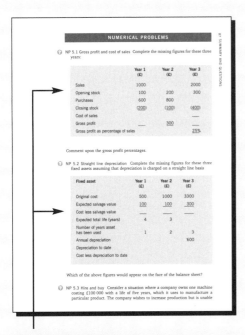

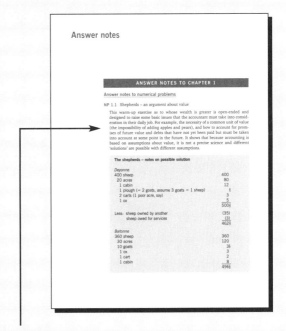

Numerical problems

appear at the end of most chapters. These questions provide an opportunity for you to try out the numerative aspects and techniques and to check your understanding.

Answers

Many answers to tasks, review questions, numerical problems and cases are provided towards the back of the book. Answers to selected complex questions will be on the password-protected section of the website so that the lecturer can work through these with you. Questions with answers in the back of the book are indicated with ❓.

Companion Web Site

Visit the *Introduction to Accounting for non-specialists* accompanying website at www.thomsonlearning.co.uk/accountingandfinance/hand to find further teaching and learning material including:

Information about the book.

Chapter overviews to give you an indication of the coverage of the book

STUDENT SIDE

Multiple Choice Questions – to check your progress as you work through the text
Additional Questions – to prepare you for your exams
Case exercises plus answers
Related links to guide you towards further study.
Glossary of key terms to refer to as you navigate the website

LECTURER SIDE

Answers to Review questions and numerical problems not answered in the book for you to work through with your students in seminars or tutorials
Additional Multiple Choice Questions to give to your students as class tests
PowerPoint™ Slides from the book to adapt for your lectures
Additional questions with answers
Case exercises with answers

Introducing the world of accounting

After studying this introductory chapter you should be able to:

- appreciate the significance that accounting information has within organisations
- describe the legal, financial and social roles of accounting within society
- appreciate the user perspective that we take within this book
- describe the main areas covered by management accounting and financial accounting.

Introduction

You may be studying this subject as part of a business, engineering or management development course, or early in an accounting programme. Whatever your interest, we believe that it is important that you take a user view of accounting (that is, consider financial information from the viewpoint of the people who will use the information when making decisions). Users may be, for example, investors who want to know about the overall performance of a company, perhaps to decide whether to buy or sell shares; or managers who need a more detailed understanding of the costs of the firm's products or activities. Accounting information hardly ever has a value in itself; rather, its value stems from the usefulness of the information provided. So decision-usefulness is one way of judging accounting information – does the information help in guiding and informing the decisions of the users?

But what is an accountant?

This is a very good question, and the following answers have been put forward:

- A financial information manager, responsible for the recording and classifying of financial transactions and the production of reports both internal and external to the organisation.

- Someone who assists management in taking decisions which have financial implications; for example, major **capital expenditure** programmes, the pricing of products, the implementation of cost control programmes.

- Someone able to revitalise an ailing company or to track down the missing funds following a 'white collar' crime – i.e. fraud.

- A magician who can make profits appear, change and disappear at will – or a spin-doctor who can change the view of financial facts by altering the perspective shown by the numbers!

There is probably some truth in each of these definitions, as the accountant occupies a series of different roles within organisations. As you study this text we hope that you will discover the variety of activities that are undertaken by accountants, and come to appreciate the significance of the role of accounting both within organisations and in society at large.

And what is accounting?

Another good question, and one best answered after you have studied this book. For now we offer some early thoughts about the major items on the accounting menu. Do not be fooled by the fact that accounting is based upon numbers. You don't have to be incredibly numerate to interpret accounting information. Nor should you be lulled into thinking that accounting is boring and is performed by grey people wearing grey (and traditionally pin-striped) clothing (although some are, and do!). You may be surprised how active many accountants are within not only the profit-making private sector but also in many areas of public life, including government, health care and education. Many decisions taken throughout the economy are based, at least in part, upon accounting information.

Anyone wanting to make a living as an accountant has to study and pass the exams of a professional accounting body and gain sufficient practical experience to be admitted as a member. Some parts of the accounting role are very highly regulated and we discuss the accounting bodies and accounting regulation in more detail in Chapters 6 and 7. Accounting has been defined in many different ways – here is a selection of definitions:

- A system which provides financial information about an organisation.

- A way of recording, summarising and analysing the transactions of a business.

- The practical application of economic theory to income measurement and asset valuation.

- The language of business.

- A method of fooling some of the people, some of the time!

As with our definitions of accountants, there is some truth in each of these definitions of accounting – for accounting can operate at many different levels. At a superficial level accounting can be seen as a **value-free** activity which merely reports events in a financial form. But at a deeper level some would argue that accounting plays an important **social role** by influencing the way in which resources are allocated within a company and within society.

Accounting information in society

All business organisations interact with other parties within society, and these interactions take a number of forms which can be classified as follows:

Legal   The entity must comply with the legal framework which society has adopted. One way that we ensure that entities are indeed meeting their legal requirements is to examine their financial statements. A valuable concession granted to companies is the concept of 'limited liability', which enables and encourages investors to invest in companies by limiting the amount that they can possibly lose. In recognition of this major concession, companies must make public their financial statements on an annual basis, and these statements must undergo an independent **audit** to ensure that they represent a true and fair view of the financial position of the company. The company cannot (at least in theory) keep secret any of its financial dealings, no matter how damaging they might be.

Financial   The business entity enters into contracts with employees, customers, suppliers, government and other stakeholders that involve the movement of goods, services and ultimately the transfer of cash. It is these financial interactions that the accounting system tracks and reports.

Social   A business entity will impact upon society in a number of ways at both local and national levels. Obvious examples of areas that may be affected are employment of local people, and pollution and waste passed into the atmosphere. One way in which members of society monitor the activities of business entities is by looking at publicly available information (including financial accounts) about the organisations.

Of course, no business organisation operates in isolation. A business is continually making formal and informal arrangements – to supply goods and services – to provide employment – to earn profits – to distribute dividends to shareholders – to pay taxes – and to act responsibly in the way in which it consumes resources. In each of these activities information flows between the business, and between other individuals and organisations. It is the responsibility of the accountant to collect, measure and record the financial aspects of the information flows and to report them in a form useful to users. One of the criticisms of accounting is that it focuses solely upon financial aspects to the exclusion of all others and, in this way, lots of valuable and vital information is overlooked, including information about the ways in which the organisation impacts on local and national communities (e.g. through the levels of pollution it creates). The other criticism is that the accountant, in using money as the sole unit of measurement, is incapable of measuring anything unless it can be reduced to a monetary value. The team spirit built up by the workforce, or the entrepreneurial flare of the management team, cannot be captured by the accountant as it is impossible to place an accurate monetary value against it. Thus, as we take you through the values and important roles of accounting information, we would also ask you to be critical and aware of the limitations of the accounting measurement systems that we will describe.

Industrial and information revolutions

The Industrial Revolution, which transformed many economic activities from small-scale rural 'cottage industries' into large factory-based organisations, radically changed the way in which society was organised, and its effects can still be seen today. We are now seeing a new revolution – an information revolution. The ways in which we record, access, order and use information continue to change at a bewildering pace. Taking a Darwinian perspective, it might be argued that, as was the case with the Industrial Revolution, those who are able to adapt and to make the new systems work will survive and prosper, while those who cannot will wither and die. Accounting information is part of this information revolution, and those who understand and can access and manipulate accounting information will be in a position of strength. So, whether or not you intend to specialise in accounting, be aware that financial information plays a critical part in many of the decisions taken within your society; accounting is an important arbiter in social and economic decision-making.

Plan of the book

Exhibit 1.1 provides an overview of the book and explains the way in which we see accounting and its links to the organisation. The areas in Exhibit 1.1 that lie outside the larger circle contain those groups (sometime referred to as stakeholders) with whom the organisation interacts and/or has some responsibility towards. The book begins in familiar territory (with Stage 1 – products and services) and considers the ways in which accounting can inform management plans and decisions (Stage 2). These two stages cover what is often referred to as **management accounting.** The book goes on (in Stages 3 and 4) to look at the methods that accountants use to record and report the transactions and activities of the business. This reporting function is referred to as *financial accounting*. In Exhibit 1.1 we explain the elements of accounting, how they relate to business activities and where they can be found within the text. Exhibit 1.1 will help you to locate the detail of the chapters within an overall view of the subject, and we suggest that you refer back to it as you work through each chapter.

Following this first introductory chapter, Chapter 2 offers a background to your study by examining financial aspects of the products or services which businesses supply. Accounting exists (as the name suggests) to provide an account of activities or events. A possible definition of the word 'account' is 'a statement explaining one's conduct', and in one sense business organisations are operated by managers who are seen as being accountable to shareholders (who own the business) for their actions. Financial reports, which shareholders study, represent a summary of all the financial activities carried out by the managers during the recent past, and many of these activities relate to the products or services provided by the firm. Thus it is important, at an early stage, to gain an appreciation of some key financial terms related to the products and services which provide the starting point for most economic events.

Chapter 3 continues the management accounting theme, and builds on the product focus by considering the part that accounting information may play in the decision process. Business decisions are rarely taken on purely financial grounds; money and financial analysis are often at the heart of the decision, and here you will be introduced to some of the key criteria used for decision analysis.

In Chapter 4 we move into the financial accounting area and look at the ways in which the various decisions and transactions that managers set in train are recorded within the accounting system, and we lay out the basic ground rules used by accountants when preparing financial statements. As when you visit a foreign country, a good working knowledge of the local language helps you to get around, so it is with accounting. In the accountant's world words have a very particular meaning that is not always obvious or intuitively sensible! For example, the word 'profit' carries different meanings for the accountant, the economist and the layperson. Without a basic grasp of the 'language' you will struggle to understand and interpret the numbers which you come across.

In Chapters 5 and 6 we take a closer look at some of the ideas raised in Chapter 4 in order to deepen your understanding of profit and financial position. We look critically at the balance sheet and profit and loss account and raise questions about the meaning and limitations of these statements. We also consider in more depth the conceptual underpinning for accounting reports – the 'rules of the game' that accountants play by.

Chapter 7 looks again at published accounting statements and describes the role of the accounting profession in policing company reports. This chapter also completes the 'triangle' of key accounting statements by adding the cash-flow statement to the balance sheet and the profit and loss account, and emphasises the importance of cash flow and liquidity management within the firm.

In Chapter 8 we ask the question 'What can we learn about a business from an examination of its published accounting reports?', and we look at the key indicators (or ratios) of performance and assess their value and limitations. Following this theme of performance measurement, Chapter 9 examines the way in which accounting information can help managers to understand and cope with the

Exhibit 1.1

Accounting in
the organisation

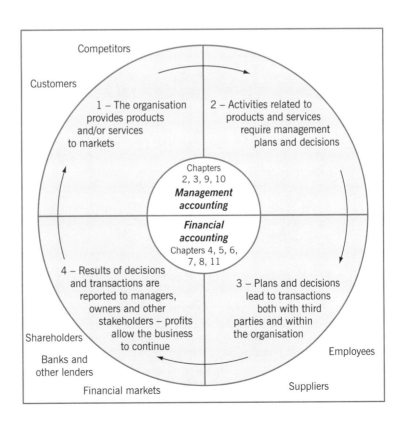

future. The main focus here is the budgeting process – a key financial tool for planning and control in most firms.

To some extent Chapters 1 to 9 provide, we believe, a self-contained (if introductory) picture of the world of accounting. However, two further chapters provide you with insights into aspects of the subject which you may encounter in later studies or in practice. Depending upon the course which you are taking, you may wish to consider these chapters at some stage. Chapter 10 extends the ideas about accounting-for-decisions we began to discuss in Chapter 3 into the realms of the long-term and investment decisions of the organisation. Finally, Chapter 11 emphasises the inherent dynamic of accounting – that it is a changing study and cannot be viewed in isolation from its social and economic environment. This final chapter raises issues about corporate governance and draws your attention to some of the challenges and issues currently facing business and the accounting profession.

Please turn to the back of the book for detailed answers to questions marked with a ❓. Answers to the other questions can be found on the companion website at www.thomsonlearning.co.uk/accountingandfinance/hand

REVIEW QUESTIONS

RQ 1.1 Do you have any preconceived ideas about accountants? If so, what are they? What evidence and life experiences have shaped your beliefs?

RQ 1.2 Can you quote examples from your own experience where financial information has been important for decisions which you or others have made?

RQ 1.3 What do you understand by the term 'true and fair'?

NUMERICAL PROBLEM

This warm-up exercise as to whose wealth is greater is open-ended and designed to raise some basic issues that the accountant must take into consideration in their daily job. For example, the necessity of a common unit of value (the impossibility of adding apples and pears), and how to account for promises of future value and debts that have not yet been paid but must be taken into account at some point in the future. It shows that because accounting is based on assumptions about value, it is not a precise science and different 'solutions' are possible with different assumptions.

❓ **NP 1.1 Shepherds – an argument about value** In the high mountains of Chatele, two shepherds, Deyonne and Batonne, sit arguing about their relative positions in life, an argument which has been going on for years. Deyonne says that he has 400 sheep while Batonne has only 360 sheep. Therefore, Deyonne is much better off. Batonne, on the other hand, argues that he has 30 acres of land while Deyonne has only 20 acres; then, too, Deyonne's land was inherited, while Batonne had given 35 sheep for 20 acres of land 10 years ago, and this year he gave 40 sheep for 10 acres.

Batonne also makes the observation that of Deyonne's sheep, 35 belong to another man and he merely keeps them. Deyonne counters that he has a large, one-room cabin that he built himself. He claims that he has been offered 3 acres of land for the cabin. Besides these things, he has a plough, which was a gift from a friend and is worth a couple of goats; 2 carts which were given to him in exchange for a poor acre of land; and an ox which he had acquired for 5 sheep.

Batonne goes on to say that his wife has orders for 5 coats to be made of home-spun wool, and that she will receive 25 goats for them. His wife has 10 goats already, 3 of which have been received in exchange for 1 sheep just last year. She also has an ox which she acquired in a trade for 3 sheep, plus a cart which cost her 2 sheep. Batonne's two-room cabin, even though smaller in dimensions than Deyonne's, should bring him 2 choice acres of land in a trade. Deyonne is reminded by Batonne that he owes Tyrone 3 sheep for carrying up his lunch each day last year.

Can you resolve the dispute about whose wealth is the greater? State any assumptions you make in your analysis.

WEB RESOURCES

www.thomsonlearning.co.uk/accountingandfinance/hand

The companion website has free additional resources for you to use along-side this book. If you are a student you can access material to help with revision, including practice questions with answers to test how much of the material you have understood. There are also useful hyperlinks to compa-nies and information sources mentioned in the book as well as interactive quizzes. There are additional resources for lecturers using this book on their courses; the details can be found in the preface at the front of this book.

CHAPTER 2

Accounting in context: focus on the product

LEARNING OBJECTIVES

The chapter focuses upon products and services to provide a way into the understanding of business accounting. After studying this chapter you should be able to:

- contrast types of products and services and discuss the ways in which product costs can be measured
- understand the way in which an accountant may view product costs and appreciate ideas of cost behaviour, including the distinction between fixed and variable costs
- describe and calculate key numbers, including contribution, break-even points, relevant range and margin of safety
- analyse the relationship between costs, profits and volumes
- draw elementary graphs that describe costs, revenues and profits
- distinguish between full cost and marginal cost
- relate costs to prices and describe key approaches to pricing of products and services.

Introduction

Before we take you into the world of accounting reports we think it important to provide a context for your study by beginning with something with which you can identify. You may know nothing about accounting, but you almost certainly know something about the **products and services** which businesses supply – if only as a consumer of them! Accounting needs placing in context in order to make sense – and the usual context for accounting is an organisation which is providing products or services to customers. In this chapter we introduce some financial aspects of these products or services, and this product focus allows us to introduce key financial terms (particularly 'costs' and 'profit') which will prove useful throughout your study.

All firms provide a service or a tangible product to customers. Look around you and notice the wide variety of services/products which you come across in any one day in and around your own college, workplace or home (for example food and drink, computers, entertainment, newspapers, educational courses, books, travel, clothes, cars). Managers of the organisations which provide these products are faced with a continuous stream of decisions, for example:

- What price to charge?
- How many units of the product or service to supply?
- Whether to invest in new technology?
- How many people should be employed in making the product or service?

A challenge for the accountant is to provide information about the product or service that will inform the managers when making such choices.

Think about the real products which were mentioned above. What do you think is the relationship between the costs of those products and the price charged to the customer? How does the retailer or manufacturer decide where to pitch the price? Is it by reference to costs or to 'what the market can bear', or a combination of both?

In this chapter we will try to answer some of these questions, and will offer you some useful frameworks for analysing the financial aspects of services and products which you see around you.

We will use the word 'product' to refer to either tangible items (houses, cans of beans, computers, cars, furniture, beer, clothes, food and so on) or intangible services (banking, consultancies, insurance, air travel, holidays and the like). For Interbrew the product could be a litre of lager – for Nissan, a family saloon car – for Thomsons, a package holiday – and for the Open University, a course of study.

Management accounting and financial accounting

In the plan of the book (Chapter 1) we noted that the study of accounting is often divided into two areas: management accounting and financial accounting. In this book we wish to stress that all forms of accounting and business activities are closely linked, and that the borders between management accounting and financial accounting are fuzzy. Having said that, the subject of this chapter and of Chapter 3 would, conventionally, be located within the study of management accounting.

Unique products or one of many?

Notice that the products quoted above fall into two general groups: products which are produced and sold in large quantities, and where one item is pretty much the same as any other (paint, beer, swimwear, package holidays, houses), and products which are unique 'one offs' (ships, hospitals, bridges). This difference has important implications for the way in which we consider the costs and prices of the product. If a shipbuilder such as Harland & Wolff is building a 'one-off' vessel it is likely to be a very large project lasting more than a year and taking place in one location – crucially many of the costs will be fairly easy to trace to that particular ship. At the other extreme, Britvic is bottling thousands of bottles of fruit juice in one week and will only be able to trace costs to an individual can in a very general sense. Simply put, the Britvic accountants will record all costs on the fruit juice production line for that week and divide by the number of bottles produced to give a unit cost.

Product costs and cost behaviour

To make sense of product costs and **cost behaviour** you need to grasp some key ideas about cost types. In particular we introduce here the notion that costs may be seen as either fixed or variable.

Variable and fixed costs – a crucial distinction

It can be helpful (even though a simplification) to think about costs as either fixed or variable. What does this mean? Let us consider a retailer, such as Next plc, selling clothing. Next's main variable costs are the price of the shirts, tops, scarves, etc. bought from the suppliers. Next's main fixed costs will be those related to its retail and office premises, and staffing costs. These fixed costs will remain at pretty much the same level whatever the level of clothing sales. They are fixed in the sense that activity levels (measured by how many clothes they sell) do not change them (obviously the rents and staff costs may go up with inflation but that is another issue altogether). The cost of the clothes are variable in the sense that if the Next shop sells 100 tops (say) then the cost (in total) will be double that for 50 tops.

From this illustration we can attempt two general definitions:

Variable costs are costs which rise or fall in line with activity. Examples could be bought in components, raw materials, power and some forms of direct labour where labour is paid according to items produced.

Fixed costs are costs which tend to remain the same even though output may change. Examples of fixed costs would be managerial costs, rents, insurance and labour costs paid according to time rather than output.

TASK 2.1

A retailer's costs?

Making whatever assumptions appear to be reasonable, draw up an imaginary set of cost headings (not amounts) for any retailer that you know.

Which of these costs would be fixed, and which would be variable?

ILLUSTRATION 2.1

Costs of a product – a pottery

One of the most important questions for managers (but annoyingly, one of the most difficult to answer!) is:

What does this product (or service) cost?

We can begin to explore both the simplicity and complexity of this question through the illustration (that is continued through this chapter) of a small local pottery making a plate of simple design.

Let us assume that the main variable cost is the basic raw materials (clay etc.) which costs £250 for sufficient to make 1000 plates, and that other variable costs (power for example) are £0.10 per plate. The pottery has a normal output level of 1000 plates per day, although daily output varies between 800 and 1200 plates. Fixed costs are as follows:

▶

- labour costs for operating the pottery are £500 each day
- machinery costs £300 per day to operate
- other daily fixed costs are £200.

TASK 2.2

Plate-making costs

1. What are the total daily fixed costs for the plate-making?
2. What is the variable cost of one plate?
3. What is the total cost of one plate at normal output levels?
4. How does the total cost of one plate change at the minimum and maximum levels of output?

Contribution

Having introduced the distinction between fixed and variable costs, we can now consider the important concept of **contribution**. Contribution, for accountants, means the amount left over (after paying all variable costs) which contributes towards paying for the fixed costs and giving the business a profit. Contribution puts the focus, not on the full cost, but on the variable cost of the product. In the 'plate' example the variable cost was £0.35 in all (£0.25 raw materials and £0.10 for other variable items). If the selling price was, for example, £2.50, we could see that each plate made and sold would bring in a contribution of £2.15 (£2.50 − £0.35).

Thus, contribution = **revenue** less variable costs, and can be a helpful figure when we are attempting to relate profit figures to volumes of output.

ILLUSTRATION 2.2

Contribution and gross profit margin in a sandwich bar

A simple way of seeing the idea of contribution is in a retailer's business. Here there are no manufacturing costs, only the costs of buying the food, clothes, or whatever it is that the shop sells. The retailer adds a profit margin (called the gross profit margin) onto the original cost and sells the products at this higher price. Say, for example, that you run a sandwich bar and that you buy in all of your sandwiches from a local supplier already wrapped and ready to sell. Whatever you pay your supplier for the sandwiches you decide to double before selling them to your customers. In June you buy £3000-worth of sandwiches and sell them all for £6000. You have made a gross margin (or gross profit) of £3000 which will go towards paying for your rent, insurance, wages and other fixed costs. You could describe your gross margin in at least two ways:

1. as 100 per cent **mark-up** on your buying costs – i.e. you have doubled the cost
2. as a 50 per cent gross profit on your sales figure – i.e. for every £1 of sales you 'make' £0.50

If we assume that there are no other variable costs for your business (except for the costs of the sandwiches) then you could also say that you have a contribution of 50 per cent of sales – thus for a very simple retail business, contribution would be the same measure as gross profit margin.

TASK 2.3

Margins and mark-ups

1. A newsagent buys greetings cards for £1 each and adds a mark-up of 100 per cent – what is his gross margin?
2. An antique dealer reckons to make a gross margin of 20 per cent on all furniture that she buys for resale. What is her mark-up?

Break-even points

A critical piece of information for any business is to know the level of sales at which it can break even (i.e. where all costs have been covered): the **break-even point.** For the low-cost airline EasyJet it would be critical to know how many passengers must be carried for the cost of each flight to be covered. Above this point the business begins to make profits, but if operating below that level then major problems (i.e. losses!) will be encountered.

TASK 2.4

Pottery break-even

Returning to our pottery:

1. What is the daily output level of plates where there will be no profit and no loss? (In other words, the break-even point, where total costs equal total revenues or, to put it another way, total contribution equals total fixed costs.) You will find that the simplest way to calculate the break-even point is to divide fixed costs by the contribution per unit.
2. How will that break-even point alter if the following independent changes occur:
   – variable costs rise by £0.10 per plate
   – fixed costs rise by £100 per day
   – selling price falls to £2.20 per plate?
3. What happens to the break-even point if all three changes occur together?

Graphic analysis of product costs

Sometimes it can be helpful to sketch the relationships between costs, contribution, profits and volumes through simple graphs – a **graphic analysis** often sheds more light on a problem than mere numbers. Before we take this other view we include a note of explanation if you are not familiar with the use of graphs.

Expressing relationships graphically

A graph can be used to express relationships between two variables. On the horizontal line of the graph is plotted the **independent variable,** and on the vertical line we draw the **dependent variable.** Take, for example, the use of a car and the fuel used by the vehicle. There should be some relationship between the miles travelled and the petrol used up. We could draw the relationship on a graph with miles travelled (the independent variable) on the horizontal axis and petrol used (which is the dependent variable) on the vertical axis. Exhibit 2.1, although not here drawn to scale, suggests the kind of relationship that would exist between fuel consumption and miles travelled. On the graph we show three different vehicles ranging from one that is fuel hungry (the 4 × 4) to one that is very fuel efficient (the smart car). The steeper slope for the 4 × 4 vehicle shows that fuel consumption is much more rapid than for the smart car (see Exhibit 2.1). The mileage here is used as an activity measure, whereas for a business graph activity could be units of product produced or hours worked.

Returning to our pottery, let us now consider graphs which would show the sales revenues and costs of the business in relation to volumes of plates. It is important to realise that this type of graphical model is only two-dimensional and can only show the way in which costs, revenues and profits behave in response to volume (or activity) changes. Thus the horizontal axis normally shows some measure of activity (maybe volume of sales output). For our plate firm the graphs of sales revenue and total variable costs would appear as in Exhibits 2.2 and 2.3.

We can see that both sales revenue and variable costs behave in a strictly linear or 'straight-line' fashion (i.e. increases to outputs bring about proportionate increases to revenues or costs). If output is 1000 plates the sales revenue is (£2.50 × 1000) = £2500, at 100 plates £250 and so on. The lines are straight because the change in cost or revenue is in proportion to the change in activity levels.

However, if we look at the plate firm's fixed costs a very different pattern emerges (see Exhibit 2.4).

By definition the fixed costs should not change as output alters; thus the line is parallel with the horizontal axis. Whether activity is 100, 400, 600 or 1000 plates the fixed costs (labour, machinery and other costs) remain at £1000.

Exhibit 2.1

Vehicle fuel consumption

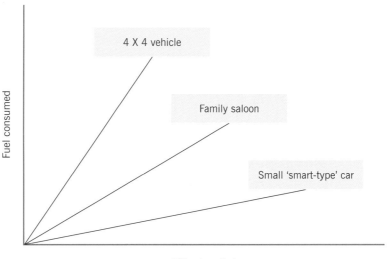

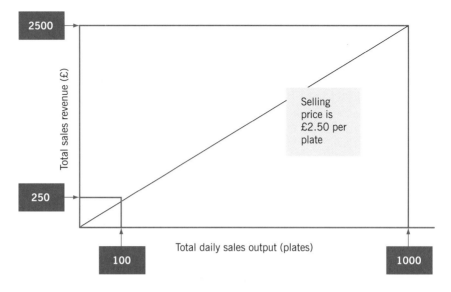

Exhibit 2.2

Plate revenues

Total sales revenue (£)

Selling price is £2.50 per plate

Total daily sales output (plates)

Exhibit 2.3

Variable costs

Total variable costs (£)

Selling price is £0.35 per plate

Total daily sales output (plates)

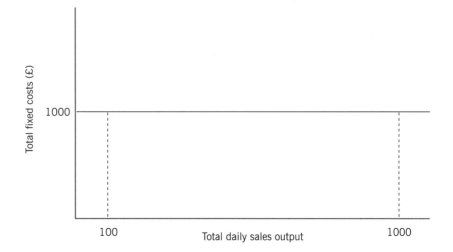

Exhibit 2.4

Fixed costs

Total fixed costs (£)

1000

100   Total daily sales output   1000

TASK 2.5

Costs of running a car

Think about the running costs of a car. Your road tax and insurance would be fixed costs: whatever your mileage (within reason) these costs would stay the same (although your insurance may go up if you travel a very high number of miles).

Estimate the fixed and variable costs that you would incur in a year for a car which travels 12 000 miles a year. Plot these numbers onto a rough graph. You will have to make assumptions about the costs, but the accuracy is not so important as considering the shape of the graph lines.

Cost, volume and profit

Now that we have considered the shapes of revenue and cost graphs for the plate firm, it is possible to combine this information into an overall **cost-volume-profit analysis** (often called CVP analysis) from which we are able to see important financial aspects of the business. Sometimes this type of graph is called a **break-even chart** because it provides a view of the level of output where the firm makes no profit and no loss (the break-even point).

For our plate firm the general shape of the CVP or break-even chart (without numbers, and not to scale) is shown in Exhibit 2.5.

From such a graph (if drawn to scale and with numbers) we could read off levels of possible profit or loss as the 'gap' between the revenue and total costs lines, and the break-even point is the output where costs exactly equal revenues. We are also able to consider two other useful pieces of information: the **margin of safety** and the **relevant range.** Each of these measures provides a way of thinking about the levels of uncertainty that may operate within the business.

Margin of safety

The margin of safety measures the gap between our actual output achieved (here the number of plates) and the break-even output, and is normally expressed as a

Exhibit 2.5

The general shape of a break-even chart

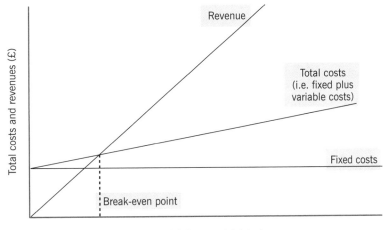

percentage of the actual output level. If, for example, a Travel Lodge hotel breaks even if 80 bedrooms are occupied, and is currently letting 100 rooms, then the margin of safety is:

$$\frac{(100 - 80)}{100} \times 100\% \text{ or } 20\%$$

i.e. the firm can lose only 20 per cent of turnover before it fails to cover its fixed costs.

Relevant range

The relevant range relates to the levels of activity with which the firm has some recent experience; in other words, those ranges which are relevant to the business. It may be (theoretically) interesting to know the profit at 100 per cent activity, or at as low as 10 per cent activity. But such levels are rarely experienced. Only the ranges of activity experienced by the firm are strictly useful (i.e. relevant) to decisions and plans. The relevant range of a 100-room hotel in the Lake District may be in practice between 30 rooms in the quiet season to 100 at peak holiday time, thus 30–100 would be the relevant range.

TASK 2.6

Margin of safety and relevant range

Referring back to Task 2.4 Part I, what can you say about the margin of safety and relevant range of the pottery?

Marginal and full cost

We have spent some time considering the difference between fixed and variable costs. Another related and important idea in product cost analysis is the difference between marginal and full cost. The **marginal cost** is (literally) the cost at the margin, or the cost of making and selling one extra unit – and will often (though not always) equate to the variable cost per unit. For our pottery the marginal cost is £0.35 except for the very first plate – moving from zero to one unit costs £1000.35! But that is a fairly theoretical output point. For practical purposes it seems sensible to consider £0.35 as the marginal cost. If the plate firm were working at full capacity, however, and could only generate a further 200 daily plates by taking on extra fixed costs of £300 (say to run an extra machine) then the marginal cost of those extra plates would be the variable costs (£0.35) plus the new increase in the fixed costs:

$$\frac{(£300)}{200} = £1.50)$$

or £1.85 in total.

From this discussion of full and marginal cost we begin to see why it may be difficult to be precise when answering the question that was raised right at the beginning of this chapter, namely: 'How much does it cost to produce one unit?' In turn that difficulty leads towards a discussion about how prices are set.

▨ ▪ ▪ ▨ Pricing, costs and profitability

We live in an exchange economy where everything appears to be given a price. The determination of price is a critical function within any market economy, for price signals how we value a commodity and also reflects how it will be allocated within the economy. We can be aware of prices from the moment we wake (the cornflakes at breakfast), as we move around (petrol, bus fares), when we stop to relax (coffee and snacks), when studying (the price of this book!) and so on. Some prices even make news headlines: the price of shares on the Stock Market, house prices, the price of money (i.e. interest rates), the price of currencies in relation to other currencies (e.g. the weakness or strength of the pound).

Why is pricing important for the manager?

At a personal level, prices (and in particular price rises) can mean the difference between happiness and misery, as noted by Charles Dickens in the novel *David Copperfield*:

> *Annual income twenty pounds, annual expenditure nineteen shillings and six pence, result happiness. Annual income twenty pounds, annual expenditure twenty pounds nought and six, result misery. (Chapter xii)*

For most companies the pricing decision is crucial for survival and profitability. Over-pricing may lead to loss of business, and under-pricing to loss of profits. At a **corporate** level striking the 'correct' price can mean the difference between success and failure. Low-cost airlines such as bmibaby faced this decision when setting up their initial fare structures. Too high and the customers would not be attracted in sufficient numbers, too low and the planes might be full but losing money.

Pricing policy is an interesting study in itself, but within this introductory accounting text our concerns about pricing are:

- that it is a key financial management decision which has major implications for the firm
- that pricing often relates closely to product cost analysis and activity levels which we have discussed earlier in the chapter.

Pricing theories

Pricing may be considered from many different angles. Alternative **pricing theories** exist which attempt to explain how selling prices are worked out. Some economic theories, for example, emphasise the links between demand, supply and price. If demand is at a certain level then as supply rises so price is expected to fall; similarly if supply is at a fixed level then if demand rises so will price. If the firm has a monopoly, it will be able to charge practically any price it likes and make super-profits, while firms in a competitive market will have to be price-takers. Under a behavioural analysis, pricing is seen to be just another management decision. This means that to understand pricing decisions we need to see them as a set of negotiations undertaken by individuals or groups who have vested interests in the outcome (e.g. the sales manager may ask for a low price to increase his/her sales volume; the accountant may ask for higher prices to safeguard profits and cash flow). Under a behavioural approach we need to examine the people in the organisation and ask about their motives and relative positions of power. A third approach, the marketing angle, stresses customer behaviour and preferences and opens up the issues surrounding what exactly the consumer is buying, and why, and the price that the market and customers may be prepared to pay.

Accounting and pricing decisions

When a pricing decision is left to the accountant it is sometimes supposed that the price will arise from a close examination of the costs of the product; that the accountant will say something like: 'Well, this product costs us £10 to make, and we need a profit of 10 per cent, so I suggest that we sell it for £11.' Certainly it is true to say that accountants often stress the need for the firm to cover all costs in their product price. This 'cost-plus' approach to pricing takes the variable and fixed costs of the product at some 'normal' level of output and *adds* a reasonable profit to arrive at a suggested selling price. The approach is certainly tidy and produces a simple answer to the pricing question. For example, looking back to the pottery example, assume that 1000 plates is the normal level of output and that managers have decided on a profit margin of 30% on top of all costs. Then the price to be charged could be calculated as:

	Pounds sterling
Variable costs	0.350
Fixed costs ($\frac{\text{£1000}}{1000}$)	1.000
Full cost	1.350
'Reasonable' profit (30%)	0.405
Suggested selling price	1.755

Some problems become apparent with this approach. How, for example, can we determine 'reasonable' profit? And what if your local competitor is selling plates for £1.50? Finally we can recall that the £1.00 fixed costs (per plate) is a function of *output* – if output levels change then the £1.00 figure needs to be altered.

TASK 2.7

Pottery-selling prices, profits and costs

1. For the pottery, what would be the profit for a 10-day period assuming that the selling price was set at £1.75, that variable costs and total fixed costs were as predicted, and that output fell to 800 plates per day?
2. How would this profit differ from the profit at 1000 plates per day for a 10-day period?
3. Explain the difference in your two profits.

How do firms actually make pricing decisions?

It is not always easy to understand how pricing decisions are made. Perhaps the pricing decision is not really a 'decision' at all (because prices are determined by the marketplace). Or does the cost structure influence the price charged? The information about how firms actually arrive at a price is both partial and conflicting. Some research studies have suggested that firms base their prices on the costs of the product, while others indicate that firms do take account of the market price. Perhaps a way into the puzzle is to recognise that no two organisations are exactly alike, and that several variables will determine the influence which a firm has over its prices, including:

■ the type of market in which the firm operates (e.g. a monopoly with one producer, a highly competitive market with lots of buyers and sellers or an oligopoly with a few large players)

■ the beliefs and traditions within the business, and the different levels of power wielded by individual managers

■ the quality of information which the firm has about its markets and about its own cost structure.

FINAL COMMENTS

The plate-making pottery example which has been used throughout this chapter is limited to a single-product firm, and costs are perceived as either fixed or variable. The real world is seldom this simple: multiple products, inflation rates and more complex cost behaviour mean that few firms can consider cost predictions in such a simplistic manner. Nevertheless, the notions of cost behaviour and contribution are quite robust and, if used carefully, can offer real insights into the relationships between output levels and profits.

We can also see that there are many inputs into the pricing decision. Consumer responses, competitors' decisions, capacity to produce, cost structures, general economic conditions and government policy all relate to, and have an impact on, the pricing decision. Most pricing decisions probably contain an element of economic, financial and behavioural analysis.

Supplementary notes about cost behaviour

These extra comments are not essential for an early understanding of product costs, but are offered to supplement and deepen your learning. We suggest that you consider these extra points now and then return to them when you are studying Chapter 9, which is related to budgets.

Two variants on the basic fixed and variable cost types are **stepped fixed costs** and **semi-variable costs.**

Stepped fixed costs

These are costs which are fixed within particular ranges of activity – when activity moves outside of that range the cost may rise or fall. For a building firm like Barratts this could be for site supervision; for a supermarket such as Tesco an example might be regional warehouse rental costs. On a much smaller scale, for a market trader who became very busy and had to employ one or more assistants then this would be a stepped cost, rising by the cost of one assistant at critical levels of activity. For a manufacturing firm, warehouse rental could be an example of a stepped fixed cost. Perhaps the firm could store up to (say) 200 000 units in existing warehouse space at a cost of £5000. If more space were needed the firm would have to take on a whole new area for (say) a further £1500. The cost 'steps up' by £1500 and the new fixed total becomes £6500. Graphically, the shape of such stepped costs would be along the lines shown in Exhibit 2.6.

Semi-variable costs

Some costs may have both a variable and a fixed element. One example could be the salary of an employee who is paid partly at a fixed rate, plus a variable element of commission for sales made. Similarly, telephone and faxing costs may behave in a semi-variable fashion. If a manufacturer paid a flat rate for the hire of telecommunications equipment of (say) £100 per month plus a cost per unit used of (say) £0.10 then clearly the fixed element is £100 at any level, and the

Exhibit 2.6

Stepped costs

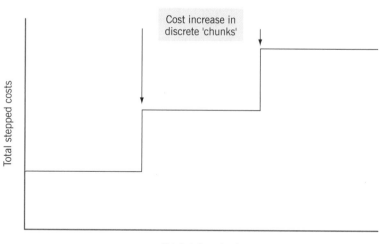

variable part depends on how many units are used. At 500 units the total cost would be £100 fixed plus (500 × £0.10) £50 = £150 total semi-variable cost. Again the graphic view of such costs would be as in Exhibit 2.7.

Exhibits 2.6 and 2.7 demonstrate how there can be degrees of 'fixedness' and variability in some costs which make cost behaviour less straightforward than the simpler fixed/variable elements.

SUMMARY

In this chapter we have placed the costs of products within a context of markets and management decisions. The following concepts and techniques have been covered:

- The products and services context for accounting.
- Cost behaviour – fixed, variable, semi-variable and stepped costs.
- Contribution, including gross margin and mark-up.
- Graphical depiction of costs, revenues and profits.
- Cost volumes and profit, break-even points, relevant range, margin of safety.
- Pricing and costs.

Please turn to the back of the book for detailed answers to questions marked with a ❓. Answers to the other questions can be found on the companion website at www.thomsonlearning.co.uk/accountingandfinance/hand

REVIEW QUESTIONS

RQ 2.1 Explain the meaning of the following terms:

- average full cost
- marginal cost
- contribution

Exhibit 2.7

Semi-variable costs

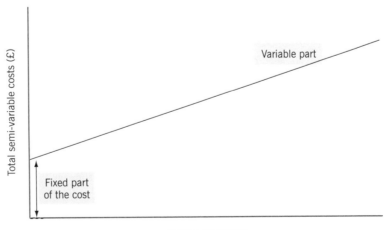

- break-even point
- margin of safety
- relevant range.

RQ 2.2 Discuss the assertion that: 'selling prices are all to do with what the customer will pay, and nothing to do with the cost of the product'.

RQ 2.3 What are the major strengths and limitations of break-even analysis by the use of cost-volume-profit graphs?

RQ 2.4 Take any consumer product/service of your choice and consider the following:

1. How would you describe the characteristics of the market in which the product exists (e.g. the extent of monopoly or competition in the marketplace)?
2. What are the implications of the market for pricing and profitability?
3. What do you think is the rough cost structure of this product/service? Distinguish between fixed and variable costs of making and selling the product/service and attempt to assess the relative importance of each in the cost structure.
4. What might be the relationship between output levels, costs, prices and profitability?

NUMERICAL PROBLEMS

NP 2.1 Restaurant costs and break-even A restaurant spends around £5000 each week on fixed costs (staff, rents, insurances, energy etc.). For each meal served an average of £6 is spent on variable costs (mainly the food and drink provided). Although the menu varies, customers spend on average around £16 for one meal. The restaurant owner knows from past experience that it is normal for an average of 600 meals to be served each week, although during quiet spells this may be as low as 300. It is unusual for more than 700 meals to be served.

1. Calculate the following information:
   - contribution per meal
   - break-even point
   - relevant range
   - total contribution and profit for 300, 400, 600, 700 meals
   - margin of safety.
2. How would the break-even point and relevant range change if the following happened at the same time:
   - prices were put up by £2 per meal
   - normal output dropped to 550 meals
   - fixed costs increased to £5400?

NP 2.2 Swift – CVP and break-even analysis The managers of Swift Engineering are considering *making* a component which is currently *bought* from an outside supplier at a cost of 5p per unit. Two alternative methods of manufacture are being considered:

- by semi-automatic machine
- by fully automatic machine.

Costs are expected to be as follows:

	Semi-automatic	Automatic
Annual fixed cost	£3 000	£5 000
Variable cost per unit	£0.020	£0.015

To help the management of Swift Engineering in reaching its decision you are asked to produce the following information:

1. For each machine, the minimum number of units that must be made and sold in order to have the total annual costs equal to outside purchase costs.
2. The most profitable (i.e. lowest cost) alternative for 300 000 units annually.
3. The most profitable alternative for 600 000 units annually.
4. The volume level that would produce the same total cost regardless of the type of machine owned.
5. A graph which shows the information in questions 1–4 above
6. A discussion of the implications of your analysis.

NP 2.3 Kaplan – CVP analysis Kaplan plc is a manufacturing company facing a decision regarding the choice of buying one of two machines to make its product. Machine A is a basic piece of low-technology equipment which will require relatively high operating costs. Machine B is more advanced and requires lower operating costs, but carries a much higher level of fixed costs. The product which either machine will produce sells at £10 per unit in a fairly competitive and unstable market – demand is quite unpredictable but is expected to be in a range of between 7000 and 10 000 units each year. The running costs of the two machines are given below:

	Machine A	Machine B
Annual fixed costs	£20 000	£50 000
Variable cost for each unit produced	£7	£4

You can assume that production quantities are equal to sales quantities throughout your analysis – i.e. there are no unsold stocks to complicate the calculations.

1. Calculate, for each machine, the maximum and minimum annual contribution and profit.
2. Calculate, for each machine, the number of units produced that will give a break-even position.
3. Draw a break-even chart for each of the machines.
4. Discuss the calculations and your graph derived from 1., 2., and 3. Discuss the usefulness and limitations of break-even analysis for decisions such as this.

NP 2.4 Eden Holidays – costs and prices Eden Holidays is a medium-sized firm which sells one-week European package holidays at the cheaper end of the market. Adam, Eve and Cain, the executive managers of Eden, are reviewing the results for the year just ending, which show:

		£m
Sales revenue – 70 000 holidays at £100 each		7.0
Variable costs of £20 per holiday		1.4
Contribution		5.6
Fixed costs		
Holiday centres	3.0	
Promotion	1.2	
Administration	0.9	5.1
Profit		0.5

For reasons outside the control of individual companies, the industry is suffering from very high cost inflation, and the managers of Eden are discussing pricing policy for next year when inflation is expected to cause all costs to rise at the rate of 10 per cent (i.e. the variable cost of a holiday will be £22 and annual fixed costs will become £5.61m).

Adam remarks:

> *The industry is likely to be quite competitive next year with a fall-off in demand for foreign holidays and the renewal of the UK as a holiday destination. Let's say that we can only sell 65 000 holidays next year. We want to hold our profit at £0.5m and therefore we will need a contribution of £6.11m (that is to cover the fixed costs of £5.61m and profit of £0.5m). From 65 000 holidays that's around £94 of contribution from each holiday. This means our selling price should be £116 per holiday. I suggest that we charge £120 in order to give a profit improvement.*

Eve is unconvinced by Adam's argument and produces market research information which suggests the following relationships between price and demand, for the coming year:

Price of holiday	Likely customer demand for holidays
£120	50 000
£110	60 000
£100	70 000
£90	85 000
£80	90 000

Eve suggests, therefore, that price reductions will be necessary if the firm is to make any profit at all!

Cain puts forward a third suggestion:

> We are not a large firm, but we have a good name and a lot of our customers take holidays with us every year. We need to encourage this customer loyalty. I suggest that we add a further £0.5m to our promotion budget (in addition to inflation rises – taking fixed costs up to £6 110 000). We can reduce customer resistance to our prices if we emphasise quality and value for money. Assume that, with the extra promotion costs, we only lose 10 per cent of last year's customers. I think that a profit target of cost plus 5 per cent would be reasonable, and our prices should be calculated on that basis.

Consider the following issues regarding Eden Holidays:

1. What flaws or problems are evident within Adam's calculations and assumptions?
2. What price do Eve's data suggest? What are the drawbacks to her approach?
3. What price would Cain's approach suggest? Comment on his approach.

NP 2.5 Goodtime Holidays – prices, costs, volumes and profits Goodtime Holidays, a holiday firm based in the Midlands, sells holidays in France. In the approaching budget year Goodtime is facing a downturn in demand due to the recession. The management accountant has extracted figures for the year just ended as follows:

- total sales revenue for 100 000 holidays = £22 million
- air travel costs – £50 per holiday
- costs incurred in France are variable costs of £80 per holiday and fixed costs of £2m annually.
- costs of the UK offices are variable costs of £20 per holiday and fixed costs of £3m annually.

Assume that the firm sells only one type of holiday, and that all holidays are of equal length and price.

The management accountant is producing a financial forecast for the approaching year and has gathered the following information:

- Demand for Goodtime's holidays is expected to drop by 10 per cent from the current level.
- The industry will be very competitive, and Goodtime's holiday prices can only be increased by 2.5 per cent.
- All costs (except for air travel) are expected to rise by 4 per cent next year. Air travel costs, due to increased risks and costs of air travel, are expected to rise by 5 per cent.

1. Produce a two-column table under the following column headings:

   - for the year just ended
   - for next year.

Each of the columns should show selling price per holiday, variable cost per holiday, total contribution for the year, total fixed costs for the year, profit for the year.

2. Using only the figures from the column 'for next year' above for this part of the question:

   - Calculate the break-even point in volume and sales value.
   - Calculate the profit if demand falls by 20 per cent instead of 10 per cent.
   - What is Goodtime's margin of safety?
   - If the lowest volume experienced by Goodtime in recent times is 70 000 holidays, what is the relevant range?

3. Comment upon Goodtime's performance as suggested by the question and by your analysis in (1) and (2) above.

WEB RESOURCES

www.thomsonlearning.co.uk/accountingandfinance/hand

The companion website has free additional resources for you to use alongside this book. If you are a student you can access material to help with revision, including practice questions with answers to test how much of the material you have understood. There are also useful hyperlinks to companies and information sources mentioned in the book as well as interactive quizzes. There are additional resources for lecturers using this book on their courses; the details can be found in the preface at the front of this book.

CHAPTER 3

Using accounting for managers' decisions

LEARNING OBJECTIVES

After studying this chapter you should be able to:

- describe the relationship between accounting information and managers' decisions
- calculate relevant cash flows for decision analysis, and appreciate the significance of opportunity cost in decision-making
- conduct a financial analysis to support a range of business decisions
- appreciate the ways in which uncertainty may affect the data for decision analysis.

Introduction

In Chapter 2 we considered product-based issues related to cost, volume, price and profit. In the current chapter we stay within the management accounting area of accounting to develop the managerial uses of accounting information. In particular, we take a closer look at decisions that managers may face and the ways in which financial analysis may inform their decisions. To some extent this chapter develops a deeper understanding of concepts already discussed (for example, contribution). But the chapter also introduces new ideas (for example, relevant cash flows) which will help you to gain an understanding of the financial analysis of decision-making. The word 'decision' suggests a commitment to action, a choosing from among alternatives. In corporate life decisions are an important part of managers' work and definitions of management often stress the decision-making aspect of the task. A key question to have 'up front' throughout this chapter is: 'How may accounting and financial information improve decisions?'

Few decisions are taken simply on economic grounds, and managers use many criteria including financial analysis, personal preferences and past experience. However, it is undeniable that economic measurements do form a central part of the decision process.

In any organisation, managers are faced with a continuous stream of opportunities, challenges, and problems relating to their products and services. Examples are:

- Should we continue to make this component or subcontract it?
- Which of the different available technologies should be used?
- What is the most effective way of advertising the product?
- Should this product be continued or closed down?
- Would it be worthwhile accepting a one-off order at a special low price when we have idle capacity?

One way of beginning to answer such questions is to ask: 'What will be the impact of this action on the future cash flows of the firm?' First, then, we explain the notion of **relevant cash flows.**

Relevant cash flows

Cash is sometimes described as the 'lifeblood of the business' and few would deny the importance of clear cash flow information. For **decision analysis,** however, the manager is required to take a singular view of cash flow. Some cash flows will not be relevant to the decision (i.e. they cannot be altered by it), for example cash flows already paid or received or payments which will be the same whatever choice is made. Imagine that you are standing at a crossroads. Each path represents an alternative for you to take. The key question to ask is: 'What difference will it make to my future cash flows if I take either pathway?'

Relevant cash flows are best defined as **future incremental cash flows**. 'Future' because past flows cannot be changed by future decisions, 'incremental' because we should only be concerned with the extra cash flows generated by the decision. If cash flow will be unchanged irrespective of the decision then it is not relevant.

TASK 3.1

Personal relevant cash flows

Can you make a rough estimate of the relevant cash flows of your course of study? The answer will of course be specific to you, but is likely to include the cost of books and computing equipment, travel, and course and exam fees. These are obvious cash outlays that many students incur, but a further (and often more significant) cost could be income given up by the decision to study. If you were not undertaking this course, could you be earning more income? If so, then that income sacrificed is a further relevant cash flow.

Opportunity costs

The idea of 'income given up' leads us to the important concept of **opportunity cost**, which is defined simply as 'benefits sacrificed by choosing one alternative over another'. Any decision involves choice. The value of the next best alternative represents your opportunity cost. If taking your course of study means giving up part-time income of £100 each month, then this is a very real opportunity cost of your decision.

At an organisational level, decision-makers could ask questions about the relevant cash flows of:

- hiring or buying vehicles or plant
- selling off a plot of land, or developing it
- opening a new retail outlet
- closing down a division or a plant
- using subcontractors rather than employees to do the work.

We now look at a light-hearted illustration that provides examples of these ideas.

ILLUSTRATION 3.1

Reckams – a Christmas story

The festival of Christmas is celebrated in many countries in a variety of ways and a strong tradition of consumer spending has become associated with the festive season. Businesses see Christmas not so much as a religious festival but as a market opportunity. The figure of Santa Claus is important for this development. Children also play a key role as prime consumers of Christmas presents. Many large retailers install a 'Santa' in their stores during the Christmas period to entice children (and their parents of course) into the shop. Our example concerns one such retail store – Reckams – which is considering the economic viability of bringing in Santa.

The general manager of Reckams, a large city-centre retailer, is making plans for the approaching Christmas period, which is always a critical time for sales. Reckams, like most other large retailers, has always put an area of the store aside for a 'Santa Claus Grotto'. Some of Reckams' managers, however, have suggested that the presence of Santa does not improve profitability and may, in fact, reduce profits because of the special costs involved.

It is expected that the Grotto area will operate as follows: each child visiting Santa will pay £2.50 and, after a short talk with Santa, will receive a small gift which costs Reckams a total of £1 each. Santa's Grotto will operate for 40 shopping days immediately prior to Christmas, and an average of 150 children each day is expected to visit. Fittings and decorations which cost £2500 last year can be used again, but extra decorations will have to be bought for £900. The job of Santa Claus will be undertaken, on a rota basis, by four managers who each cost Reckams £22 000 per year. Having Santa in store is expected to cost £2800 in extra part-time staff for the 40-day period. Reckams owns a Santa Claus costume which cost £200 three years ago. Repair work plus a new beard will cost £60 this year. Reckams expect to spend £500 in advertising the coming of Santa, and incidental costs will be £1000. A major effect of the Santa operation will be the loss of floor space for the sale of other goods. Fifty square metres will be taken up by Santa and the normal gross profit per square metre per day is £25.

The big unknown in all this is: How much extra trade will Santa generate by bringing extra people in who will spend money on other goods? A relevant cash-flow analysis may help to clarify the decision.

Relevant cash flows for Reckam's Santa	£
Fittings and decorations Only the new expenditure of £900 is relevant. The £2500 spent previously cannot be changed by the decision and is irrelevant	900
Managers' salaries The mangers would be employed anyway. This decision does not change their salaries and hence the relevant cash flow is zero	0
Costume repairs	60
Advertising	500
Incidental costs All of these three items will be new (and therefore relevant) expenditure	1 000
Loss of floor space Santa will cause the loss of 50 square metres for 40 days at £25 per square metre per day lost gross profit	50 000
Total relevant costs	52 460
Less the net inflows from gifts – from 150 children for 40 days × (£2.5 − £1) £1.50 will give relevant inflows of	9 000
Thus the net relevant cash outflow of bringing in Santa (based on these various assumptions) is	43 460

You will notice that the analysis ignores certain costs – the fittings and costume costs previously paid out, along with the salaries of managers employed by Reckams. These are examples of **sunk costs**. Sunk costs are those which have already been incurred and which are therefore not relevant to the decision.

The concept of opportunity cost is demonstrated by the loss of profits on floor area given up to Santa. The whole analysis is based on relevant cash flows, in other words cash flows that will be changed by the decision.

The analysis suggests that Santa will cost Reckams £43 460. The general manager can now consider whether that kind of extra profit is likely to be generated for the store by the presence of a Santa. This represents around £1086 per day for 40 days. Can she expect to recover that level of profit through extra sales? If not, is the store prepared to stand this loss for other, qualitative reasons such as future goodwill? A decision such as this would rarely be taken solely on financial grounds. The image of the store, traditional practice and likely policies of other competing stores would all be important for the decision.

Notice also that the analysis is based upon predictions, not hard facts. The more predictable items are those of least consequence (fittings, costume etc.). A large sum in the analysis relates to the number of visitors to Santa, and this would perhaps not be easy to predict.

Ranking decisions

The Reckams problem could be described as an **accept or reject decision**. The choice was simple: have a Santa or don't have a Santa! A different type of decision that managers often face is the **ranking decision**. Here the decision-maker may be selecting best or better alternatives – taking the best and leaving out the worst. While the accept or reject decision implies that choices are mutually exclusive (e.g. Reckams' decision to have a Santa automatically rules out not having a Santa) the ranking decision implies that there are many things that the decision-maker would like to do but is forced, because of constraints on resources, to choose some and not others. In such circumstances the notion of contribution again can be useful.

Our next example demonstrates how the concept of contribution that we introduced in Chapter 2 may be useful in ranking decisions

ILLUSTRATION 3.2

Beardsley – a difficult choice

Beardsley is a small building firm that offers specialised work within the local area. Skilled labour is in very short supply; in fact, Eric (one of the employees) is the only person in the firm who is capable of carrying out the glazing work that is often called for and he is paid £20 per hour. Two customers, Oscroft and Baines, want essential and specialised glazing jobs done immediately. If Eric cannot do them next week they will go to a competitor. Financial information about the two jobs is as follows:

Job	Oscroft	Baines
Number of Eric's hours	20	15
Materials cost (£)	500	300
Labour cost for Eric @ £20 per hour (£)	400	300
Subcontract costs (£)	600	200
Total costs for the job (£)	1500	800
Price for the contract to be paid by the customer (£)	2400	1600
Leaving contribution (£)	900	800

What can we make of Beardsley's choice? Though Oscroft's job offers the largest contribution Baines' job is the one to accept. Why? Because it gives the best return on the scarce resource – Eric's labour (sometimes called the **limiting factor** in that it limits the firm's ability to grow).

Specifically		
total contribution is (£)	900	800
and Eric's labour hours are	20	15
thus – contribution per labour hour (£)	45.00	53.30

Beardsley begins to open up our understanding of contribution and opportunity costs. The next illustration (Matheson) is more complex and takes the ideas of choices, ranking and limiting factors further.

ILLUSTRATION 3.3

Matheson

Matheson imports children's toys and sells them to UK retailers. Currently there are only three toys imported: Zaps, Gigs and Pronks.

	Zaps	Gigs	Pronks
The expected annual demand (in units) is	4 000	4 000	4 000
Each toy is sold to the retailer for	£10	£11	£14
The import cost of each toy is	£7	£7.50	£10
The contribution for each toy can therefore be calculated at	£3	£3.50	£4

Matheson's other costs are fixed at £20 000 per year, and will not alter, whatever the mix of total sales.

1. We could begin by working out Matheson's profit if there were no complications and all demand could be satisfied.

	Zaps	Gigs	Pronks	
The contribution for each toy is selling price less variable costs	£3	£3.50	£4	
The expected annual demand (in units) is	4 000	4 000	4 000	
Thus total contribution for Zaps, Gigs and Pronks will therefore be	£12 000	£14 000	£16 000	
We can see then that Matheson's total contribution is				£42 000
less fixed costs				£20 000
leaving a profit of				£22 000

2. Matheson might therefore expect a profit of £22 000 if there were no constraints on either demand or supply. But what decisions would be needed if, for example, new information suggested that Matheson's share of the market for these kind of toys would not exceed 10 000 units in total and 4000 units for any one model during the year?

The relative contribution of each product could be examined viz:

	Zaps	Gigs	Pronks
The contribution for each toy is selling price – variable costs	£3	£3.50	£4
and the products could be ranked	3rd	2nd	1st

▶

The ranking would suggest that Matheson should aim to sell the maximum number of Pronks (4000) and Gigs (4000) which would take up 8000 units of demand, leaving 2000 Zaps to make up the 10 000 maximum.

	Zaps	Gigs	Pronks
Total sales	2 000	4 000	4 000
Total contribution	£6 000	+ £14 000	+ £16 000 = £36 000
less fixed costs			£20 000
Profit			£16 000

The market restriction is seen to be costing Matheson £22 000 − £16 000 = £6000. This would suggest that the firm could consider looking for ways of increasing market share (e.g. through advertising) as long as that does not cost more than £6000. In the short run, the contribution analysis helps to pinpoint the products which are more profitable.

TASK 3.2

Input constraints for Matheson

Now, if we assume that there are no demand constraints i.e. Matheson can sell up to 4000 units per product, but that supply is restricted, we can look at contribution in a slightly more subtle way. If an input is providing a constraint, the key measure becomes not simply contribution, but contribution per unit of that scarce resource (as seen in the Beardsley illustration where labour was scarce). If, for example, Matheson were restricted to £80 000 of imported goods (perhaps because of cash-flow pressures, or that the toys were in short supply) you could calculate the contribution per £ of import cost. Try this by filling in the gaps below (marked with a ?).

	Zaps	Gigs	Pronks
The contribution for each toy is selling price less variable costs	£3	£?	£4
The import cost of each toy is	£?	£7.50	£?
Thus, contribution per £ of import cost =	£?	£?	£?
and the ranking becomes	2nd	1st	3rd

(Check that your ranking is the same as this before proceeding)

| What would be the preferred sales programme for each product? | 4000 | ? | ? |

Check – so far you should be concluding that Gigs and Zaps can be sold up to maximum demand, which only takes up import costs of £58 000 (4000 × £7 = £28 000) + (4000 × £7.50 = £30 000).

▶

This would leave £80 000 – £58 000 = £22 000 of money to buy in Pronks.

The number of Pronks which could therefore be imported and sold is

$$\frac{(£22\,000)}{£10} = 2200.$$

What then is the contribution for each product?

Total contribution is	£34 800	£?	£?	£?
less fixed costs	£20 000			
Profit	£14 800			

The input constraint can be seen to be costing Matheson £22 000 (the original maximum profit) minus £14 800 (the level of profit calculated above) i.e. £7200. This can be proved by checking that 1800 fewer Pronks are to be sold at a contribution of £4, i.e. £7200. This is a significant loss of profit and could lead the managers of Matheson to consider ways of lifting the resource constraint (e.g. by extra borrowing if it is cash shortage that is restricting the supply).

Product viability

For Matheson all products were profitable, but choices were forced on the firm because of constraints of demand or supply. Sometimes organisations have doubts about the viability of their products or departments. The question for management is: 'Should we continue with this activity?' Our next illustration demonstrates how contribution may help to inform such difficult decisions.

ILLUSTRATION 3.4

The Jackson Hotel – viability of activities

Jackson Hotel is a small, family-owned hotel with 50 bedrooms. The owner/manager of Jackson Hotel is concerned about profit levels, and has done a rough analysis (see Exhibit 3.1) of how the annual costs and revenues of the hotel are broken down between the two main activities: room letting, and restaurant and bar.

In Exhibit 3.1 variable costs are those that relate directly to the activity. For room lettings this will include cleaning costs, free drinks, and repairs to fittings in the rooms. For the restaurant the variable costs are the drinks and food sold. Fixed costs are not so easily split between the two activities. Although some of the fixed costs can be directly traced (mainly staff wages), there are many costs of a more general nature (insurance, some management staff wages, energy, local rates and so on) that cannot be easily split. In the analysis above the amounts (for fixed costs) have been allocated to rooms or restaurant in a very approximate manner based on revenues as follows:

	£000		
Total fixed costs	700		
Revenues	1000	750	250

The amount of fixed costs 'charged' against the two activities is therefore assumed to be in proportion to sales revenues. For room letting this would give

$$\frac{(£700 \times 750)}{£1000} = 525$$

and for the bar/restaurant

$$\frac{(£700 \times 250)}{£1000} = 175$$

The profit or loss is therefore misleading as we only get a loss for the bar/restaurant if the split of fixed costs is accurate – but we have seen that it is very approximate. More critically, it is likely that many of the fixed costs are general costs (e.g. insurance) and do not relate to the specific activities. The profit and losses reported are therefore misleading and our notion of contribution is more helpful to the owner/manager. The contribution for each activity would be just the revenues minus the variable costs, i.e. £650 000 for room letting and £150 000 for the bar and restaurant.

Exhibit 3.1	£000	Total	Room lettings	Restaurant and bar
Analysis of the Jackson Hotel's revenues, costs and profits	Revenues	1000	750	250
	Variable costs	200	100	100
	Fixed costs	700	525	175
	Profit (or loss)	100	125	−25

The point of this illustration is that when managers look at the costs and profitability of different products or departments or services, care is needed when considering how the costs are allocated. A superficial glance at the Jackson numbers might lead us the think that the hotel would be better off without the bar and restaurant as it seems to be 'losing' £25 000 each year. But this is probably not true as this part of the business is at least providing a contribution (£150 000) towards the fixed costs. Closure would lead to a drop in contribution of £150 000 and some saving in fixed costs but almost certainly not by that amount, as many are general costs.

Our next illustration follows up Jackson Hotel in considering this tricky question about how fixed costs can be allocated to the various products, activities or departments of the business. As we see from Jackson, the tendency to treat these fixed costs as though they are one given sum for the business is flawed. In reality fixed costs are a difficult area for accounting treatment because they (generally) do not relate to particular products. Some costs are directly associated with one product or service (raw materials, bought-in-components, and some direct labour costs are examples of costs which are often incurred for a particular product) while many are not and can only be traced to the product in an indirect way (e.g. rent, costs of running machinery, managers' salaries, vehicle running costs). Traditionally, the accountant has devised ways of charging a 'fair' amount of these fixed overheads to the product. Overheads are said to be 'absorbed' or 'recovered' into the product cost. In Jackson the rate of absorption was based on sales revenue. This illustration provides a basic description of how **overhead recovery** or **allocation of fixed costs**) may work.

ILLUSTRATION 3.5

X and Y – the allocation of fixed costs

A firm makes two products, **X** and Y. The following information is given:

	X	Y
Units made and sold	1000	2000
Direct materials (£)	20	30
Direct labour (£10 per hour)	30	20
Direct labour hours per unit	3	2

In addition to the variable costs noted above, the firm incurs £140 000 of fixed costs (rent, telephone, insurance, managers' salaries, etc.) in making the two products.

The accounting problem here is: What is a fair amount of fixed overheads to allocate to each product? We could simply charge each product with half of the £140 000 but this seems unfair as product Y has twice the output of X and takes up 4000 hours, against only 3000 hours for X. Perhaps a 'fairer' approach is to look at the time taken up and charge £20 per hour (£140 000 ÷ 7000 hours) for the fixed element of costs. This would lead to costs of:

(£)	X	Y
Variable costs	50	50
Overhead allocated	3 × 20	2 × 20
	= 60	= 40
Total cost	110	90

But is this reasonable? Should product X be regarded as more 'expensive' than Y? The short answer is that we don't have enough information about the way the fixed costs are used up. For example, product X may be more complicated in terms of setting up the production line or in dealing with suppliers – if so, perhaps it should bear more of the set-up and buying fixed costs.

TASK 3.3   **Allocating overheads to products**

1. Can you suggest other ways of sharing these overhead costs between the two products?
2. How useful do you think it is to charge overhead costs to individual products?
3. How might the calculation shown above impact on the selling price charged for **X** and **Y**?

We see again (as in Chapter 2) that the question: 'What does this product cost?' is not easy to answer, depending as it does upon assumptions about the way in which certain costs are spread across products. Perhaps a more sensible approach is to say that we may be able to measure fairly accurately the variable cost of a product or service, but that any calculation of full or total cost (i.e. including fixed costs) should be regarded with caution – different assumptions will lead to different answers.

We return to the allocation of overheads further in Chapter 10, where we consider long-term decisions. There we can consider issues about long-run costs (which is what most overhead allocation is about) and will see how the long-run cost view links into the organisation's plans about future directions and strategy.

Long-term and short-term decisions

A common feature of our examples so far has been the time scale. The period under consideration has been relatively short. For Reckams the decision spanned a few weeks, for Beardsley one week, for Matheson one year. Clearly a short time horizon is very limited and unrealistic for many decisions. When an airline buys new aircraft, when a supermarket builds a new store, when a theatre invests in new seating, managers are concerned with the impact of the decision over several years, and not just for the current period.

To label some short-term and others long-term decisions is to oversimplify the real world of business. All decisions connect at some point (however distant) and it is probably more helpful to think of a continuum. At one end are those decisions which have very short-term implications and which can be altered without too much pain. These would include an hotel re-ordering routine items of cleaning materials for stock, an electrical retailer offering a discount on selling price for one week only or a textile firm employing temporary staff. At the other end of the scale are those decisions which involve much time, commitment and, probably, cash. Such long-run decisions may only be altered at considerable expense and include a care agency entering a fixed-price contract to supply care services over one year, a university hiring permanent staff, a pottery replacing an expensive kiln and a large public company building new office accommodation.

Long-term decisions tend to set frameworks within which later short-run decisions take place. An organisation is a dynamic location for a continuous stream of decisions and none of these decisions can be isolated. Each must be seen in the context of other decisions previously taken or yet to be considered. In Chapter 10 we return to some of these issues and examine the special financial aspects of longer-term decisions.

Uncertainty in decision-making

To say that most decisions are subject to uncertainty is to state the obvious. Surely if there were no uncertainty there would be no choice and no decision – the solution would be clear to all. However, much that is written about accounting for decision-making plays down the fact that a whole range of outcomes are possible for many decisions.

How then can we handle the inherent uncertainty? We suggest that the introduction of uncertainty into the calculations should leave decision-makers better informed about the range and riskiness of possible outcomes. In effect, uncertainty analysis should force the decision-makers to consider their confidence in predictions and attitude towards risk.

Best or worst?

A first step could be to use **best or worst analysis**. Ask for more than one set of predictions; for example, pessimistic, optimistic, and most likely. While a simple decision analysis may inform the decision maker that 'profit will be £12 000 if all assumptions hold up', it must be more useful for a decision-maker to be told 'your profit (from this decision) may be £10 000, £12 000, or £15 000 depending on (for example) levels of market demand'. By providing a worst/most likely/best range of predictions the accountant is encouraging discussion about the decision and about the important variables that will determine the outcome.

What if?

The widespread availability of spreadsheets has opened up new dimensions for uncertainty (**what if**) **analysis**. Spreadsheets allow the manager to alter the key variables within the decision model and to observe the effect on the outcome (whether measured by profit or contribution). 'What if?' questions can be asked and multiple solutions generated. A dynamic view of the decision is more useful than a 'single-point' estimate. This has been an exciting development. At the same time the ever-changing spreadsheet model may leave managers feeling uncomfortable – for the decision outcome cannot be summarised on one sheet of paper with a single 'bottom-line' outcome. Through the spreadsheet managers are confronted with the complexity and uncertainty inherent within many decisions.

FINAL COMMENTS

This chapter has focused on the crucial, yet often difficult, area of decision-making. But what distinguishes a 'good' decision from a 'bad' decision? Perhaps we can only make the distinction correctly with the benefit of hindsight. However, one crucial factor in determining whether a decision is likely to be good or bad is the quality of information provided for the decision-makers. Is the information accurate? Unbiased? Timely? Clearly presented?

The role of accounting information, in this context, is to reduce uncertainty in the mind of the decision-maker. Uncertainty cannot, by definition, be eliminated. Yet timely, relevant and well-presented accounting information can aid the decision process by lowering levels of uncertainty related to the decisions. This chapter has looked at some of the ways in which the accountant can support the decision process through financial and economic analysis.

SUMMARY

In this chapter we have introduced and illustrated the decision-making process and the uses of accounting information by managers. The following concepts and techniques have been covered:

- Managers' decisions, relevant cash flows, and sunk costs.
- Opportunity costs in decision analysis.
- Types of decisions – accept or reject, ranking, viability.
- The use of contribution within decision analysis, and limiting factors.
- Treatment of fixed overhead costs in decision analysis.
- Uncertainty in decision-making.

Please turn to the back of the book for detailed answers to questions marked with a 🌐. Answers to the other questions can be found on the companion website at www.thomsonlearning.co.uk/accountingandfinance/hand

REVIEW QUESTIONS

RQ 3.1 Can you think of decisions which you have witnessed or taken recently, which have been informed by financial information? How significant do you think the financial information was for the decision?

RQ 3.2 It has been suggested in this chapter that only relevant cash flows matter for decisions. Do you believe this? Can you think of situations where *past* cash flows may influence *future* decisions?

RQ 3.3 Business financial reports only account for their internal costs when making decisions – i.e. the impact on their own costs and revenues. Who pays the other external or social costs of these decisions?

NUMERICAL PROBLEMS

NP 3.1 School catering A school currently has all of the pupils' food supplied by a local catering firm at no cost to the school as the caterers keep all money received from the meals. The new finance manager of the school is putting forward a plan to manage the meals within the school as this would give the pupils more choice, create employment opportunities within the local community and provide much needed extra income for the school. A summary of the initial forecasts show the following:

Number of pupils having a meal on average each day	500
Number of school meal days in each year	200
Average price charged for a meal	£1.50
Average variable costs of each meal (mainly food and energy)	£0.80

Annual fixed costs

| Staff employed to prepare and serve the meals | £30 000 |
| Other costs directly brought about because of the meals service | £10 000 |

General school costs (e.g. energy, insurances,
administration salaries etc.) charged to the school meal service £20 000

(It is estimated that £15 000 of the general school costs would be
incurred whether or not the meals are managed by the school).

- Produce a financial analysis to show whether or not it makes sense to
  bring the meals service within the school.
- If you were advising the head teacher and governors of the school about
  this plan, what points would you bring to their attention?

NP 3.2 GH Ltd – making or buying? GH Ltd manufacturers a component that is
used in several of its finished products. Cost records show the following details
for each unit of this component:

	£
Direct materials	1.40
Direct labour	0.50
Variable overhead	1.00
Total variable cost	2.90
Fixed overhead – this figure is to cover GH's overall overheads and does not directly relate to this particular component	1.00
Total cost	£3.90

The company's annual demand for this component is 20 000 units.
Z Ltd has written to the production director of GH Ltd, offering to supply these
components at a price of £3.50 complete and delivered.

1. Produce an analysis explaining whether the company's profit will
   increase or decrease if they accept Z Ltd's proposal, under the following
   totally independent circumstances:
   - assuming that GH Ltd would have no other use for the facilities at
     present used in the production of the component and that closure of
     this production line would save £8000 of fixed costs
   - assuming that the resources released by subcontracting the
     component could be used to produce 10 000 units of another

product, with a unit contribution of £2, in which case there would be no savings in fixed costs.

2. What other factors, in addition to those listed above, would have to be considered in reaching a decision?

NP 3.3 MNO – a special order MNO produces and sells for £250 an office machine for which there is a heavy demand and which the company is prevented from meeting because of a shortage of skilled labour. The direct material and labour costs of the machine are £100 and £50 respectively. The labour force is paid £12.50 per hour. All other costs may be regarded as fixed.

The company's European representative has been invited by one of his customers to supply, for a price of £20 000, a batch of machines of modified design and capacity which the customer wishes to incorporate into his own product, a large multipurpose machine.

MNO has calculated that, to execute the order, 200 direct labour hours would be required and the cost of material would be £8500 excluding the cost of special switches, which could be bought in for £1000 or, alternatively, made by the company for material cost of £400 and labour time of 20 hours.

■ Advise the management of MNO Ltd whether to accept the European order. Your answer should be supported by relevant calculations and should include comments on any other matters which you consider should be taken into account.

NP 3.4 Carbonia – the cost of coal Carbonia is a small country with a long-established coal mining industry. Coal is extracted from three mines and is sold, within Carbonia, to general consumers and to the Carbonia Electricity Board. Demand for coal in Carbonia is expected to be five million tons each year into the foreseeable future. Each of the three mines is operating near to full capacity, but excess demand can be satisfied by importing coal which costs £100 per ton. The coal industry is wholly nationalised and is operated by the CNCB (Carbonia National Coal Board). The government of Carbonia has set a target for CNCB of £3 per ton profit after deduction of *all* costs detailed below. The following data relates to annual projected revenues and expenses of the three mines (North, South and West) that, between them, produce the whole of CNCB output.

	North	South	West	Total
Coal produced and sold (millions of tons)	1.5	3.0	0.5	5.0
		£		
Selling price per ton, set by the government of Carbonia	90	90	90	
Variable costs of extracting coal (per ton)	30	35	50	
Annual fixed costs for each mine	60m	107m	17m	184m

In addition to the above mine-specific revenues and expenses there are £80m of central CNCB-fixed costs to be allocated on the basis of coal tonnage produced. For example, South mine should bear $\frac{3}{5}$ of these costs as that mine has $\frac{3}{5}$ of the tonnage. The costs covered by the £80m include managerial costs and central head office services and would not reduce if volumes of coal changed nor if one of the mines were to close.

It has been suggested, on the basis of the above information, that West mine is uneconomic and should be closed if CNCB is to achieve its profit objective.

Produce a financial analysis that takes account of the above information and that will inform the managers of CNCB and the government of Carbonia about the viability of each of the mines.

CASE STUDY: COUNTRYSIDE DAIRIES

This case study covers the following areas:

- management accounting information for pricing
- product costs
- short-run decisions and their relationship to long-run business strategy
- marketing and accounting information
- the 'people' aspects of decision-making.

There are four managers in this case: Chris Edwards (chief executive), Alex Andrews (accountant), Mo Mason (marketing manager) and Phil Mullins (production manager).

The four people are in a meeting to decide on the initial price of a new product (fruit juice). Although the chief executive will have to make the final decision, he is a democratic manager who would prefer the group to agree on a pricing strategy if possible. However, conflict is built into the scenario.

Background to the case

Countryside Dairies (CD) is a family-controlled company operating in the South Midlands. The firm has a proven record of milk processing and delivery and has been showing fair, if unexciting, profits and cash flows for a number of years. The traditional methods of 'doorstep deliveries' have always been important for milk sales and CD maintains a fleet of milk delivery vehicles. However, there has been a noticeable switch towards sales to supermarkets in the past three years, and this now accounts for around 50 per cent of all milk sales. CD has a number of large delivery vehicles which take milk to supermarkets in the region. Two years ago CD changed all of its product packaging from glass bottles to disposable cartons.

The milk market has become much more difficult in recent times with supermarket chains squeezing the margins of suppliers – CD is looking for a diversification of products to provide a much-needed boost to profits and cash flows. The switch towards supermarket sales and disposable packaging has led, indirectly, to the perception of a new market opportunity which CD is about to exploit – the production and sale of fruit juices. The initial venture (and the decision today) involves only sales of juice directly to supermarkets. However, later developments could incorporate direct sales to consumers.

The company's executives believe that CD's milk management expertise equips the company for a move into this complementary market. In particular, the processing technology is very similar (and some plant is under-utilised at present), and spare capacity on delivery vehicles can be used (both for supermarket deliveries and later for 'doorstep' provision).

The markets

The milk market is quite fragmented. The nature of the product lends itself towards regional operations. Recent deregulation of the milk market has brought a lot more uncertainty into the marketplace. There is considerable price competition for supermarket sales.

The juices market is quite complex and is dominated by a handful of large players (55 per cent of the market is held by three international companies). However, local production is also quite common – most areas of the country have local producers who trade (in part) on a good local reputation for quality products – CD believes that this is where its own market opportunity may lie. Regional firms such as CD can offer a local service and a strong local image along with some cost advantages (delivery costs, for example, will be lower than for national distributors). It is accepted, however, that the large firms have a cost advantage in terms of routine production costs. Marketing surveys are unanimous in their predictions: the market for quality fruit juices is expected to grow at between 2 and 4 per cent each year over the next three years following the trend towards healthier diets. Mo Mason suggests that, given CD's good reputation and the expanding market, 5 per cent of the South Midlands market (around 120 000 to 130 000 litres per month) may be achievable in the first year assuming that CD offer a reasonably competitive price.

The people

What follows is public knowledge within the company.

Chris Edwards – chief executive

Chris is one of the founders of the firm. The Edwards family has a controlling interest. Chris is well regarded by other managers and is seen as a strong leader who is not afraid to take risks. He has been enthusiastic about the juices venture from the start and sees it as a way of taking the company out of the doldrums.

Alex Andrews – accountant

Alex qualified two years ago, and was appointed at CD only six months ago. This is Alex's first position of real responsibility. Unused to being involved in decision-making, until now she has merely provided figures for others to deal with. But Alex is a confident individual who has made a good initial impression with other managers.

Mo Mason – marketing manager

Mo has been with the firm for three years, is seen as the prime mover behind the new juices venture, and has a very personal interest in its success. Known to be an aggressive marketer, she believes price will be critical in consumer choices.

Phil Mullins – production manager

Phil has been at CD for around 15 years and is very loyal to Chris Edwards. Seen as a solid individual but perhaps rather conservative, Phil is known to believe that the firm's production function is *the* most important aspect of the business. Phil also worries about the dangers of moving into a new market, and of the general move towards a more 'market-oriented approach'. He will be expected to oversee the production of juices as well as milk – although there will be an under-manager for juice production who will handle the routine operations.

Accounting numbers

Competitors prices in the juices market range between 50p and 60p per litre (that is the price charged *to* the retailer), and Alex Andrews, the accountant, has drawn up figures which suggest that CD's price needs to be at the top end of that range. Alex's calculations follow. Production and sales levels are assumed to rise to 100 000 litres per month within a few months of the start of operations (assuming a price of 59p per litre charged to the retailer). Monthly fixed costs of the juice operation are expected to be £40 000, made up as follows:

1. Overhead costs specific and relevant to the product

	£
Production	20 000
Marketing	5 000
Administration and finance	5 000

2. Share of general company costs allocated by estimate to juices (e.g. distribution, warehousing, and central management) = £10 000

These above costs are expected to remain broadly unchanged within monthly volumes of between 80 000 and 140 000 litres. Direct product costs are 10p per litre (mainly for the juice and packaging). The normal profit margin for CD's existing products is 15 per cent of selling price. Taking account of the above data, Alex's suggested price is made up as follows:

	Pence per litre
Direct costs	10
Fixed costs $\frac{(£40\ 000}{100\ 000)}$	40
Total product cost	50
Profit (approx 15% of selling price)	9
Selling price	59

Marketing numbers

The marketing manager, Mo Mason, is sceptical about Alex's assumptions and suggests that this product is subject to quite strong price competition. After studying competitors' prices and market research studies, Mo has produced a schedule of predicted price/volume relationships as follows:

Price per litre (p)	Monthly volume (litres)	Direct cost per litre	Contribution per litre (p)	Total monthly contribution (£s)
50	130 000	10	40	52 000
51	130 000	10	41	53 300
54	100 000	10	44	44 000
55	100 000	10	45	45 000
59	85 000	10	49	41 650
60	85 000	10	50	42 500

The above analysis suggests to Mo that the optimum price is at the bottom end of the range rather than the higher 59p suggested from Alex's numbers.

Your brief

Assume that the meeting takes place as described. Imagine yourself in that meeting and answer these questions:

1. What price would you set for the new product? And why? There is no right or wrong answer here but you must be prepared to justify your answer in terms of financial analysis and market-based information.

2. How do you think that the meeting would develop? What arguments do you think each of the managers would use? What price would they each be promoting? Whose arguments do you think would prevail?

3. What other information would you like to have available?

4. And finally, what does the Countryside Dairies case study tell you about the value and limitations of accounting information?

WEB RESOURCES www

www.thomsonlearning.co.uk/accountingandfinance/hand

The companion website has free additional resources for you to use alongside this book. If you are a student you can access material to help with revision, including practice questions with answers to test how much of the material you have understood. There are also useful hyperlinks to companies and information sources mentioned in the book as well as interactive quizzes. There are additional resources for lecturers using this book on their courses; the details can be found in the preface at the front of this book.

A framework for accounting reports

After studying this chapter you should be able to:

- describe the special nature of the accounting views of an organisation – in particular views of financial position and progress
- understand the key financial classifications used by accountants to report the activities of a business
- appreciate how accountants begin to determine the profit earned by a business and how accounting values are attached to the assets of the business
- understand the content and structure of the profit and loss account and the balance sheet
- apply simple rules for recording **transactions** within an accounting framework.

Introduction

Chapters 2 and 3 focused on the decisions that are taken in managing the business. Managers' decisions result in business transactions, and these transactions require a systematic method for recording and reporting. This recording and reporting area of accounting is often referred to as **financial accounting**.

One of the major purposes of financial accounting is to report back to the owners of the business (for a company this means the **shareholders**) on how their investment has been managed during the recent past. Such reporting fulfils the **stewardship** role of accounting, for the managers of the business are stewards who look after the owners' investment in the business. As part of this process all businesses are legally obliged to keep **books of account**, which are records of the financial transactions that have been undertaken by the business. The production of what are sometimes called the 'final accounts' (including the profit and loss account and the balance sheet) is governed by company law and by accounting standards. Don't worry too much if you have not come across any of these terms before, as we will explain them in much more detail later in the book. Suffice to say that at this stage management accounting is an internal function and service to the business and its reports are retained within the business. Financial accounting must satisfy external obligations by producing reports which will be published externally.

Recording and reporting financial transactions

In this chapter we want to provide you with an understanding of how the profit and loss account and balance sheet are created through the particular rules and language that accountants use. As a learning device we will introduce you to the Accounting Quadrant, which provides an overview of the main accounting reports and which should also give you some insights into the way in which transactions are recorded by the accounting system.

In Chapters 2 and 3 we were concerned with management accounting questions and were looking at the micro-level of reporting (e.g. for specific decisions or products). In Chapter 4 we will be looking at the 'big' picture which the accountant draws of the whole organisation and how this picture can be used both internally within the business and externally by people who are interested in the performance of the business.

All accounting begins with the recording of financial transactions, which today usually means the use of computers allied to specialist software packages. It was not always so. The recording of financial transactions has been with us for centuries. Some of the earliest known records are to be found on papyrus belonging to the Phoenicians living between the seventh and fifth centuries BC, while the first known textbook to be written on accounting was by the mathematician Luca Paccioli in 1494.

We can assume then that accounting must fulfil some basic purpose if it has survived and stood this test of time. There are in fact two fundamental purposes for accounting. First, to report to external interested parties, particularly owners, on how well the business has done over a particular time period. This is the *external* reporting function, and falls within the area of financial accounting. Secondly, accounting provides information to managers about the financial health of the business on an ongoing basis so that the managers can react accordingly (the *internal* planning, decision-making and control function often described as management accounting).

Accounting is based upon the recording of transactions in terms of money, and has its roots in the value and use of money. So we need to begin by examining the role of money in business and accounting.

Money – the common measure

Most of the economies in the world have moved from a barter to a money-based system of trade. Money is used as a medium of exchange in the acquisition and disposal of resources. Without money an economy could never handle the vast quantities of transactions common to any 'developed' country. Money is also used to store wealth which can at a later stage be invested into a particular enterprise or process.

Entities such as individuals, governments and businesses all use money (although most of the accounting in this book is about businesses). Three key money measures are regarded as important:

1. Measuring the flow of money during a period of time.
2. Measurement of financial position at a chosen moment in time.
3. Measurement of management's use of economic resources.

We will now take a closer look at each of these three measures.

Measuring the flow of money during a period of time

First, flow measurement is important in order to ascertain whether the entity is running successfully. We need to know the total size of the flows; what are their constituent parts in terms of money flowing out of and into the business. We also need to know about differences between cash inflows and cash outflows. You will often read in the financial press that a particular business is suffering a cash-flow crisis which means that, for some particular reason, the business has more money flowing out of the business than is coming in. This is a very serious situation and one which a business can only sustain for so long. Eventually it will run out of cash, will be declared bankrupt and will cease to exist.

Measurement of financial position at a chosen moment in time

Financial position is also a measure of the money (or money equivalent) which the entity owns or owes at a particular moment. Business entities are often assessed upon the size and type of the assets which they own. A key question often asked is: Can the entity meet its liabilities as and when they fall due? If not then it may be declared insolvent. That is to say that the business owns assets but does not have sufficient cash to meet immediate obligations.

You may have heard of the 'Footsie 100'. Published in the *Financial Times* (FT) each day this is a list of the top 100 companies quoted on the Stock Exchange (SE), hence FTSE 100 index or 'footsie'. This index is a ranking of companies according to their market capitalisation (or market value), and in effect represents the economic value of money and other assets which the company controls. The largest UK companies at the top of the footsie at the time of writing were as shown in Exhibit 4.1.

The values in Exhibit 4.1 are only one measure of financial position – an economic value (i.e. the value that people are prepared to pay for their shares at that

Exhibit 4.1	Position	Company	Sector	Market value at September 2003 (£billion)
Top UK companies by market value	1	BP	Oil	98
	2	HSBC	Banks	89
	3	Vodafone	Telecoms	83
	4	GlaxoSmithKline	Pharmaceuticals	76
	5	Royal Bank of Scotland	Banks	49
	6	Astrazeneca	Pharmaceuticals	46
	7	Shell	Oil	39
	8	Barclays	Banks	31
	9	HBOS	Banks	28

date). However, accountants calculate financial position in a different way – financial position based upon costs incurred rather than upon current economic values. The reason for this is that economic values are subject to rapid change and are difficult to prove (we would expect, for example, that by the time you read this book the values in Exhibit 4.1 will have changed quite significantly), while the financial accountant is concerned with working with values that can be clearly demonstrated and are capable of independent audit.

Measurement of management's use of economic resources

Thus flow and position measurement is an important element within the accounting framework of reports and we deal in more detail with these measures later in this chapter and in Chapters 5, 6 and 7. The final element of measurement is to judge the way in which managers have used the economic resources within the business (always related back to a monetary value). This element can be measured in a variety of different ways, including:

- the extent of the accounting profit or loss
- measuring accounting profit as a percentage return on assets
- the growth of sales, cash flows or profits
- the ability of the directors and managers to hit the targets set by the owners.

This performance measurement aspect is considered in Chapters 8 and 9.

Our study of accounting in this text is concerned with all three of these elements – the presentation of flows, financial positions and the use of economic resources by managers. The power of accounting rests on its ability to be utilised within a broad range of economic entities from something as simple as your local newsagent, right through to BT and Hanson Trust. The beauty of accounting is that the basic accounting rules remain the same. Therefore, once you have learned the rules you can apply them to a range of different enterprises and, providing you treat your analysis with a degree of caution, you will be able to form an independent view as to how a particular business is performing. You will also be able to make informed comparisons between different businesses.

Pictures of an organisation

If you were asked to describe any business organisation that you can think of, you could probably provide a number of different 'pictures':

- a *physical* picture: the buildings, equipment, fittings, motor vehicles
- a *people* picture: numbers, ages, gender, types of personnel
- a *products* picture: what is made or provided for customers
- and, after studying this text, we hope that you could paint a *financial* picture: the accountant's description.

All of these pictures tell only part of the story and the accountant's view is no different. When studying accounting we tend to focus just upon the financial picture, and accountants produce a series of financial statements at the end of the year which purport to represent a **true and fair** view of the business. Keep in mind that, as the accounting statements are presented only in money terms, they will give an incomplete view of the business.

TASK 4.1	**Pictures of an organisation**
	Which of the above 'pictures' may not be represented within the accountant's financial picture?

■ ■ ■ ■ The financial views of a business

In painting this financial picture the accountant uses a generally agreed system of classification which can be summarised as in Exhibit 4.2.

Exhibit 4.2 is based upon are three of the major accounting statements produced by an accountant for a business at the end of a **financial year**. Assets and Liabilities along the top layer are represented on the balance sheet. The middle layer, containing Expenses and Revenues represents the profit and loss account, and the bottom layer, which focuses upon Cash Inflows and Outflows, the cash-flow statement. At the moment, do not be too worried about the terminology or how these statements might work, since we will explain these as we work through the examples. In this chapter we will focus upon the first two statements – the top and middle layers.

Exhibit 4.2	Aspects of the organisation		Accounting reports
Financial views of a business	**ASSETS** Things that the business owns – would include land, buildings, machines, computers, vehicles, cash	**LIABILITIES** The amounts owed to others – for example creditors, loans, and owners funds	**POSITION** Called the balance sheet – a static view of assets and liabilities at one moment in time
	EXPENSES Resources used up in running the business – would include rents, cost of goods sold, wages, energy costs, insurances	**REVENUES** Mainly the sale of goods or services	**PROFIT/LOSS** Called the income statement or profit and loss account – a moving picture over a period of time of revenues and expenses
	CASH OUTFLOWS Outflows of cash, including payments to suppliers, new vehicles, payment of dividends or tax, payment of wages	**CASH INFLOWS** For example, receipts from customers, tax refunds received from government	**= CASH SURPLUS or Deficit** Called the cash-flow statement – a moving picture over a period of time of all cash flows

For the moment, notice that the model represents an important system of coding which enables users and preparers of the accounts to communicate with one another. It is vital to your progress in accounting that you understand these general classifications and can apply them consistently. We will use the Accounting Quadrant to help in your early understanding of the basic concepts which underlie these crucial business reports.

■ ■ ■ ■ Links between decisions and financial reports

One way of viewing published accounting reports is as a set of financial numbers which simply tell us about all previous decisions made by the firm's managers. Essentially this is a process which links decisions and accounting reports. The broad strategic decisions about the firm's markets, products and resources lead to the detailed operational decisions which actually cause things to happen within the business. These fundamental decisions cause the firm to enter into transactions with other people and groups (for example, suppliers and customers).

Consequently, transactions are recorded in the financial accounting system and give rise to the following major headings within the system:

ASSETS and LIABILITIES which appear in the balance sheet

and

EXPENSES and REVENUES which are shown in the profit and loss account.

Finally, business performance as reflected in the balance sheet and profit and loss account, leads to refinement and revision of future strategy for the business.

It will be helpful, at this stage, to understand the basic principles upon which transactions are processed within the accounting system and upon which the financial reports are based (although we are *not* aiming to turn you into an accountant!). We will introduce a simple model (the Accounting Quadrant – see below) and use this model to demonstrate the recording of transactions in the accounting system.

The key aspects of this quadrant are the top layer, which represents the balance sheet, and the bottom layer, which represents the profit and loss account. To use the quadrant you need to understand fully the meaning of the four key words: assets, liabilities, revenues and expenses.

ASSETS	LIABILITIES
EXPENSES	REVENUE

ASSETS   Assets are items which are owned by the firm and have been acquired at sometime in the firm's past. Some assets can be seen as *fixed* (e.g. land, vehicles, machines, computers); these are kept and used over a period of years. Other assets are *current* (e.g. **stock**, **debtors**, cash); these are of a more temporary nature, are constantly changing and are probably only held by the firm for a short time.

LIABILITIES   Liabilities are any amounts owed by the firm, perhaps loans to the bank or unpaid bills. This section of the quadrant also includes the (at first sight) slightly odd liability to the *owner* of the business. If the owner invests £100 into the business, in accounting terms the business owes that money back to the owner. We can see the logic of this in that (should the business fold up) its value is paid back to the people (owners) who made the original investment in it. From a legal perspective the business and the owner have different legal personalities.

REVENUES   Revenues represent the value of goods and services sold to customers. Revenues are not the same as cash received but are related to the point of sale for our particular product. Very often this will represent the moment when the customer takes possession of the goods or service. In a supermarket the point of sale when revenue is recorded will be the same as the moment when cash changes hands. However, for an airline the revenue is earned (and recorded) when the ticket is sold, even though the cash may not be paid until later.

EXPENSES   Expenses are the resources used up by the firm in generating the revenues and could include wages, costs of materials, rents, energy costs or insurance. As with revenues, the cash flow (which is called 'expenditure') may not be in the same period as the recording of the expense. For example, an hotel may use £3000 of electricity during August (which is the month that the accountant would record the expense) while it may be a month later that the cash is actually paid to the energy company (the cash expenditure point).

Notice that, on the quadrant, the four main sections appear in a very particular order. Viewed horizontally, assets and liabilities form the balance sheet, or financial position, while expenses and revenues give us a picture of the profit (or loss) of the firm. Looking vertically, a business has to gain money (either from revenues from the sale of products or from borrowings and liabilities) and uses that money (either by buying assets or by running the business – expenses).

The best way to understand the quadrant is probably through the use of illustrations, and we will now take you through one illustration, and then offer further examples for you to consider.

ILLUSTRATION 4.1

53 LINKS BETWEEN DECISIONS AND FINANCIAL REPORTS

The quadrant in action

1. A retail business begins with £1500 of owners' (shareholders') money – all of this capital is represented by £1500 cash in the bank.
2. The firm invests £500 of this cash in fixed assets.
3. £1000 of raw material stocks are supplied on credit (i.e. not yet paid for).
4. £700 of the stocks are sold for £1400 cash.
5. Other expenses of £100 are paid for cash.

Let us try to record these transactions onto the quadrant to see the effect which each transaction has on revenues, expenses, assets and liabilities. Because we are considering transactions, notice that there will be two aspects to each item; in other words, the firm is involved in an *exchange* and the quadrant must reflect this – hence the two-sided aspect to each transaction.

The resultant quadrant is shown below. Notice the following aspects of these transactions and how they have been recorded:

1. The owners put in £1500 of their own money. So the cash asset increases by £1500 and the business 'owes' the same amount to its shareholders (owners). It may seem odd that the business owes money to its owners, but remember: the firm has a separate legal existence from its shareholders – the firm belongs to the owners, thus all of the value in the business is, legally, owed back to the owners.

ASSETS				LIABILITIES
Cash	1500	Shareholders		1500
EXPENSES				REVENUE

2. The £500 of cash invested in fixed assets means that we are trading cash for other assets, so cash goes down and fixed assets goes up.

ASSETS				LIABILITIES
Fixed assets	500	Shareholders		1500
Cash	1000			
EXPENSES				REVENUE

3. £1000 of raw material stocks are supplied on credit – the business has gained a current asset (stock) in exchange for a liability to a supplier.

ASSETS				LIABILITIES
Fixed assets	500	Shareholders		1500
Stocks	1000	Creditors		1000
Cash	1000			
EXPENSES				REVENUE

4. £700 of the stocks are sold for £1400 cash. This transaction has two separate outcomes:
   - First, stock of £700 has now disappeared from our assets, so stock asset is reduced. The goods have been sold and the £700 now represents an *expense* (cost of goods sold). We have used up £700 of our resources in generating the sale.

ASSETS				LIABILITIES
Fixed assets		500	Shareholders	1500
Stocks	(1000 − 700)	300	Creditors	1000
Cash		1000		
EXPENSES				**REVENUE**
Cost of goods sold		700		

- Secondly, the goods were sold for £1400 to the customer. Thus our revenue (sales) increases by £1400 for the value of goods provided to customers. The other side of this transaction is that cash has increased by £1400.

ASSETS				LIABILITIES
Fixed assets		500	Shareholders	1500
Stocks	(1000 − 700)	300	Creditors	1000
Cash	(1000 + 1400)	2400		
EXPENSES				**REVENUE**
Cost of goods sold		700	Sales	1400

5. Other fixed expenses of running the business are £100, and cash reduces by the same amount.

ASSETS				LIABILITIES
Fixed assets		500	Shareholders	1500
Stocks	(1000 − 700)	300	Creditors	1000
Cash	(2400 − 100)	2300		
EXPENSES				**REVENUE**
Cost of goods sold		700	Sales	1400
Other expenses		100		

▶

TASK 4.2	Reviewing the quadrants

Go back and total each side of each quadrant vertically. You will find that the totals are the same. Why do you think this might be?

The final quadrant for Illustration 4.1 now appears as follows (with transaction numbers given in brackets).

ASSETS				LIABILITIES	
Fixed assets		(2)	500	Shareholders	1500 (1)
Stocks	1000	(3)		Creditors	1000 (3)
	(700)	(4)			
			300		
Cash	1500	(1)			
	(500)	(2)			
	1400	(4)			
	(100)	(5)			
			2300		

EXPENSES			REVENUE	
Cost of goods sold		700 (4)	Sales	1400 (1)
Other expenses		100 (5)		
TOTALS		**3900**	**TOTALS**	**3900**

TASK 4.3	What if?

How would the quadrant in Illustration 4.1 have changed if:

1. instead of selling the stocks for cash (£1400) we had allowed the customer some time to pay?
2. we had taken out a long-term loan of £500?
3. we had paid off £250 of our liability to the supplier?

TASK 4.4

Footballers – expense or asset?

Look up on the club's website or write to any Premier League football club for their accounts and see how players are recorded.

Are they an asset on the balance sheet or has the cost of purchase been written off to the profit and loss account as an expense?

Why do you think different clubs have treated the expense of players in different ways?

Reflections on the Accounting Quadrant

We can see from these early illustrations and tasks that the Accounting Quadrant provides a mechanism for drawing up the 'accountant's picture' of the business, showing assets, liabilities, revenues and expenses. The quadrant provides a structured approach to the key accounting statements: profit and loss account and balance sheet. Every transaction will have two aspects (because of the exchange nature of the transactions) and the quadrant reflects this.

We should emphasise here that the quadrant is a powerful educational tool which should aid your understanding of the way in which accounting reports work. But it is *not* an accounting technique (for complex businesses it would be impossible to record the thousands of transactions onto a quadrant, and you would not find quadrant information within the accounting systems of real businesses).

Notes about the quadrant for students with some previous experience of accounting

If you have studied accounting previously you may have worked with **debits** and **credits** without using the quadrant and may be wondering whether it is really necessary. You should consider the links between the quadrant and 'double-entry' bookkeeping: asset and expense accounts are (primarily) debit balances, while revenues and liability accounts would normally be expected to show a credit balance. The double-entry system is merely a fuller and more detailed form of the quadrant – clearly once we get beyond a handful of transactions it is not possible to record everything onto one page, hence the need for separate 'accounts' of each type of asset/expense/revenue/liability.

The first point, then, is that there is *no* conflict between the quadrant and double-entry bookkeeping. Even though you may have studied bookkeeping, did you understand *why* the accounts worked as they did? We believe that the quadrant provides insights into the underlying logic of double entry and should help to deepen your understanding of the mechanics of accounting.

Secondly, the quadrant provides an holistic view of the accountant's picture – by placing all transactions onto one page we can see the inbuilt simplicity and elegance of the accounting system – each new transaction provides (if we need it) a fresh balance sheet, and we can readily see the effect of exchange. In particular, the quadrant explains some of the less obvious aspects of accounting as assets become expenses (stock becomes part of the cost of sales, and later we will see how fixed assets costs are spread out as a **depreciation** charge).

This text places more emphasis on your ability to use and interpret accounting information than upon your skill in using double-entry bookkeeping to produce financial statements. The quadrant challenges you to explain how and why the accounting system operates rather than working at the superficial level of number manipulation.

TASK 4.5

A second quadrant example

Produce a quadrant for these transactions:

1. Start a business, receiving £1000 of cash from shareholders.
2. Buy some equipment (fixed asset) for £500 cash.
3. Buy stock valued at £400 on credit (i.e. without paying immediately) from the supplier.
4. Pay your supplier £350 in cash.
5. Sell all of the stock for £700, but receive no payment.
6. Customers pay £500 in cash in part-payment for the sales above.

Here is a hint to help you in tackling this task – we suggest that the method you use is as follows:

■ Work through the transactions from 1 to 6 in order.
■ Each transaction (1–6) should be represented by two entries – mark each one with the transaction number in brackets.
■ Decreases in amounts should be marked in brackets, e.g. (500) means decrease by 500.
■ Produce a total for each of the four sections of the quadrant.
■ Add the two sections of the quadrant on the left-hand side (ASSETS + EXPENSES), and the two sections of the quadrant on the right-hand side (LIABILITIES + REVENUES) – the totals should be the same.

If you record the transactions correctly you should obtain totals of £1750 on

Clearly the quadrant is not the format that would be used by an accountant to present the information to users. If you were to examine a number of published accounts of **public limited companies** you would soon discover that the layout adopted is in a very prescribed format. This aids comparison and analysis. The layout of the accounts as we shall later discover is governed by a whole series of rules and conventions. Using the information from this last task a more typical layout of the profit and loss account and balance sheet would appear as follows:

Profit and loss account	
Sales	700
Less cost of goods sold	(400)
Gross profit	300
Less other expenses	0
Net profit	**300**

Notice that this is merely a summary of the bottom half of the quadrant, bringing together expenses and revenues. The intriguing question to consider is: What happens to the **bottom-line** or **net profit** of £300? A moment's reflection should tell us that this profit belongs to the owners (shareholders) so in the balance sheet which follows we will add it on to the owners' stake in the business. In effect the business (in financial terms) has grown by £300 so that the owners' initial stake has jumped from £1000 to £1300.

Balance sheet				
Equipment		500	Shareholders' funds (1000 + 300 profit)	1300
Stocks	0			
Debtors	200			
Cash	650			
	850			
			Creditor	50
	1350			1350

Notice a couple of important aspects of this statement:

1. To re-emphasise a point already made, the balance sheet is *in balance*; each side totals to the same number. This is not surprising as we have recorded an *equal* and *opposite* amount for each transaction. In some accounting texts you will see this 'natural balance' position as the accounting equation:

$$\text{Assets} = \text{Liabilities} + \text{Capital}$$

2. The profit was £300, while the cash balance has fallen by £350 (£1000 − £650). So *profit is not cash* – each is a measure of performance but they are rarely the same number.

Looking back on the two initial quadrant examples it is worth noting that accountants have developed profit and loss accounts and balance sheets as standard reports to transmit financial information. These reports are designed primarily for the owners of the business, which in the case of a **limited company** will be the ordinary shareholders. It is assumed that the owners will need to know how much profit has been earned and to form a view as to the financial stability of the business.

TASK 4.6

County Brewery

Finally, we suggest that you complete a much fuller example (County Brewery) which has other types of transactions. These numbers are loosely based upon the Midlands-based brewer, Mansfield Brewery, prior to their takeover by Wolverhampton and Dudley.

County Brewery's initial quadrant at the end of Year 1 looks like this:

▶

ASSETS			LIABILITIES
	(£m)		(£m)
Property	100	Shareholders' funds	110
Machines and vehicles	50	Long-term loans	23
Stocks	8		
Debtors	11	Short-term creditors	40
Cash/Bank	4		
EXPENSES			REVENUES

The bottom part of the quadrant has no values as the business has yet to commence trading in this particular financial year.

Summary of transactions for the current year

	(£m)
Investment in new machines (for cash)	32
Sales to customers (on credit)	125
Cash received from customers	117
Materials bought from suppliers on credit	30
Cost of materials used in sales	25
Other production costs (on credit)	55
Marketing and administration costs (on credit)	20
Cash paid to creditors	96
New loan taken out	15
Interest paid on all loans	6

1. Update the initial quadrant for these transactions.

Additional information

2. The following additional information is now given about County Brewery for Year 2. Include this additional information in the quadrant and prepare a balance sheet and profit and loss account.

■ *Depreciation on machines and vehicles is £6m.* Depreciation is a measure of the amount of fixed asset value 'used up' in earning the sales revenue. Businesses calculate the depreciation for the year and treat it as an expense in arriving at the profit calculation. For the balance sheet the business then calculates *all* depreciation since the assets were first bought and shows the full amount of depreciation as a deduction from the fixed assets on the balance sheet. Depreciation is an example of why cash and profits are not the same measure. For cash flows the original

▶

cash outflow will be recorded when the asset is purchased; for profit a share of that cost (i.e. the depreciation) will be shown in each year that the fixed asset is used. (See Chapter 5 for a more detailed discussion of depreciation.)

- *Tax on this year's profits is calculated at £4m.* Tax is the government's share of the profits. Thus we must show a 'before' and 'after' tax figure for profit. Notice that although this is calculated at the end of the year it is not paid in cash until the following year, but is a liability at the end of the year. Tax is a further example of why profit and cash are not the same measure – in any one year the tax for that year should be shown as a deduction against profits, but the cash will not flow out of the business until the following year.
- *£2m of dividend is declared on this year's profits.* This is the cash which will be paid out to shareholders as a short-term return. As with the tax charge the dividend will be paid in the following year.

3. What do you think about the performance of County Brewery based on these figures?

Hints on this task
If your calculations are correct the following figures should emerge:

	(£m)
Profit before tax	13
Profit after tax	9
Retained profits (profits left after allowing for all tax and dividends)	7
Total assets	210
Total liabilities (except for owners' liability)	93
Owners' stake	117

Reflections on profit and loss accounts and balance sheets

Our concern in this chapter has been to emphasise the two major financial statements: the profit and loss account and the balance sheet. It may be worth recapping and reflecting on some of the important issues which have been raised.

Profit and loss account

The profit and loss account is a statement that gives a financial picture of the revenues matched with the relevant expenses of an enterprise for a past period (normally one year). Assuming that the revenues are greater than the expenses, the business will show a profit. If the expenses are greater than the revenues then a loss will result. Assuming a profit has been earned then the business will first of all have to pay tax to the government (called corporation tax). This is an important source of revenue for the government. During a recession corporation tax has the effect of lowering corporate profits and therefore less company tax is paid into the Exchequer.

After the tax has been paid the directors must then decide what to do with the 'after tax profits'. Usually a proportion is paid to the shareholders (called a dividend). The vast majority of profit, though, remains in the business and is used for investment in new assets and to help the business to grow. Profits are a vital source of finance for businesses and a sign of a successful business is that it is financing much of its own growth internally from profits. But profits are not an amount of spare cash which the business has lying around. The only cash the business will have will be shown on the balance sheet under the cash and bank items.

Balance sheet

The balance sheet is a financial snapshot of the business. It is a position statement – a list of the assets and liabilities which the business has on the last day of a given period of time. It is essentially a stewardship statement, showing the ways in which monies invested in the business have been used by managers. A balance sheet does not necessarily give a current value of assets and liabilities. Fixed assets and stocks, for example, will often be shown at original acquisition cost even though the assets may have been bought some time previously. This 'historic cost' approach may seem odd, and can certainly lead to difficulties when we attempt to interpret a balance sheet, but be clear at this early stage: a balance sheet is *not* a statement of current economic values. One view of the balance sheet is as a kind of 'dumping ground' for all the 'left-over' balances – those items which have not yet been allocated to the profit and loss account or which have some financial value at the end of the period.

The format of accounting reports

For the Accounting Quadrant we have adopted a layout in the accounting statements with the sole intention of facilitating your understanding of accounting. To conclude this chapter we need to devote some space to the detailed presentation of our key accounting reports.

Partly from tradition, partly from legislation, accountants usually adopt what is termed as the vertical layout (each statement reads from top to bottom, in contrast to the horizontal view we have seen in the quadrant) in presenting the annual statements of profit and loss account and balance sheet. The vertical layout, it is argued, makes it much easier to present comparative information on a year-by-year basis. Although the vertical layout (because it moves away from the basic principles of the quadrant) may look strange at first sight, the content and accounting principles used are just the same.

To demonstrate the vertical format we will use an illustration of an imaginary company called Sparkes plc. We suggest that you review carefully the contents of Sparkes' profit and loss account and balance sheet and familiarise yourself with the layout and content. To assist you in this process we have numbered certain items and provided notes for a fuller explanation.

ILLUSTRATION 4.2

63 THE FORMAT OF ACCOUNTING REPORTS

Sparkes plc

Sparkes plc – profit and loss account for one year ending 31 December

		(£)
Sales		33 260
Cost of goods sold		22 170
1. Gross profit		11 090
Cash expenses		
Wages and salaries	4 970	
Rent and rates	840	
Heating, lighting	296	
Insurances	150	
Vehicle expenses	200	
Miscellaneous expenses	440	
	6 896	
Non-cash expenses		
Depreciation on		
furniture	400	
vehicles	250	
	650	
		7 546
2. Profit before tax		3 544
Taxation		1 500
3. Profit after tax		2 044
Dividends		600
4. Profits retained		1 444

Looking at Sparkes' profit and loss account you will notice that it shows four different levels of profit:

1. Gross profit is the difference between the sales revenue and the cost of all goods/services sold.

2. Net profit before tax is the **surplus** after deducting both cash and non-cash expenses from the **gross profit**. This gives the level of profit before allowing for that part of the profit which is taken by the government in tax.

3. Net profit after tax is the surplus which is available for retention or for the distribution of dividend.

After deducting dividends (the monies given back to the owners of the business by way of return on their investment) from profit after tax, we arrive at:

4. Profit retained which is profit kept within the business to help the business expand. We note again that this is not the same as cash!!

▶

Following the profit and loss account let us now consider Sparkes' vertical balance sheet:

Sparkes plc – Balance sheet at 31 December

	Cost (£)	Depreciation (£)	Net (£)
5. Fixed assets			
furniture and fittings	4 000	1 760	2 240
vehicles	1 700	550	1 150
	5 700	2 310	3 390
6. Current assets			
stock		2 060	
debtors		5 350	
cash		4 236	
		11 646	
7. Current liabilities (less than one year)			
creditors	4 300		
taxation	1 500		
dividends	600		
		6 400	
8. Working capital			5 246
			8 636
9. Less long-term loans (those not repayable for at least one year)			1 000
10. Net assets			7 636
11. Share capital			2 000
Retained profits (4 192 accumulated profits from previous years + 1 444 retained this year)			5 636
12. Equity			7 636

5. Fixed assets are assets which are expected to last for more than one accounting period. These are listed in the order of permanence. Following the deduction of all depreciation this leaves us with the net book value of the fixed assets.

6. Current assets are assets which the business anticipates will normally be consumed within one accounting period, and are listed in reverse order of liquidity (the speed with which they can be converted to cash) with the least liquid first and the most liquid last.

7. Current liabilities are the amounts owed by the firm which will be repaid within one year.

▶

8. Working capital sometimes called net current assets, is the difference between current assets and current liabilities. This is a significant figure for understanding the liquidity and financial stability of the firm, and is discussed in more detail in the chapters on cash-flow management and ratio analysis (Chapters 7 and 8).

9 and 10. Net assets represents the net investment in all assets of the business by the owners, and is merely the fixed assets plus **working capital** less **long-term loans**.

Thus the **net asset** total provides a value (albeit at cost) of the business. The remainder of the balance sheet in Sparkes shows how the shareholders have funded that investment.

11. Share capital is the amount invested by the owners in the business in terms of the shares that were originally purchased at face value.

12. Equity is the total investment by the owners represented by their original investment in **share capital** together with the balance of reserves which have been created by non-distributed profits. The shareholders own the business and therefore any undistributed profits belong to them and are included within the **equity** total. Note that equity (the shareholders' investment) must be equal to net assets (the assets owned).

The Sparkes example has used a vertical layout, and this is the common format used by accountants when producing external published reports. Although at first sight it may appear a little strange to you, having grown familiar with the quadrant, on closer inspection you will note that items are grouped together in the usual way. The main difference is that liabilities, instead of being shown separately, are deducted from assets. This format is used to make the information more 'friendly' to naive users of accounting information. To reinforce your understanding of the vertical presentation we ask you to carry out one more task.

TASK 4.7

Vertical layout for County Brewery

Return to the County Brewery task from earlier in this chapter. Now re-present your profit and loss account and balance sheet in a vertical format following the Sparkes illustration.

SUMMARY

Having completed this chapter you should now understand the following key points:

- Money is the only unit of measurement used by financial accountants.
- The transactions of an organisation are classified and recorded in the accounting system under series of key headings – assets, liabilities, revenues and expenses. The transactions reflect the 'exchange' nature of business and, as such, each transaction has two equal and opposite aspects.

- A profit and loss account is a period statement which shows how well the business has performed during a particular year. Within the statement we see a list of revenue and expense items which, after matching, shows the relevant profit or loss for the period.

- A balance sheet is a position statement which shows the assets and liabilities of the business. The values shown are based on historic cost and do not reflect current economic values.

- 'Profit' in the profit and loss account does not equal the 'cash' figure in the balance sheet. However, having enough cash to pay the bills is vital for the survival of any business and we pursue this issue further in Chapter 7.

Please turn to the back of the book for detailed answers to questions marked with a 🛟 . Answers to the other questions can be found on the companion website at www.thomsonlearning.co.uk/accountingandfinance/hand

REVIEW QUESTIONS

RQ 4.1 What important information is excluded from the financial statements of a business?

🛟 **RQ 4.2** What does a balance sheet tell you about an organisation?

🛟 **RQ 4.3** Why does a balance sheet balance?

🛟 **RQ 4.4** Give three reasons why profit is not the same as cash within a company's accounts.

NUMERICAL PROBLEMS

🛟 **NP 4.1 Albert Adey – a quadrant problem** On the 1 January Albert Adey started a business buying and selling a variety of goods for the growing leisure market. The following events took place in the first few days of January.

1 January – Albert opened a business account at the Church Street branch of the bank, paying in a cheque for £1000 drawn on his private account. After a long discussion with the branch manager, overdraft facilities for up to £10 000 were agreed, Albert depositing the deeds of his private residence with the bank as security for the overdraft.

1 January – A small building was rented for £2000 (this rent would cover four months or 120 days) and paid for by cheque.

6 January – Office equipment was purchased for £400 (paid by cheque).

7 January – Stock for resale was purchased at an agreed price of £10 000 to be paid not later than 28 February.

10 January – £5500 of stock (which had cost £5000) was sold to two customers. The first paid £1000 in cash, and the second agreed to pay £4500 in one month's time.

11 January – Albert visited two other prospective customers. Both expressed interest in his products and he was delighted to receive a firm order for the balance of his stock (which had cost him £5000) at a price of £6000, to be delivered on the 31 March. Cash was to be paid on delivery of the goods.

From this information you are asked to produce:

1. An Accounting Quadrant for these transactions.

2. A balance sheet on 11 January, after all of the transactions have been completed, and a calculation of the profit for this period.

NP 4.2 Adam Asteron – opening and closing financial positions Adam Asteron had only the following assets and liabilities at the opening of business on the 1 September:

	(£)
Cash in the bank	975
Stock in hand	4274
Creditors	953
Debtors	328

1. What is Adam's opening equity?

During September the following transactions took place:

	(£)
2 September – Telephone bill for September paid	246
5 September – Paid to creditors	352
7 September – Stock purchased for cash	256
9 September – Rent for September paid	165
12 September – Purchases bought from suppliers on credit	1153
16 September – Stock costing £423 was sold for cash	525
22 September – Stock costing £890 sold on credit	1135
28 September – Salaries paid in cash	250

2. Prepare two Accounting Quadrants to reflect the financial position of the business at the beginning and end of September.

WEB RESOURCES

www.thomsonlearning.co.uk/accountingandfinance/hand

The companion website has free additional resources for you to use alongside this book. If you are a student you can access material to help with revision, including practice questions with answers to test how much of the material you have understood. There are also useful hyperlinks to companies and information sources mentioned in the book as well as interactive quizzes. There are additional resources for lecturers using this book on their courses; the details can be found in the preface at the front of this book.

CHAPTER 5

A deeper understanding of the balance sheet and profit and loss account

LEARNING OBJECTIVES

This chapter covers a range of issues which help to explain why accounting is not just **bookkeeping** – judgement is needed in the preparation of financial accounts. After studying this chapter you should be able to:

- understand how judgements made by the **directors** of a company can affect the view of the users of accounts
- discuss how profit differs from cash, including issues of **revenue recognition** and cost allocation
- discuss the importance of stock and fixed assets in the accounts, including issues of valuation in the accounts
- understand and demonstrate techniques of deriving figures for the accounts where judgement is required.

Introduction

In the last chapter we explained the general picture regarding financial reports and finished with the Sparkes plc example to show how companies publish financial accounting information. This chapter continues in the financial accounting area and sets out to deepen your understanding by returning to issues which have been only lightly touched upon so far. A theme of the chapter is the subjective nature of some accounting measures. There is more judgement involved in the calculation of profit and of asset values than you might have imagined.

Accounting numbers sometimes relate to 'facts' which are beyond dispute (e.g. last month's rent cost) but are frequently about imprecise measures (e.g. 'How much is this stock actually worth now?' or 'How long will this fixed asset last for?'). In this chapter we will focus on two major areas in which accountants are called particularly to exercise skill and judgement; the valuation of two kinds of asset which appear in the balance sheet but also affect other areas of the accounts: stock and fixed assets.

We will explain further how the valuation of these two assets has a major impact upon reported profit. But first let's take the big picture view and see how the balance sheet and the profit and loss account, which we introduced in the last chapter, interrelate with each other. The balance sheet is a snapshot, a picture of the assets and liabilities of the business, at a point in time. The profit and loss account fills in the gap, if you like; it outlines the story of the events that take place between the two balance sheets. So when you look at a set of **published accounts** you see two balance sheets, *as at* the start and the end of the year in question, and the profit and loss account *for the year ending* on the later of the two balance sheet dates (see Exhibit 5.1). Together with the other information in the accounts (which we will discuss in a later chapter) you can then build up your understanding of what happened during the year.

Before we examine this issue in more detail we must first be clear as to what the term 'profit' means.

Another look at profit

Profit is a word which is commonly used but generally misunderstood. Some people might suggest that the term 'profit' is too vague to be of use to financial managers or investors. It is, though, a concept that investors are clearly interested in when evaluating and ranking investment opportunities. Managers are clearly aware of the importance of reporting the profit figure of the business as it may well have an impact upon the level of salary that they may receive as well as the rating that the **Stock Market** will award to the company. The Stock Market ranks highly those companies which manage to make consistently good profits. Therefore managers are under some pressure to present an ever-increasing level of reported profit. In response to these pressures the standard setting body of the accountancy profession is trying to educate users away from a simplistic approach towards profit by requiring the disclosure of a range of profit figures which can be used to evaluate businesses. (We will discuss the 'interpretation of accounting statements' issue further in Chapter 8).

Exhibit 5.1

A pictorial view of the links between the main accounting statements

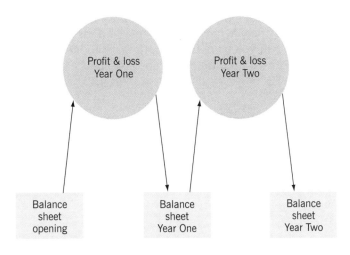

We have already seen that accountants define profit in a very specific way:

PROFIT = REVENUE LESS EXPENSES

Where REVENUE is the value of goods and services provided to customers and EXPENSES are the costs of resources used in creating the revenues. However, there are other views of what profit is.

Economics, profit and capital maintenance

Economists are also interested in the concepts which surround capital and income. They take a very different view to that of the accountant. An economist would view income as being the product of capital and would hold that we must only consume income, retaining the 'real' stock of original capital – the capital maintenance concept. Put another way: we may eat the fruit off the branch (income) but we must not consume the branch (capital). This is analogous to Hicks's definition of income. Another economist, Fisher, has provided a different definition of income: that it is the surplus left after maintaining the purchasing power of the original stock of capital.

TASK 5.1

Hicks and Fisher

Can you compare and contrast the difference between Hicks's and Fisher's definitions of income?

The question of capital maintenance does enter into debates about what accounting information should show. In particular, many critics suggest that accounting reports should incorporate inflation-adjusted figures; if this were done, they argue, then accountants could calculate the real economic profit, and the financial capital of the business would not suffer from depletion. The argument goes on to suggest that presenting accounts which use figures at their original historic amounts (how much was originally spent or earned) misleads users of accounts by not providing for capital erosion which is a natural consequence of inflation and the falling purchasing power of money. This is a topic that many people have spent a great deal of time researching and discussing. For now we ask you to notice simply that the measurement of profit and asset values is confused because of the unstable nature of money measurement.

TASK 5.2

Capital maintenance

You had £500 this time last year. You earned £2000 during the year, and spent £1900. Inflation ran at a rate of 5 per cent during this year. How much better/worse off are you?

Profit measurement and time

The measurement of profit (P) measurement is a key task for the accountant. Generally the measurement entails the matching of revenues (R) and expenses (E) for a given time period (often one year), and graphically can be shown as in Exhibit 5.2. The subscript numbers in Exhibit 5.2 are designed to illustrate different time periods, in this case years. For the accountant profit is a result of measuring revenues and expenses for a particular time period and the matching of one against the other. So the allocation of revenue and expenses to time periods is important because of the effect on reported profit for those periods.

Revenue recognition

Recognition is the process of incorporating an item into the financial statements. Revenue recognition is often, but not always, straightforward – being the value of all sales made in one accounting period. But when exactly is a sale made? As a consequence of this question accountants have developed rules which are to be adopted when assessing the relevance of a particular transaction. Rules for revenue recognition (the realisation concept) have been developed to cover different situations:

1. Revenue may be recognised during production

This applies to items which take a long time to complete; for example, building a road or an office block. Often the construction period covers more than one accounting period; there is an agreed contract for when instalments of the purchase price will be paid and when particular elements of the build will be completed. It would be misleading to the reader of accounts to ignore the project until it was completed and then put a big chunk of profit (or loss!) into the profit and loss account. This would not reflect the activity that had been going on throughout the earlier period(s). Far more sensible then, to allocate to the revenue and expense items in the profit and loss account for each period affected the revenue earned and matching expenditure on materials and wages etc. so that the reader is aware of what activities have been occurring in the period.

Exhibit 5.2

Profit is derived from matching the revenue and expenses in a period

Year 1	Year 2	Year 3
$R_1 - E_1 = P_1$	$R_2 - E_2 = P_2$	$R_3 - E_3 = P_3$

2. Revenue may be recognised at the point of sale

The vast majority of transactions fall into this category. Think, for example, about doing the weekly shop at the supermarket or sending for items on mail order. The retailer will have a system (often computerised) for accumulating the value of all the sales made in a period to form the sales (or turnover) figure that you see in their profit and loss account at the end of the year. This applies to sales on both cash and credit terms; in other words it refers to when the goods change hands regardless of when the money is received. If the customer is given a period of credit the seller records the sale but also keeps a note of what the customer owes them (refer back to Task 4.3 for an example of this).

3. Revenue may be recognised after the sale is made

This approach may be appropriate for goods sold under a hire purchase agreement which generate hire purchase interest over a number of years after the sale has been made. If you are the seller you continue to own the goods, legally speaking, until the person making the purchase has fulfilled their part of the bargain by paying all the instalments; at which point you have received not only the full cash price but also the extra interest part of the instalments. The argument for the accounting approach is that you have earned the cash price once you hand over the asset although you don't receive it at once, and you earn the interest as you allow the purchaser to take the agreed time period to pay off the instalments.

Although these seem clear general principles, each transaction type needs to be assessed on its own merits in order to decide what is most appropriate for each company's accounts. The decisions might depend on how similar transactions have been treated by the company in the past or on what other companies in the same business do.

Matching expenses

We noticed, in Chapter 2, that managers distinguish between fixed and variable expenses (costs); they are able to do this as they have access to the information. In a set of published accounts, however, only the global view of costs and expenses is reported. The only information which external users are entitled to receive is the total of expenses in categories defined by the Companies Act formats. We have previously mentioned in the text the importance of matching, which affects the measurement of expenses. We have also seen that expenses incurred are not necessarily the same as cash paid out of the business. In the remainder of the chapter we will consider expense measurement more deeply through looking at the way stocks and fixed assets are treated in the accounts

Why are stock and fixed assets important?

These are areas which require the accountant to exercise subjective judgement, which is very different from the traditional view of the accountant being ultra-objective and merely recording financial transactions. A major aim of this chapter is to consider in more depth these areas of subjective calculation.

TASK 5.3

Stocks and depreciation effect on the balance sheet

Look at a set of published accounts – you can find a set on our website (www.thomsonlearning.co.uk/accountingandfinance/hand) if you do not have one handy. What would be the impact upon the profit and loss account and the balance sheet if the items of closing stock and depreciation for the year were subject to an error of plus or minus 50 per cent?

Cost of goods sold and stock values

For businesses selling tangible products, cost of goods sold (COGS) is the most significant expense. Before you start this section you might like to review the Sparkes plc example (Illustration 4.2 in the previous chapter).

COGS may be calculated as follows:

*Costs of finished products in the business at the beginning of the period (*opening stock *value)*
Plus *cost of products purchased or manufactured during the period*
Less *cost of products in the business at the end of the period (*closing stock *value).*

ILLUSTRATION 5.1

Cost of sales

We could think of COGS in terms of goods flowing through a warehouse. Exhibit 5.3 illustrates this with numbers. We can see from this illustration that at the start of the period we had opening stock in the warehouse of £8000. We then purchased more stock of £200 000 of which £20 000 remained unsold at the end of the period. Thus we can deduce that the stock we sold had originally cost us £188 000 (8000 + 200 000 − 20 000).

Exhibit 5.3

Cost of sales

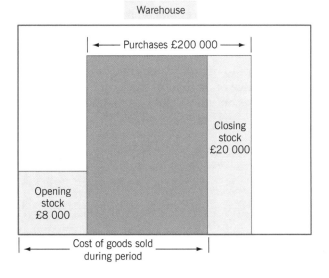

In the illustration above we can see that the closing stock values will directly affect the calculation for COGS and hence the level of reported profits. The importance of 'getting the stock figure right' is clear; overstated stocks = overstated profits which may lead to unjustified dividend and tax payments in the current year; but remember that this year's closing stock is next year's opening stock, so the cost of sales next year will also be affected.

TASK 5.4

The effect of different closing stock values

In the warehouse example given above, what would be the likely effect on profits, dividends and tax if the £20 000 closing stock had been valued at:

1. £25 000?
2. £15 000?

So the valuation of stock is important in arriving at profit. Valuation depends on how many stock items and how much each one is worth. The next section looks more closely at issues related to the valuation of this important asset.

Stock valuations

Almost all businesses, particularly those in the manufacturing and retailing sectors, will keep some amount of stock. There are various reasons why firms hold stock. It could be that they keep a certain level of raw materials to even out production flows or to ensure that they are not caught out by sudden price rises in the cost of the raw material. They may keep some level of finished goods to ensure that they are always able to meet a customer's order. Stocks (sometimes referred to as inventories) are normally split into the following categories:

- raw materials – items unprocessed by the company
- work in progress – products or services which are part completed
- finished goods – products ready and waiting for sale.

One of the most vexing questions for an accountant is: 'What is the "correct" valuation for the stock on hand at the end of the year?' At first it might seem obvious just to count the stock and multiply the number held by the cost (i.e. the purchase price of an item of stock on the relevant date of the transaction). Unfortunately it is not that simple, as the following story will show:

ILLUSTRATION 5.2

Brazil nuts and stock values

At Christmas in particular, people in the UK buy bags of Brazil nuts. These nuts have been originally collected from the floor of the Amazonian jungle – at that point they have zero cost as they are a 'natural' resource to the local people. The nuts are collected and moved to the coast and shipped to the UK. At each stage of the distribution chain their 'cost' (and hence accounting value) increases due to the labour, transportation and packaging costs being added, up to the point of final sale in your local supermarket. The cost of the stock is arrived at by taking the original purchase price together with any additional costs associated in bringing the product to its current state and in its current position.

At each stage, if the owner of the nuts were to value them, they would have a different figure of cost.

Changes in stock prices

A further complication that may arise in valuing stock is that the purchase price of the stock may have risen or fallen during the period and so there may be a range of cost figures which could be applicable to those units of stock on hand at the end of the accounting period. Thus 'cost' may need to be estimated in an appropriate way depending on what has happened to prices during the period. This is a separate issue from the order in which the stock was *actually* used.

First In First Out (FIFO) assumes that stock is used steadily, the oldest items first; what is left at the end of the year is the most recently purchased and should therefore be valued according to the most recent price(s) incurred. Of course, we may not know when the actual items were used (if stock items look identical – items of hardware, for example) and this is more to do with finding a fair and consistent method of 'matching' costs against revenues. For FIFO the balance sheet is left with more recent stock **purchases** and hence has a more up-to-date value.

ILLUSTRATION 5.3

FIFO

Suppose stock was purchased in four equal batches of 100 units at prices of £1 per unit for Batch 1, £1.25 per unit for Batch 2, £1.50 per unit for Batch 3 and £1.75 per unit for Batch 4. Each time stock is used the oldest price of unused units is attributed to COGS.

If there were 120 units left at the end of the accounting period then closing stock, under the FIFO principle, would be valued at:

$$(100 \times £1.75 + 20 \times £1.50) = £205$$

Used	Used	80% used	Left over
100 × £1.00	100 × £1.25	100 × £1.50	100 × £1.75
1	2	3	4
£100	£125	£150	£175

Exhibit 5.4

FIFO

The **Last In First Out (LIFO)** technique of valuation charges the most recently purchased items first against profits. LIFO means that the profit and loss account is more up to date in that it is charged with recent prices, but what is left unused at the end of the year (and therefore on the balance sheet) is valued at the oldest price(s).

ILLUSTRATION 5.4

LIFO

This technique seems reasonable if you imagine a situation where the stock is not perishable and is perhaps kept in a big pile so that the later purchases are in fact used first; although, as we have pointed out the choice of FIFO or LIFO is not so much to do with actual usage of stocks as the matching of costs into the profit and loss account. In terms of rising prices, LIFO gives a much lower valuation to closing stock and a higher value to cost of sales.

$$20 \times £1.00 + 20 \times £1.25 = £125$$

Left over	80% used	Used	Used
100 × £1.00	100 × £1.25	100 × £1.50	100 × £1.75
1	2	3	4
£100	£125	£150	£175

Exhibit 5.5

LIFO

WAC (weighted average cost) involves keeping a running calculation of purchases, weighted by the number of units acquired. Each time stock is used the current average price is used for the COGS value and any stock left on hand at the end of the period is thus valued at an amalgam cost. This may be a good approach if there are a large number of purchases and uses of stock in the year – it can be too difficult to keep track of each movement in and out as FIFO and LIFO require. The drawback is that the average price may never actually have been paid – it is not a real experience.

This is not an exhaustive list of possible ways of approximating the cost of stock held. Any technique that management think is appropriate can be used, although the aim is to get close to actual cost. So some techniques may be rejected by the Inland Revenue as not being fair approximations and hence not giving a fair picture of taxable profit (usually LIFO, because low stock value leads to low reported profit; thus, the LIFO technique is less commonly used in practice than FIFO and WAC). You may also have noticed that there is quite a difference between the FIFO and LIFO values in the examples above. This is not always the case, but if you go back and look at Task 5.4, the choice of method could make a big difference to reported profit in a time of rapidly inflating or deflating prices.

The basic accounting rule which has been developed is always to value the closing stock at its cost or net realisable value (NRV), whichever is the lower. NRV can be defined as the net amount the business would receive if they were to sell the stock at its current market value. NRV represents the sales price less any costs of conversion to bring the stock into a saleable condition less any marketing costs.

In most situations the cost figure will be lower than the NRV (this is logical if you think that most businesses intend to make a profit and therefore sell their goods at a price greater than original cost). However, in special circumstances (e.g. at the end of a craze for a novelty, such as Spice Girls dolls, or upon the introduction of a new model of machine) the business cannot sell its merchandise for the price it originally planned and the NRV may fall below cost.

The notion of NRV is also relevant if you think of the common situation that could occur where stock is damaged (e.g. has been dropped) or has deteriorated in some way (e.g. has been nibbled by mice!). The stock should only be valued in the accounts at the value at which it can be disposed of if that is now less than the original cost. Any difference (or 'write down') is a cost to be borne by the business in the profit and loss account.

Expenses – accruals and prepayments

Most of the expenses of a business will be paid out in cash at regular intervals, or as the bills are received (e.g. salaries, electricity, telephone). Sometimes the cash outflow will not coincide with the accounting period, i.e. the total cash outflow in the period will not equate to the actual consumption of the item of expense by the business. For example, motor insurance is paid annually in advance but the insurance year is unlikely to coincide perfectly with the accounting year.

Accountants have to ensure that the items of expense and revenue within the profit and loss account are an accurate reflection of the economic activity by the business during the accounting period. Adjustments will have to be made to convert the cash outflows into expenses; for instance, insurance premiums tend to be paid in advance (at the start of the period to which they apply), electricity is normally paid in arrears. Such adjustments are made in order to ensure that the current accounting period fully reflects all expenses incurred, even if the cash paid does not match the usage derived.

ILLUSTRATION 5.5

Allocation of insurance expense using the quadrant

Suppose you start a business in January. The business is so successful that you buy a van on 1 February (a fixed asset cost) but you also need to insure it (an expense) and you pay £600 for one year's insurance (up to 31 January of the following year).

The initial entry to record the insurance expense on the quadrant would be to decrease cash and to increase the insurance expense by £600.

However, when you came to prepare the accounts at 31 December, it would not be fair to match a payment of £600 for 12 months' of insurance (up to 31 January next) against the revenues gained by having the use of the van for only 11 months (from 1 February) this year.

Therefore you should make another quadrant entry which would decrease the insurance expense and increase a prepayment (a current asset) by £50 (the one-twelfth of the insurance bill already paid for but which will not be 'used' until next year). Thus only only 11 months' of insurance cost are 'matched' against this year's revenues.

Quadrant illustrating insurance prepayment	
ASSETS Cash − 600 Prepaid insurance + 50	LIABILITIES
EXPENSES Insurance + 600 − 50 = + 550	REVENUE

Thus, a **prepayment** is where you pay for something in advance and do not gain the benefit until the following year. It shows as an asset in the quadrant above because the business will get the benefit of that payment in the next accounting year. You can link this example back to Exhibit 5.2. The cash paid out in Year 1 is actually in respect of expenses that apply to Year 1 and Year 2.

The converse situation is where you have already had the benefit but have not paid for the item of expense. This is called an **accrual**. The amount outstanding would be shown as a current liability as it will require payment in the following period.

It is worth noting that the accountant goes to a lot of effort to ensure that these adjustments are as accurate as is possible. All that is happening is that adjustments (allocations to time periods) are being made which will alter the figure of profit for one year, but will not alter the total profit earned by a business over the long term (i.e. expenses are being shifted from the period in which they were paid to the period in which they are used by the business).

TASK 5.5

Quadrant entries reflecting accruals and prepayments

Suggest quadrant entries for the following:

1. Pay rent on 1 July £360 for the year July–June; accounting year end is 31 December.
2. At the end of the year recognise that no entry has been made for unpaid business rates of £100.
3. Recognise that wages of £500 are owed but have not been paid out.

Depreciation

Expenditure which occurs when a business purchases fixed (or non-current) assets is referred to as capital expenditure (i.e. expenditure that is shown as an asset on the balance sheet), whereas normal running costs, such as rent, are called 'revenue expenditure' (i.e. the expenditure that is charged against revenues to determine profit). Fixed assets (such as machinery, plant, vehicles and equipment) are bought in one year but used over several years; they are purchased with the intention of being used (consumed) over time to produce products or services for resale. With a fixed asset, the full impact upon cash flow normally occurs at the commencement of the life of the asset (it is paid for in full on Day One) but the asset will be used for some years afterwards.

To arrive at the full costs of running the business for a single accounting period we must include, as part of expenses, an element which represents the consumption of the fixed asset. We call this expense 'depreciation'. Unlike other types of expense which appear in the profit and loss account, depreciation does not represent a cash outflow for the current period. It is for this reason that depreciation is called a 'non-cash' expense.

Depreciation is the technical accounting process of allocating cost to accounting periods so as to charge a fair proportion of the cost of an asset to each accounting period, according to its usage. Assets with differing patterns of usage will require different patterns of depreciation. For example, computer equipment is constantly being superseded by new models and most businesses will upgrade frequently so the equipment loses a lot of its original value in the early years; whereas a commercial aircraft owned by British Airways will be used for many years and is depreciated according to the number of hours it flies during a time period. As a result, accountants have developed a number of accounting bases for depreciating fixed assets.

The rationale for depreciation

We have already established that there is a logical argument for accountants, when calculating profit, to make a charge for depreciation in the profit and loss account, and that if non-cash expenses were not put in the profit and loss account for a particular accounting period the reported profit could be shown as significantly higher.

There are a number of reasons why it has become accepted practice to depreciate fixed assets.

- In the case of a limited company this practice has now been incorporated into the Companies Act – there is a legal requirement to depreciate all fixed assets (other than land) each year; to show the annual charge in the profit and loss account; and to show the accumulated depreciation to date on the balance sheet.

    One reason for this legal requirement is an interesting story from the time of the early railway companies. Some unscrupulous owners would not replace the wooden carriages as often as they should have done. They showed the full cost of the carriages as an asset in the balance sheet but never depreciated them, thus showing as much profit as they possibly could in subsequent years through not having any depreciation expense in the profit and loss account. Then, when major investment was required to replace the carriages, they would sell the business to new unsuspecting shareholders. Some of the more responsible companies *did* depreciate their carriages and so the system was changed to apply to them all in attempt to stamp out such devious behaviour.

- As we have already seen, when a fixed asset is used or consumed in the course of business, depreciation is the expense that must be matched against the sales revenues of the products that the fixed asset has produced. This is the application of the matching concept (see Exhibit 5.2 again) which is done in an attempt to derive as accurate a figure of net profit as possible.

- Looking back to the earlier discussion about capital maintenance you might also take the view that charging the cost of the asset against the profit made during the periods of its useful life also goes some way to ensuring the asset can be replaced when necessary. For example, if your business needs a packing machine to be able to operate successfully there is no point in distributing so much of the profits you make from using it that you cannot afford to buy a new machine when the old one is worn out. Thus it can be argued that charging depreciation in the profit and loss account allows you to maintain the *financial* capital (the same amount of money). However, if you expect that by the time you come to replace the asset it will be more expensive in money terms, perhaps because of inflation, then you would also need to make sure you set aside *more* money to enable you to actually buy a new machine.

Choosing a method of depreciation to suit the circumstances

Once purchased by the business there are various reasons why a fixed asset will no longer be worth its original value:

- wear and tear
- use and abuse
- lack of maintenance
- obsolescence
- the passage of time.

Different types of fixed assets will, of course, depreciate at different rates. Some will depreciate very quickly; for example, a motor vehicle will be depreciated perhaps over four or five years. We are familiar with the idea that if you return a new car to the showroom very shortly after you have purchased it you will not receive the original price that you paid. It will have instantly depreciated by a significant amount. Plant and machinery will usually last much longer and could be depreciated over 10 to 20 years. Some textile mills in the UK are still using machines bought in the 1950s!

The pattern of depreciation may also be different. Some assets depreciate very quickly in the early stages of their lives. Again vehicles, or computers, would be a good example; whereas other assets, such as fixtures, will depreciate at a very steady rate. As a result the accounting standard allows the accountant to choose any method of depreciation, depending upon the type of fixed asset, which will accurately reflect the use of the asset during its useful life.

Commonly used methods of depreciation

Straight line method

This is the simplest method to adopt. It assumes that the asset will be used up evenly over its expected lifetime. A formula can be used to calculate depreciation, as follows:

$$\frac{\text{(original cost of the asset) less (expected scrap value)}}{\text{(number of years' expected use)}}$$

TASK 5.6

Straight line depreciation calculation

A company purchased office furniture at a cost of £10 000. It was assumed that the furniture would last for five years, and would then have a scrap value of £1000.
Calculate the annual charge for depreciation under the straight line method.

This method is named the 'straight line' method because, if you were to plot the amount charged in the accounts for depreciation on a graph each year, it would produce a straight horizontal line. Exhibit 5.6 illustrates this.

Exhibit 5.6

Straight line depreciation

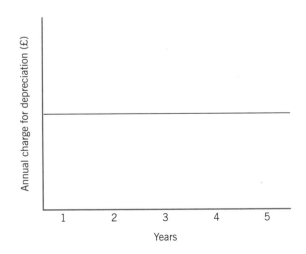

Exhibit 5.7	DATE	COST	ANNUAL CHARGE	DEPRECIATION TO DATE	NET BOOK VALUE
Straight line depreciation example	YR1	10 000	1800	1800	8200
	YR2	10 000	1800	3600	6400
	YR3	10 000	1800	5400	4600
	YR4	10 000	1800	7200	2800
	YR5	10 000	1800	9000	1000

TASK 5.7

Effect of alternative assumptions

What would be the impact of the following changes to our original assumptions about the annual depreciation charge on the office furniture in Task 5.6?

■ The estimated asset life may have been misjudged and the asset lasts for a period of, say, ten years.
■ The estimated disposal value may prove to be incorrect and we are unable to recoup any value at all.
■ The furniture proves to be of a lower quality than we anticipated and by the end of the third year it needs to be replaced.

The annual charge represents an allocation of the cost of the asset to be charged against profits for the assumed life of the asset. Using the previous task, with an annual depreciation charge in the profit and loss account of £1800 you could tabulate the effect of the depreciation process on the balance sheet as shown in Exhibit 5.7.

The net book value is the original cost less all the depreciation charged so far, or the amount of original cost that has not yet been matched against the revenue earned, and this is the amount which would appear on the balance sheet at the end of the accounting period.

However, bear in mind that all of the above is based on estimates, and a number of things could go wrong with the asset purchased in Task 5.6.

Reducing balance method

Some assets tend to depreciate at a greater rate in the early stages of their lives and at a lesser rate as they get older. A good example of this would be a motor vehicle which depreciates very substantially within the first years of its life and then the level of depreciation slows. In recognition of this accountants use the reducing balance method of depreciation.

The effect of this method when represented on a graph is that of a descending curve: a high charge in the early years and a lower charge in later years (see Exhibit 5.8).

Exhibit 5.8

The reducing
balance
technique

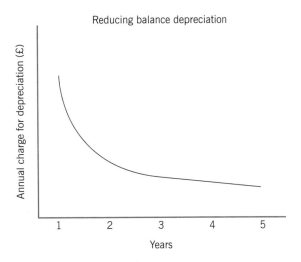

Reducing balance depreciation

ILLUSTRATION 5.6

Reducing balance

A company buys a lorry for £200 000. Because the lorry is expected to lose much of its value early on, the accountant decides to depreciate it at a rate of 40 per cent of the net book value (i.e. a balance which reduces each period).

The numbers would then go like this:

The annual charge would be calculated by applying the reducing percentage to the undepreciated value brought forward thus:

Year 1   200 000 × 40% = 80 000
Year 2   (200,000 − 80 000 = 120 000) × 40% = 48 000

and so on, as shown in Exhibit 5.9.

Exhibit 5.9

Reducing
balance
example – the
whole picture

YEAR	COST	ANNUAL CHARGE	DEPRECIATION TO DATE	NET BOOK VALUE
1	200 000	80 000	80 000	120 000
2	200 000	48 000	128 000	72 000
3	200 000	28 800	156 800	43 200
4	200 000	17 280	174 080	25 920
5	200 000	10 368	184 448	15 552

Note that, with the reducing balance method, it is mathematically impossible to depreciate the asset down to a zero net book value. But the choice of the depreciation percentage is made in order to approach as closely as possible the expected amount that will be realisable at the end of the estimated life of the asset.

Other techniques of depreciation may be used; for example, allocating machine cost by the number of hours a machine is used each year. As with stock valuation the accountant is expected to choose the most reasonable method which approximates the amount of the asset that should be matched against the revenues generated through using the asset in the year.

Revaluations

Depreciation is about reducing, or writing down, the accounting value of the asset in a measured way as it is utilised in generating revenue for the business. But what about movements in the worth of the asset either down or up? If a fixed asset, for example a property, has shown an increase in value we believe to be permanent, then we are allowed (but not required) to carry out a **revaluation** exercise. If it has gone down in value we are expected to reduce the amount shown in the accounts as a matter of prudence. The asset will be valued, often by independent outside valuers, and will be adjusted in the balance sheet to reflect the new valuation. A net increase will be placed into the Reserves section of the balance sheet and called 'Revaluation Reserve' (part of the owners' capital). This is to reflect the fact that the revaluation has resulted in an increase in the net book value of the business, which then means that the amount of capital has also increased. The revalued amount will now be depreciated over the remaining life of the asset.

This capital increase belongs to the owners of the business (shareholders). However, given that this 'profit' has not arisen because of a cash-based transaction, we must not use this *unrealised* profit to pay out a dividend. As the revaluation is taken straight to reserves it does not pass through the profit and loss account. In quadrant language a revaluation would cause fixed assets to increase and owners' liability to increase by an equal amount. If the asset subsequently fell in value the revaluation downwards would first be written off against the Revaluation Reserve; then, when that was used up, any remainder would be charged to the profit and loss account.

ILLUSTRATION 5.7

Revaluation

The business owns commercial premises which currently have a value of £200 000. Following a revaluation exercise they are now valued at £300 000.

Balance sheet extracts for the revaluation would show:

	Before revaluation	After revaluation
In the top half of the balance sheet FIXED ASSETS Premises	200 000	300 000
In the bottom half of the balance sheet SHARE CAPITAL and RESERVES Revaluation Reserve	—	100 000

▶

Both halves of the balance sheet are affected by a revaluation. The business still owns a fixed asset which is now considered to be worth more and so this is reflected in the fixed asset section of the top half of the balance sheet. The growth in value is unrealised profit (the asset has not been sold yet) and so the Revaluation Reserve holds the 'profit' made by shareholders rather than putting it in with the profit and loss account, from which dividends could be paid.

Depreciation – a recap

All businesses are required to depreciate their fixed assets and, depending upon the type of asset, may choose different methods of depreciation. Whatever method is chosen the essential process is one of expense allocation. The accountant is trying to make an estimate about:

1. the probable fall in value of the asset due to the use
2. the benefit which the business has derived from the asset during a particular accounting period.

At best, the annual depreciation charge can only be an estimate on the basis of the information available. However, it is better to make as accurate a guess as possible than not to depreciate at all! We must be aware that this is an area in which the numbers are open to judgement, error and (in some unfortunate cases) manipulation. As a result the figures of profit and the net book values in the balance sheet are not as precise as they may appear to be. Users need to treat the net book value of any fixed asset with a degree of caution.

FINAL COMMENTS

This chapter has gone into more depth about the measurement of profit and asset values. In particular we have looked at two important areas of the accounts to show you some of the practical applications of accounting techniques that accountants and managers have to undertake on a day-to-day basis. We have shown that accounting profit is often about the exercise of subjective judgement.

SUMMARY

Having completed this chapter you should now understand the following key points:

- Fixed assets and stocks (inventory) affect the picture shown both by the balance sheet and the profit and loss account
- There is no single right answer as to what the stock figure should be since the number you put in the accounts is a product of *how much* stock you have and *what it cost you* and sometimes both of those things involve estimates and judgement.
- The general approach is to value stock at *the lower level of cost and net realisable value.*

- We need to allocate expenses incurred in a single period across any periods in which revenue is earned through using the resources that those costs made available. This is the application of the matching (or accruals) concept.

- Fixed assets are non-current assets or assets that are intentionally held by the business for more than one accounting period, such as buildings and machines.

- The balance sheet shows the part of fixed assets that have not yet been used up in operating the business – the original cost (or subsequent valuation) less any accumulated amounts of depreciation.

- Depreciation is the process of allocating the original cost (or subsequent valuation) of a fixed asset to the expenses section of the profit and loss account; it is acknowledging that part of the fixed asset has been used to generate revenues during the period, although the asset is still owned by the business.

Plese turn to the back of the book for detailed answers to questions marked with a ❓. Answers to the other questions can be found on the companion website at www.thomsonlearning.co.uk/accountingandfinance/hand

REVIEW QUESTIONS

RQ 5.1 What particular stock valuation problems might be faced by a manager in the following types of business

- supermarket
- department store
- fashion boutique
- construction company
- wholesaler
- delicatessen?

❓ **RQ 5.2** What method of depreciation would you choose for the following items:

- sales representative's car
- microcomputer
- ink-jet printer
- packing machine
- photocopier
- lease on land and buildings?

Give reasons for your answers.

❓ **RQ 5.3** List and discuss three reasons which cause profit measurement to be a matter for subjective judgement. Does this subjectivity matter?

RQ 5.4 What will be the general effect of inflation on the balance sheet of a firm?

RQ 5.5 Does the choice of policy in terms of depreciation and stock valuation affect the total profit that a business will earn throughout its life (assuming that the particular business has a life of ten years)?

NP 5.1 Gross profit and cost of sales Complete the missing figures for these three years:

	Year 1 (£)	Year 2 (£)	Year 3 (£)
Sales	1000		2000
Opening stock	100	200	300
Purchases	600	800	
Closing stock	(200)	(100)	(400)
Cost of sales	____	____	____
Gross profit	____	300	____
Gross profit as percentage of sales	____	____	25%

Comment upon the gross profit percentages.

NP 5.2 Straight line depreciation Complete the missing figures for these three fixed assets assuming that depreciation is charged on a straight line basis

Fixed asset	Year 1 (£)	Year 2 (£)	Year 3 (£)
Original cost	500	1000	3300
Expected salvage value	100	100	300
Cost less salvage value	____	____	____
Expected total life (years)	4	3	
Number of years asset has been used	1	2	3
Annual depreciation			600
Depreciation to date			
Cost less depreciation to date			

Which of the above figures would appear on the face of the balance sheet?

NP 5.3 Hire and buy Consider a situation where a company owns one machine costing £100 000 with a life of five years, which it uses to manufacture a particular product. The company wishes to increase production but is unable to purchase a new asset. It is decided, therefore, to hire an additional machine at a cost of £30 000 p.a. How would the usage of these machines be reflected within the accounts of the business?

(You may find it useful to run this illustration through the Accounting Quadrant.)

NP 5.4 Calculation of depreciation charge A fixed asset cost £10 000 with an expected life of four years and an expected scrap value of £400. There is expected to be an even phasing of wear and tear on the asset throughout its life.

1. Calculate the annual depreciation charge.
2. Calculate the balance sheet value of the asset at the end of:
   (a) Year One
   (b) Year Three.
3. Discuss the implication for capital maintenance if prices for such assets have risen by 10 per cent in each year.

NP 5.5 John Franks – depreciation and profit calculation John Franks has decided to start a business to manufacture switching equipment for the telecommunications industry. He started out with capital of £25 000 which he promptly invested in high-tech machinery. He operated from a small industrial unit on which he paid rent of £12 000 for the year (this figure includes all his light, heat and power requirements). At the end of his first year's trading he has the following list of balances:

Item	£
Revenue: sales	120 000
Expense: cost of goods sold	40 000
Asset: machinery	28 000
Expense: rent	12 000
Other expenses	30 000
Liability: capital	25 000
Asset: vehicle	20 000
Asset: bank	4 800
Drawings (withdrawals by owner reducing liability of business)	5 200
Asset: closing stock	5 000

He wants you to advise him. He does not know how much profit he has made. He feels he may have had a successful year as he has withdrawn £100 per week and still had money left to pay his business expenses, and also had a healthy bank balance at the end.

The machinery he bought was second hand, at half the current price. John anticipates it will last for four more years (i.e. five years in all) and will have a scrap value of £3000. Straight line depreciation is normally applied to this kind of machinery. The vehicle was bought new and carries 30 per cent reducing balance depreciation.

1. Draft a profit statement to show the amount of profit earned by Franks in the current year.

2. Assuming that Franks wants to expand the business, advise what depreciation policies he should consider if market prices of fixed assets are expected to continue to rise.

NP 5.6 Stanley – depreciation Stanley Ltd was established on 1 January of Year 1 to manufacture a single product using a machine which cost £400 000. The machine is expected to last for four years and then have a scrap value of £52 000. The machine will produce a similar number of goods each year and annual profits before depreciation are expected to be in the region of £200 000. The financial controller has suggested that the machine should be depreciated using either the straight line method or the reducing balance method. If the latter method is used, it has been estimated that an annual depreciation rate of 40 per cent would be appropriate.

1. Calculate the annual depreciation charges and the net book values of the fixed asset at the end of Year 1, Year 2, Year 3 and Year 4, using:

   (a) the straight line method

   (b) the reducing balance method.

2. Discuss the differing implications of these two methods for the financial information published by Stanley for the years 1–4 inclusive. You should also advise management which method you consider more appropriate, bearing in mind expected profit levels. In what ways would you seek advice on useful lives and residual values?

WEB RESOURCES   www

www.thomsonlearning.co.uk/accountingandfinance/hand

The companion website has free additional resources for you to use alongside this book. If you are a student you can access material to help with revision, including practice questions with answers to test how much of the material you have understood. There are also useful hyperlinks to companies and information sources mentioned in the book as well as interactive quizzes. There are additional resources for lecturers using this book on their courses; the details can be found in the preface at the front of this book.

CHAPTER 6

The financial reporting framework: the rules of the game

LEARNING OBJECTIVES

This chapter covers a range of issues which underpin the financial reports that companies publish each year. After studying this chapter you should be able to:

- explain who uses accounting statements
- understand what they want to use them for and whether the accounts are suitable for these purposes
- recognise what an annual report looks like, and find your way around a real report
- outline the general assumptions that we make when reading accounts, and be aware that these assumptions are rarely stated explicitly.

Introduction

In the earlier chapters we have looked at basic accounting information and the ways in which it may be presented. Chapters 4 and 5 demonstrated how the business moves from recording the individual transactions it carries out to producing the annual financial statements and we introduced the major statements of the profit and loss account and the balance sheet. The purpose of this chapter is to consider the rules that accountants follow when they produce financial statements. We look at the different uses that people make of accounting information and explain further the distinction between management accounting (basically reports for use inside the business) and financial accounting (reports for public consumption).

There is no one 'correct' way of accounting, only conventions followed at a particular point in time. While we can dispute these rules, and debate their usefulness (for example, we can question the accounting profession's attachment to historic cost values as potentially irrelevant as it is out-of-date information) we do need to understand what they are in order to make sense of accounting statements. You can compare this to someone watching a game of (say) rugby, without being familiar with the rules; they will be unsure why things are happening and uncertain about the movement of play. So it is with accounting: a familiarity with the rules enables you to appreciate more fully the patterns and events within the accounting framework.

Markets and financial information

All businesses exist within markets – markets for customers (e.g. leisure, holidays, beer, soft drinks) and markets for resources (e.g. people, materials, services). There is one market which is common to all businesses, however – the market for **finance**; and all firms (whatever their products) compete in this market. In order to survive, to develop and expand, a firm often needs finance. Firms need to reassure the financial markets of their dependability if they are to gain the confidence of current and future shareholders and lenders.

We can sum up the links between finance, confidence from external sources and information in this way: unless there are sufficient surpluses left over from past activities to fund what they want to do next, companies need new external finance. This can come from various possible sources (but mainly the Stock Market and banks). However, all investments carry some degree of risk. Therefore investors in the financial markets need to have confidence in firms, and confidence is gained, in part, via access to financial information about the company. A major source of information is found within the annual published accounts.

What are published accounts?

You will notice that this text has been using terms such as 'accounting statements', 'annual reports' and 'financial statements' fairly interchangeably. This is common practice but you need to make a distinction between information that is kept private within the organisation and that which is 'published' or made public outside the organisation.

Internal information Often the production of internal information is known as 'management accounting'. It is often very detailed, and is, perhaps, sensitive information if it were to fall into the hands of competitors. Management accounts do not have to be presented in any particular format but are used to help management make decisions by reporting on the past or helping to model and predict the future. Chapters 2, 3, 9 and 10 contain examples of management accounting information.

Published information The annual report must be given to all shareholders and be filed with Companies House. It must be released in a specified timeframe and contain as a minimum, detailed information specified by the Companies Acts and by additional non-**statutory** financial reporting guidelines. This information can be obtained (for a small fee) by any member of the public who wishes to see it.

Who uses accounting statements?

Lots of different groups have been identified as having an interest in accounting reports, and these include:

- managers
- investors (mainly shareholders in the case of companies)
- potential shareholders
- financial analysts and advisers
- lenders (including banks)
- suppliers and creditors
- government and the Inland Revenue
- employees and trade unions
- customers
- members of the general public (including environmental pressure groups).

The professional accountancy bodies research this area periodically as accounts producers need to have a clear idea of who they are generating the accounts for and what those groups want/need to know. In 1975 *The Corporate Report*[1] was published as a result of discussions by the Accounting Standards Steering Committee which, in part, considered the usefulness of financial statements. The report concluded:

> *The fundamental objective of corporate reports is to communicate economic measurements of and information about the resources and performance of the reporting entity* useful *to those having reasonable rights to such information. (para. 1.8)*

More recently the **Accounting Standards Board** published its *Statement of Principles for Financial Reporting* (December 1999) and, again, the concept of usefulness was a significant feature in this publication.

TASK 6.1

The users of financial statements

Look at the list of user groups above. What do you think each of the groups is looking for in the financial statements and which do you think are the main groups that the producers of accounts focus upon?

Some of the above users (e.g. shareholders) have a legal right to information from the organisation. In the case of companies this is covered by requirements of the Companies Acts which specify the rights of owners, shareholders, creditors and the government. The main accounting statements (such as the profit and loss accounts and balance sheets covered in Chapter 5) tend, therefore, to focus on the needs of these particular groups and it is assumed that all other user needs are met indirectly. One of the pressures faced by the accounting profession is meeting the information needs of other groups of users whose primary requirement may not be pure financial information (e.g. for environmental issues and employment policies).

---

[1] The Accounting Standards Steering Committe (1975). *The Corporate Report*. London: The Accounting Standards Steering Committee.

The needs of accounts users

The specific needs of users will obviously vary from group to group, and even between individuals within a group. However, the following needs are probably important for all users:

1. Information will be required to assess the financial stability of the entity in terms of the resources over which it exercises control. By this we mean the use of assets in terms of profitability and the extent of future liabilities.

2. The reporting of the efficient use of economic resources back to the owners is often referred to by accountants as the application of 'the stewardship concept' (the managers are reporting how they have 'stewarded', or looked after, the business to owners/shareholders who often have little or nothing to do with the day-to-day running of the business). The stewardship concept can also be linked back to medieval times when the feudal landowners expected their agricultural tenants to account to them, often verbally, each year after the harvest. The landowner's manager was called a steward.

3. In a situation where an existing or potential shareholder is using financial information to decide whether to invest in a company, then this is termed 'the decision usefulness concept'.

Accounting statements are used to meet the needs of these two conflicting concepts of stewardship and decision usefulness. The concepts are conflicting because, if you revisit the discussion of the two concepts, you will see that the stewardship concept is concerned with the past – what has happened – whereas the decision usefulness concept is concerned with future decisions. And, as you often see in television adverts for financial products, 'past performance is no guarantee of future success'!

Although many people who read accounting statements may not be financial experts, the non-expert reader is not really catered for. The fact that many users do not understand basic accounting concepts is largely ignored by the producers (i.e. the accountants). Research has been conducted as to the level of understanding of users of accounting statements and has tended to conclude that only those who have undergone a period of accounting education are able to understand and interpret accounts! For example, researchers Chandler and Bartlett of Cardiff University[2] surveyed more than 2000 readers to find that while more than 80 per cent of them claimed to make their own investment decisions, less than a quarter studied the numerical information in the published accounts.

TASK 6.2

The skills of users of accounts

Why do you think it is that accounting reports are so specialised that they are sometimes considered unintelligible to the layperson?

---

[2] Chandler, R. and Bartlett, S. (2000) 'Heavy Reading' *Accountancy*, October, **12b** (1286): 158.

What is in a set of published accounts?

We have already seen that there are many potential users of a set of financial accounts. For most of these user groups the published accounts are the best source of financial information about the company available to them.

TASK 6.3

Look at a set of published accounts

Leaf quickly through the corporate report of a well-known plc of your choice and note the sections. If you are not sure about how to obtain a suitable set of accounts, see the guidance in RQ 6.6 at the end of this chapter.

But how is it decided exactly what should appear in these reports? In the next section we look at how the content of published accounts is regulated. Three main forces are at work: the law, accounting standards, and the Stock Exchange.

The law

A limited company is granted a separate legal existence in the eyes of the law. This enables the liability of the owners (shareholders) to be limited to the amount they have paid to buy shares. In return the directors of the company are required to prepare accounts to show what they have done with the resources provided by the shareholders. The Companies Act 1985 is the major piece of legislation which sets the framework for the annual accounts that every company must produce.

Highlights of the 1985 Companies Act:

- books of account are to be kept
- annual accounts are to be prepared
- the balance sheet and profit and loss account are to be presented in a particular format, detailed in the Act
- additional disclosure requirements are detailed for inclusion in notes to the accounts or the directors' report
- the accounts should be audited by independent accountants
- the accounts must then be available to shareholders and a copy filed with the Registrar of Companies.

The overriding requirement is that the accounts should give a true and fair view of the state of affairs of the company and its profit or loss for the period. However the phrase 'true and fair' has never been legally defined – you may think of it as a phrase which means 'following the law and best accounting practice and not designed to mislead users'.

The Companies Act 1985 consolidated piecemeal legislation which had been enacted over the past century. The law is always in the process of evolution as new business practices emerge, legal cases are fought and matters such as European harmonisation affect UK companies (most recently via the 1989 Companies Act which adds to the 1985 Act). At the time of writing a major company law review is underway and so this is clearly a developing area. Already the universal requirement for all companies to have an audit has been reduced and small companies are exempt; this may be further relaxed in due course.

Standards

The law is not the only force which shapes the annual company report. In particular the pursuit of truth and fairness in accounts is advanced by **statements of standard accounting practice** (SSAPs – issued before 1991) and **financial reporting standards** (FRSs – issued since 1991) which are formulated by the UK accountancy profession.

The piecemeal development of accountancy as a profession has meant that there are now six major accounting bodies operating in the UK and Ireland:

- the Institute of Chartered Accountants in England and Wales (ICAEW)
- the Institute of Chartered Accountants in Ireland (ICAI)
- the Institute of Chartered Accountants in Scotland (ICAS)
- the Association of Chartered Certified Accountants (ACCA)
- the Chartered Institute of Management Accountants (CIMA)
- the Chartered Institute of Public Finance and Accountancy (CIPFA).

These bodies collaborate together on matters which affect the whole UK accountancy profession, such as funding the team that develops standards. In some other countries the accounting professions have developed their own standards and some use **international accounting standards** (IASs) produced by the **International Accounting Standards Board** (IASB). So you can imagine the difficulties facing companies trying to operate and report on an international scale if they are based in one country but need to report to investors in one or more other countries.

(An explanation of how the UK professional bodies work together and how standards are set and enforced is outlined in the supplementary note at the end of this chapter; see p. 105.)

The aim of standards is to give detailed advice, which is generally agreed to be the best practice, on how to calculate and disclose figures in the accounts (for example on stock valuation – SSAP9 – and depreciation – FRS15). They also highlight some key accounting principles, some of which are included in the Companies Act 1985. The point is that standards can go into much more detail than might be desirable in the law and they can often respond more quickly than Parliament is able to do.

SSAPs and FRSs are not laws although in some cases their principles have been subsequently incorporated into law. In other cases the standards merely amplify basic rules given in the law. Therefore SSAPs and FRSs are not binding on the company directors (who are ultimately responsible for the accounts). However, they *are* binding on anyone who is a member of the accounting profession (most of the people who actually prepare and audit the accounts), and have been held to be expected best practice in legal cases. Auditors are required to detail any serious infringement of a SSAP or FRS in their **auditors' report**, which is published with the accounts.

This has always been an area of change as FRSs are able to respond to practical business changes faster than the law can move. However European Union (EU) countries have agreed to try to overcome the difficulties caused by having different reporting standards in different countries referred to earlier. From

January 2005 all EU companies that have securities traded on any EU market are obliged to report according to IASs or **international financial reporting standards** (IFRSs) as they are known. In the UK the Department of Trade and Industry has allowed, but not required, non-listed companies to also start using IFRSs and the UK's Accountancy Standards Board has announced a programme of harmonising FRSs with IFRSs.

This is worth bearing in mind since you *may* find that, depending on what UK company accounts you are looking at, different regulations are being followed. This is particularly important to know about if you are trying to compare the accounts of different companies.

The Stock Exchange regulations

Not all companies are listed on the Stock Exchange – but as this gives access to raising large amounts of capital for major businesses, some think it is worthwhile complying with the extra layer of regulation and disclosure. Again this varies from market to market.

Users and accounting concepts

The producers of accounting statements are trying to transmit complicated financial information to a wide variety of users in a form that they can all understand. This means that they should be able to directly compare two different businesses by using their two sets of accounts laid side by side. In an attempt to standardise the approach that accountants will take when preparing the accounts they are assumed to have applied certain rules, or concepts, in addition to the specifically stated SSAPs and FRSs.

The terms '**concept**', '**principle**', and '**postulate**' are often used interchangeably. But a concept is not the same as a principle. A concept is a rule not governed by scientific laws; a rule which people have agreed to abide by. Therefore a concept is a much softer definition than a principle. For example, a principle would be that at sea level water will boil at 100 degrees Centigrade, and this principle will apply under all identical circumstances. By contrast, democracy is a political concept and as such it may take different forms within different societies. Therefore we can see that a concept, although commonly understood, can be applied in differing ways under different circumstances.

In accounting some concepts are so fundamental that they are always applied and are mentioned only if they are *not* used in a particular set of accounts. Without a basic understanding of the concepts users are in no position to make any sense of the accounting information before them.

What makes information useful?

The accountancy profession's research in this area has concentrated on trying to develop a conceptual framework that regulators may refer to when setting the accounting standards that preparers of accounts must follow. By considering who the users of accounts are and what they want to know (discussed earlier in this chapter), they have tried to develop a set of underlying criteria in the Statement of Principles that help to judge whether accounting information is *useful* to any individual user.

Their initial, or threshold, criterion is that of **materiality** – basically how significant is the information? This means they consider the effect the inclusion or the omission of the transaction has on the understanding of the readers of the accounts. For example, if the business is a **multinational conglomerate** with a billion-pound turnover then the purchase of a computer for £1000 would probably be treated as an expense item and written off immediately to the profit and loss account (although strictly speaking this should be accounted for as a fixed asset). In the context of the size of the firm, it is just not worth the effort of keeping track of such a relatively small item – it is immaterial and will not affect the financial reports. For a very small business then the purchase of the same computer would be 'material' and so it would be recorded as a fixed asset. Materiality is called the threshold criterion because none of the subsequent issues now raised are important if the accounting information is immaterial to any decisions that users might make.

Two primary criteria are then highlighted by the Statement of Principles: **relevance** and **reliability**. Relevant information partly depends on who the user is and whether the information is relevant to them, but also possesses other attributes such as whether it is received in good time to be useful. Reliability is a feature that gives users confidence in the information – they need to be convinced that it is unbiased and produced by people they feel they can trust, e.g. professionally qualified accountants.

Secondary criteria which are also worth distinguishing when considering how good information is from a user's perspective are how **comparability** and **understandability**. Comparability is about consistency of information

- across time, e.g. it is prepared in the same way from one year to another;
- and from one business to another, i.e. all companies follow the same regulations

Accountants are able to choose from a range of different accounting policies. These policies are the different possible techniques which have been developed to report the effects of a particular type of event upon the business. For example, as we saw in Chapter 5, there are a number of different ways to account for depreciation or stock valuation. The choice of policy can have a short-term effect upon the level of profit which may be declared in a particular accounting period. In Chapter 5 we saw that reducing balance depreciation, for example, reduces profits sharply in the first year that the fixed asset is used. To avoid the possibility of manipulation the accountant must choose (and declare) a particular policy at the start of the life of the asset and must then consistently adhere to it. Only in special circumstances are companies allowed to change the policy and they must record the effects that the change has upon previous years' profits. This is done to aid comparability between accounting periods for a particular business. Clearly if you were trying to compare the accounts of two separate businesses then you would need to be aware of the differing accounting policies which had been adopted and adjust the figures accordingly.

Understandability is less clearly definable since it involves the preparers of information making reasonable assumptions about how well educated and informed the users of accounts are. Thus they will take this into account when deciding how to present information.

How this translates into regulations

The accounting regulators, then, have considered the Statement of Principles in putting together their financial reporting standards which they then expect preparers and users of accounting information to refer to. In the UK the regulators are the Accounting Standards Board (ASB), who have identified two accounting concepts which they believe should play a 'pervasive role' in the selection of policies to disclose financial information to users. These are the broad basic assumptions upon which accounts are prepared. We can describe them as follows.

Going concern concept

This assumes that the business will continue for an indefinite period into the foreseeable future. This means that when the accountant comes to assess the value of the assets held by the business there is no need to take the view that the business will soon be 'liquidated' (which would lead to a 'sale-price' valuation) – instead the assets will usually be recorded at their historic cost less an allowance for depreciation.

Accruals concept

This is also known as the matching concept (which was introduced in Chapter 5). Costs are accrued or matched against revenues (from product sales) in relation to the time period in which they occurred as opposed to the time period in which the actual cash outflows or cash inflows were experienced. This produces what is known as an accruals-based profit figure as opposed to a cash-based profit figure. In other words, just because the business is declaring a certain level of profit it does not necessarily mean that that amount has been received into the business as a net cash flow.

These two basic concepts assumed by accountants have been incorporated into the Companies Acts. They are also the key to the approach of Financial Reporting Standard (FRS) 18: 'Accounting Policies' 2002. This is one of the most recent statements by the UK professional accounting bodies – on how preparers of accounts should select appropriate accounting policies.

Other (unstated) concepts

This is by no means an exhaustive list of concepts and the following additional concepts, although not formally recognised in the same way, are still used by the profession when preparing accounting reports.

Entity concept

The only financial transactions which are relevant to the accountant are those which directly affect the business. The business is seen to have a life which is separate from that of the owners. If the business purchases a van which is used exclusively within the business then this will be included. If the owner of the business buys a sports car for their own personal use then this is *not* recorded.

This idea of keeping business and personal transactions separate is a concept which some small business people have difficulty applying; subsequently they may get into a lot of trouble with the tax authorities!

Cost concept

Transactions are usually recorded at their original (historic) cost. In published accounts you often see the assertion that the accounts have been prepared using the historic cost system of accounting. However, particularly if you consider the huge rise in UK property prices in recent decades, putting the original cost of a property into the accounts could be rather misleading as it certainly gives no idea of its current worth. It is permissible to revalue specific assets to bring them into line with current values. We therefore need to be aware that a balance sheet can be a mix of values which are both current and historic. This concept leads to problems when historic and current values are added together in the balance sheet to provide a meaningless total – often described as adding 'oranges and lemons'

Duality concept

This is the concept which lies at the heart of the system of accounting known as 'double-entry bookkeeping'. For those of you not familiar with this term it is a standard system of record-keeping (a more sophisticated and detailed application of the quadrant we used in the previous chapter) which relies upon the fact that each transaction represents an exchange of resources, and hence there will be two equal and opposite aspects to the accounting record.

Recall here our earlier work with the Accounting Quadrant in Chapter 4, using the headings assets, liabilities, expenses and revenues. Your entries on the quadrant were an application of this duality concept.

Money measurement concept

The accountant's basic unit of measurement will be in a unit of monetary currency. All transactions are measured in monetary terms. This is a strength, in that it is a unit that we can all relate to and it makes it easy to add together a record of the various transactions the business has undertaken. It is also a weakness in that money is not a stable unit of measurement due to inflation, meaning that what you can buy with a set amount of money varies over time. Also there are some items which do not lend themselves readily to being measured in monetary terms, such as the skill of a well-trained labour force or the level of pollution that the firm is creating.

Realisation concept

This rule governs when a business should recognise the profit earned from a particular category of transaction. The realisation concept suggests that profit should be recognised when legal title in the goods (or service) passes to the customer. For a retail firm this is easy: profit is taken when the goods are sold across the checkout. Other types of business may not find it so easy to find a 'clean' realisation point, and we discussed some of these complications in Chapter 5.

Objectivity concept

Accountants want accounting information to be as objective as possible. This means that it should be free from any bias and that it should be verifiable, that is it should be capable of independent verification by an independent third party including the auditors.

That's enough for now! Again, this is not an exhaustive list of possible concepts but when you come to analyse a set of accounts (a topic we will pick up in Chapters 7 and 8) keep these concepts in mind.

FINAL COMMENTS

Although this has been a fairly short chapter, the ideas contained in it are crucial for your understanding of the subject. Accounting concepts are not always intuitively sensible – they may even be described as quirky. But the 'rules' have developed for reasons which appeared valid in the context of business needs at the time. You may not agree with the rules and with the way in which accounting statements represent and misrepresent the economic reality of a business (indeed, we would encourage you to be critical). But, in order to find your way around the world of accounting, you must have a grasp of the rules which accountants use.

SUMMARY

In this chapter we have considered some of the background information in order to understand what is in the accounts. Having completed this chapter you should now understand the following key points:

- There is no single 'correct' way of accounting – often a variety of different policies could be used and it is the directors who have to choose which they feel is most appropriate in the circumstances.
- The annual report is the information about the company that is made publicly available each year. It must follow the requirements of the Companies Act, the FRSs (and the Stock Exchange requirements if appropriate).
- Many different groups of users read the accounts and they necessarily have a range of varied requirements of both the financial and non-financial information in the accounts.
- The owners (shareholders), creditors and government are usually seen as the main user groups.
- A distinction can be drawn between wishing to use the accounts for understanding what has happened (stewardship purposes) and wishing to use them to make a choice about future action (decision usefulness).
- In addition to the numerical accounting statements and their supporting notes, the annual report also includes lots of non-accounting information –

some for public relations purposes, some for corporate governance purposes and some are necessary requirements for being quoted on the Stock Exchange.

■ The content of published accounts is regulated by

- the law
- reporting standards
- the Stock Exchange (for plcs which seek a listing).

■ Accounting concepts are rules which people have agreed to abide by in producing financial reports and which the user needs to understand in order to interpret the annual report. Some concepts have been incorporated into the law but some are simply used without any comment so you need to remember that these ideas underpin the accounts.

Please turn to the back of the book for detailed answers to questions marked with a . Answers to the other questions can be found on the companion website at www.thomsonlearning.co.uk/accountingandfinace/hand

REVIEW QUESTIONS

RQ 6.1 From where does the Stock Market obtain the information it requires to make a judgement about the share price of a company?

What does the share price tell you about a particular company?

RQ 6.2 Distinguish between the use of concepts and principles in the physical sciences and their use in accounting.

RQ 6.3 Take a particular user group and identify the full range of information (financial and non-financial) that it would require in an ideal situation. Contrast this with the information provided by a set of accounts.

RQ 6.4 What do you understand by the term 'stewardship'? How does the word relate to a balance sheet?

RQ 6.5 Describe the regulatory regime under which the published accounts of companies are prepared.

RQ 6.6 Obtain a set of published accounts for any company and complete the worksheet on the following pages.

WEB RESOURCES   www

www.thomsonlearning.co.uk/accountingandfinance/hand

The companion website has free additional resources for you to use alongside this book. If you are a student you can access material to help with revision, including practice questions with answers to test how much of the material you have understood. There are also useful hyperlinks to companies and information sources mentioned in the book as well as interactive quizzes. There are additional resources for lecturers using this book on their courses; the details can be found in the preface at the front of this book.

Worksheet: corporate reports

The idea of this worksheet is to get you looking through a full set of accounts and finding information. Look at a set of published accounts and try to answer the questions that follow. If there are more than one set of financial statements in the report you select, look at those which are headed 'consolidated accounts' or 'group accounts' and not the others, which are the accounts of the holding company alone.

If you do not have a set of accounts handy you can get one easily:

- *By post* – look inside the back page of the Companies and Markets section of the *Financial Times*, at the end of the list of London Share Service prices. There is a telephone number you can call to request your chosen set of accounts.

- *Electronically* – look on a website such as www.carol.co.uk or request one from the *Financial Times* website http://ft.ar.wilink.com. Follow their links to the company accounts of your choice and download – but make sure you get the full company annual report, not just the highlights or short form report.

- If you are not sure which company to look at then try Marks and Spencer Group plc. The weblink to these is: http://www2.marksandspencer.com/ thecompany/investorrelations/annualreport/index.shtml.

Make sure you look at the annual report and financial statements rather than the (shorter) annual review which does not give all the detail we want to show you. If you send off or telephone for a copy you will get a glossy brochure with quite a few pictures but the Web version contains less pictures and colour so that it downloads more easily.

Attempt the questions in any order you like. The purpose of this questionnaire is to discover how much information you can extract from the accounts, and to provide you with an 'overview' of the corporate report. At a later stage within the book we will return to this topic and will study the reports in much more detail.

General background information

1. In what activities is the company engaged?
2. On a quick review does the company appear to be prospering?
3. What impression do you think the presentation of the accounts brochure is supposed to give?
4. What is the accounting year end for this company and for which year(s) do the accounts provide information?
5. How is the company organised? The profit and loss account probably just gives one sales, or turnover, figure – but look at the notes to the accounts. Do they explain how the turnover is earned from different

activities undertaken by the company or whether it is split into various operating divisions?

Chairman's and directors' reports

6. What tone has the report of the chairman to the shareholders? (Apologetic? Optimistic? Non-committal?)

7. How many directors are there? (Include the chairman.) You should see that some are designated executive and some non-executive directors.

8. Are the auditors mentioned in the directors' report. In what context?

Profit and loss account

9. What was the turnover for the year? Has this changed from the previous year? By how much in absolute and percentage terms?

10. What are the figures for operating and net profit for the current year and how have they changed from the previous year?

11. What was charged in the accounts for the following in the current and previous year

    (a) depreciation

    (b) auditors' remuneration

    (c) chairman's emoluments

    (d) interest on borrowings

    (e) UK corporation tax?

    What are the percentage changes? You may need to look into the notes to the profit and loss account to find some of this detail.

12. How much in total will the company pay out to the shareholders by means of a dividend? What percentage dividend rate is the company declaring? Do you think this is too much or too little?

13. Can you find the figure for earnings per share? Does this differ from the dividend per share? How does the earnings per share compare with the previous year?

Balance sheet

14. What types of fixed assets does the company own?

15. What is the total value of the fixed assets after they have been depreciated? Accountants call this the 'total net book figure' of the assets. Has this figure changed significantly over the last year and if so why?

16. What are the totals for the following groups of items

    (a) current assets

    (b) current liabilities

    (c) net current assets

    Again, what are the percentage changes from last year?

17. How does the value of stock compare with turnover?

18. What percentage of total assets are fixed and what percentage are represented by net current assets?

19. How many different types of shares have the company issued?

20. How much share capital has the company issued? Has the company issued any new shares this year, and if so how much?

21. How much share capital could the company issue?

22. Has the company obtained any long-term loans? These are sometimes referred to as 'debentures'. At what rate of interest are they being charged? When will the loans be due for repayment?

23. What is the total figure for shareholders' funds and what items are included in the total?

24. Of the total long-term liabilities that the company has, what percentage is represented by debt and what by share capital?

Notes to the accounts

25. Are there any capital commitments (obligations to invest large amounts in the future) mentioned in the notes?

26. Are there any contingent liabilities (uncertain future costs, maybe a legal case outstanding) mentioned in the notes?

General points

27. Auditors are an independent external firm of accountants who report to the members (shareholders) on how the directors have presented the accounts. Looking at the auditors' report – on what do they actually give an opinion?

28. Does the audit report appear to be a clean one? What does the phrase 'a true and fair view' represent to you?

29. Looking at the brochure as a whole – what is your impression? How much specialised knowledge would a shareholder require to understand the accounts? How easy was it for you to find and interpret the information?

A supplementary note on the professional accounting bodies' self-regulatory system

This note gives more detail about the system that operates in the UK. The Dearing Committee (chaired by Sir Ron Dearing), which reported in 1988, led to the setting up of the current system for issuing standards and reducing the number of alternative accounting policies that might be adopted by businesses:

The Financial Reporting Council is made up of a wide range of representatives from the profession. It aims to promote good financial reporting by making representations to government and advising the Accounting Standards Board (ASB).

The ASB manages and reviews of all the existing SSAPs and is issuing FRSs itself. It has also developed a Statement of Principles to give a more general framework to the subject of accounting. The ASB proceeds by having a panel of technical experts, who study an area, put forward what they think should be best practice (an exposure draft), collect comment from any interested parties and then issue a standard which therefore has some claim to be a collective decision.

When existing standards are unclear, or a new area of concern arises, the Urgent Issues Task Force (UITF) gives advice and rulings, which may eventually lead to the ASB issuing a new standard.

The Financial Reporting Review Panel (FRRP) is the joint body that monitors and enforces compliance with standards and has the power to review and report on company accounts that may come to its attention, perhaps as the result of their annual audit or press comments, or individual (sometimes anonymous) referral. Most issues are resolved by discussion but the panel has the power to apply to court for a revision of the accounts if it believes this is necessary.

You may well think that there appear to be a confusing number of councils, panels, and task forces at work here! To offer clarification, we suggest you study Exhibit 6.1 which portrays the links and roles of the various bodies described above.

Note that, at present, this is a system of self-regulation by the accounting profession. The UK government has decided not to make regulation of accounting or auditing a statutory task. At the time of writing the role of the FRRP is being expanded to make it the UK professional board for overseeing accounting, which will mean that it will also regulate auditors' standards, ethics and discipline.

Exhibit 6.1

UK standard setting and monitoring

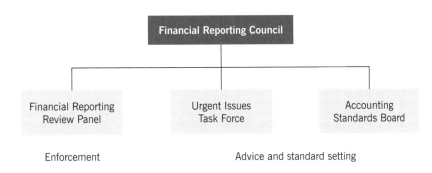

CHAPTER 7

Cash-flow statements and a broader perspective on published accounts

LEARNING OBJECTIVES

This chapter looks beyond the profit and loss account and balance sheet to the other elements of the annual financial report. After studying this chapter you should be able to:

- understand the cash-flow cycle and thus see the relevance of the view provided by the cash-flow statement
- produce a simple cash-flow statement
- identify the other information provided in a company's annual report
- discuss the potential drawbacks and limitations of published annual accounts.

Introduction

In earlier chapters we have concentrated on two financial statements which form part of a business's published accounts, the balance sheet and the profit and loss account; but in this chapter we will broaden our look at the typical published financial statements of a company.

Still in the financial accounting area, we will first focus on the use of cash in a business, which will lead us to consider the third major financial statement, the cash-flow statement; then we will review the other information contained in the published accounts; and we will end with a discussion of how useful published financial accounts are to users.

Why is cash important for a business?

A useful model to aid your understanding is to view the business as a cash-flow system. This can be shown (Exhibit 7.1) in the cash-flow cycle model, which distinguishes the long-term, often irregular, cash flows (fixed assets, share capital, dividends, taxation and borrowing) from routine working capital flows

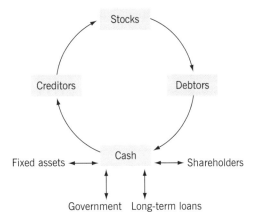

(stocks, debtors and creditors). The management of these cycles of cash flow are crucial for the survival and development of the business.

The bottom part of the model is concerned with the longer range plans of the firm, for example fixed asset investments. The top part is focused on short-run **working capital management** – it is by their performance in this area that many organisations succeed or fail.

Success in generating extra business and customers will be unhelpful unless supported by strong working capital management. Many firms, though successful at making extra sales and profits, fail to maintain adequate cash flow (for example by overstocking, or by not collecting cash from debtors); and if the cash does not come in at the right times it is then possible to fail simply because the organisation does not have enough money to pay the wages and other bills at the end of the week.

Working capital and cash flows

Let us now take a closer look at the working capital aspects of the cash-flow cycle. We will consider typical cash-flow cycles for three types of firm – manufacturing, retailing and construction – each of which has its own peculiar aspects. The accountant and other managers clearly need a detailed knowledge of the total working capital cycle of the firm in order to make sense of the effect of their own decisions upon cash flow.

In Exhibit 7.2 we see the flows for a conventional manufacturing firm. The time gap between the outflows and final collection will, in part, depend upon the nature of the industry and the product. But determined working capital management (tight stock control, rapid debt collection, etc.) can help to shorten this cycle.

For the retailer, life is relatively straightforward (see Exhibit 7.3). Not involved with making the product, and frequently selling for cash, the working capital flow is a great deal simpler. Retailers are sometimes in the fortunate position of receiving cash from customers before they have to pay the supplier! Think of Sainsbury's supermarkets. Most people pay in cash or by debit card or cheque on the spot, whereas Sainsbury's is large enough to negotiate with its suppliers so that it does not need to pay them for perhaps a month after the goods are received. But speed of turnover remains crucial, and the shelf life of products will require careful and skilled managing.

At the other extreme we can consider a construction firm, involved in long-term building projects which may take months, or even years to complete. A key feature of the construction firm's cycle (see Exhibit 7.4) is the very long gap that can occur between initial outlays and final collection of cash. In some cases progress payments (or payments on account) will be made at various stages of completion to assist the cash flow of the builder. Cash-flow problems are almost inherent within the cycle and the model goes some way towards explaining why the construction industry appears to be one of the most vulnerable to changing economic circumstances.

Exhibit 7.2

Cash-flow cycle for a manufacturer

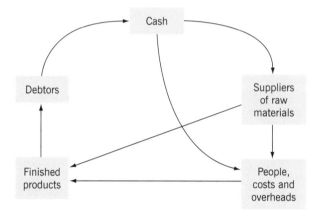

Exhibit 7.3

Cash-flow cycle for a retailer

Exhibit 7.4

Cash-flow cycle for a construction firm

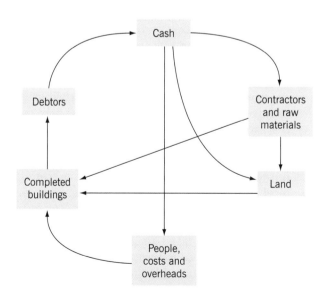

In Chapter 8 we will revisit the idea of cash-flow cycles and show how the cycle can be interpreted in terms of the number of days' trading that the cycle takes to complete. But now we will go on to look at a financial statement which attempts to give the user of the accounts an understanding of what has happened to the cash position of the business during the year.

Cash-flow statements

In the earlier chapters we have considered the balance sheet view of accounting values at the financial year end, and the income statement view of income (or profit) for the period. But there is a third statement produced by most business organisations in their published financial accounts – the cash-flow statement – which is an alternative, complementary way of looking at the performance of the business.

This third view concerns the liquidity of the business. In the earlier discussion on the importance of cash we saw that a firm, in order to survive, must make profits in the long run, even if it goes through some periods when it is unprofitable. However, an equally vital need is to ensure a flow of cash into the business at the appropriate times, sufficient to pay the outstanding bills as they arise. People will be unwilling to invest in the business for the future if they cannot see that it is likely to be able to generate enough cash to pay all the bills and have some left over to reinvest in the business and (they hope) to pay a dividend too.

We have already noted that profits do not represent cash. Thus a healthy profit and loss account (income statement) does not necessarily mean that the firm has money in the bank. Many firms have failed, not through the absence of profits, but simply from their inability to pay wages and creditors on time.

TASK 7.1

Profits are not the same as cash

Why are profits not usually equal to cash?
(Hint – refer back to Chapters 4, 5 and 6 if you are uncertain.)

The two key accounting statements that focus on the liquidity of the firm are:

- the cash-flow statement (CFS) – a retrospective statement required by accounting standards for corporate reporting purposes
- the cash budget (or forecast) – a detailed, forward-looking statement which is part of the management accounting system.

In this chapter we will concentrate on the first of these statements, the CFS. (Cash budgets are dealt with in Chapter 9 on budgeting). A general description of the CFS is:

a comparison of two consecutive balance sheets, which explains in overall terms the movement in the firm's liquid resources (i.e. cash) between the two balance sheet dates.

Events which cause cash to flow into or out of the business are classified under the following main headings in the CFS:

■ Cash flow from **operating activities** – cash flows from ordinary (trading or manufacturing) activities. This is expressed in terms of the actual cash flow from operations rather than the accounting profit made and is derived by adjusting the accounting profit for non-cash transactions.

■ Returns on investment and servicing of finance – investments made by the company, such as dividends from shares held in other companies, and interest received on money in the bank or interest and dividends paid out to investors in the company.

■ Taxation paid (or received as refund).

■ Investing activities – both capital expenditure, cash flows from buying or selling fixed assets and financial investments; and the acquisition and disposal of subsidiary companies, joint venture activities, etc.

■ Financing activities – cash received from new loans and share capital or cash paid to repay loans or share capital.

These classifications of business activities were identified by Financial Reporting Standard 1 (FRS1) 'Cash-flow statements' and are required to be used in the presentation of any CFS in a set of published accounts which is intended to give a true and fair view of the results of a business.

ILLUSTRATION 7.1

A builder's cash-flow statements

We will work through an example based upon the experience of a fictional building group of companies, Builder Group. It helps to show how a profitable company can still be desperately short of cash. Afterwards you will be able to prepare a further year's CSF in order to practise the technique.

Builder Group – income statement for three years

	Year 1	Year 2 (£m)	Year 3
Profit before tax and depreciation	32	42	55
Depreciation	2	2	3
Profit before tax	30	40	52
Taxation	1	8	19
Profit after tax	29	32	33
Dividends	7	9	13
Profits retained	22	23	20

Builder Group – balance sheets

	Year 1	End of Year 2	Year 3
Fixed assets (mainly property for rent)	54	80	94
Current assets			
stocks	214	258	299
debtors	20	26	38
cash	13	10	57
Creditors	(102)	(124)	(145)
Tax and dividends owing	(8)	(17)	(32)
Working capital	137	153	217
Loans	(46)	(58)	(70)
Net assets	145	175	241
Share capital	45	52	98
Reserves	100	123	143
Equity	145	175	241

We have constructed a CFS for Year 2 to show the sources and uses of cash in the Builder Group during this time:

Builder Group cash-flow statement

	Year 2	
Profit before tax	40	
Add depreciation	2	Converts profit to 'cash profit'
	42	
Changes in working capital:		Converts cash profit to operating
Stocks increase	(44)	cash flows
Debtors increase	(6)	
Creditors increase	22	
Net inflow from operating activities	14	
Returns on investment and servicing of finance		Dividends and interest flows
Dividends paid	(7)	
Taxation paid	(1)	

▶

Investing activities		
Fixed assets bought	(28)	The actual amount spent on new assets, so we adjusted for the depreciation effect
Net cash outflow before financing	(22)	
Financing activities		
Shares issued	7	Money from shareholders.
Loans increased	12	Extra loans from banks etc.
Net decrease in cash and cash equivalents	(3)	Difference between cost in balance sheets 1 and 2

TASK 7.2   **Builder Group cash-flow statement – Year 3**

Follow the calculations through to make sure that you are happy with how the Year 2 CFS is put together. Can you calculate the figures for year 3?

Builder Group were only able to stay liquid during this period by raising large sums from shareholders and bank lenders. The company made good profits but all of these were used up by investing in new properties and extra working capital.

The CFS statement, then, links two balance sheets and completes the traditional three-part historic accounting information set:

- balance sheet – 'snapshot' of financial position
- income statement – measure of profits/losses for the period
- cash flow – measure of liquidity of the business.

Exhibit 7.5 demonstrates the linkage between these three key accounting reports.

TASK 7.3

Use of the cash-flow statement

Why do you think that a user (of published financial reports) would need the extra view that the CFS gives?

Exhibit 7.5

Profits, position
and cash flows

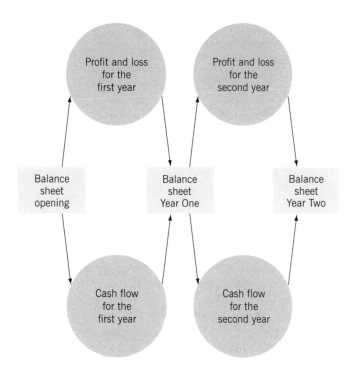

Additional information in the financial statements

We have now examined the three main financial statements that you normally see in a set of published accounts. But, as you will know from looking at real-life examples of published statements, there are normally many pages of other, finan-cial and non-financial, information published by companies in the same booklet – so now we will take a look at some of these. You might find it helpful to have another look at the annual report you used in the worksheet at the end of Chapter 5 once you have read this chapter.

Two more financial statements

The following two financial statements might be described as 'amplification' or further explanation of the picture given in the statements we have considered so far.

- **Statement of total recognised gains and losses.** Generally speaking, the profit and loss account shows **realised profits and losses**, for instance from completed transactions, and the balance sheet includes **unrealised profits and losses**, for instance from gains or losses on revalued properties. Financial Reporting Statement (FRS) 3 says that users of accounts need to know about *all* gains and losses during the period and so this statement brings the profit as shown in the profit and loss account together with all other gains and losses shown elsewhere in the accounts.

- **Statement of historical cost profits and losses.** Again, this is a requirement of FRS3, and is required if a company has revalued any of its assets. As you will recall from the previous chapter the profit is calculated using the **carrying value** (revalued figure less depreciation on the revalued figure) of any assets that have been revalued. FR3 requires this additional statement to present the profit before tax *as if* those assets had been in the accounts at historic cost all along.

Directors' report

The directors' report gives additional information which is specifically required by the Companies Acts but which cannot usually be incorporated into the main financial statements as it is often not numerical, for example the names of the directors and how many shares each one owns in the company.

Auditors' report

In the UK it is no longer the case that all companies have to have an annual audit by law. Until recently those small private companies (Ltd) with a turnover under £1m per year and a balance sheet total of less than £1.4m did not have to have one (and the Department of Trade and Industry decided that these figures should be increased so that for accounting years after March 2004 companies with a turnover of less than £5.6m do not have to have an audit). However, they often choose to do so as do some other types of organisation that are not limited companies, and all public limited companies (plcs) still have to have an annual audit. This requirement came about because it is quite common to own shares in a company, i.e. be a part owner, and yet have nothing to do with the daily running of the organisation. Thus an external firm of accountants will be employed to report on the accounts. The auditors' report gives an independent opinion to the shareholders (owners) of a company on whether the financial statements and notes to the accounts show a 'true and fair view' of the company's position, cash flow and profit and loss for the period.

Take a look at the Marks and Spencer auditors' report in their accounts for the year to March 2003 (Exhibit 7.6). As you see, the report falls into four main sections and is a report 'to the members', i.e. to the shareholders of Marks and Spencer Group plc:

1. The introductory lines identify what exactly has been audited – note that this does not include a significant chunk of the first 20 pages of the report.

2. Responsibilities of directors and auditors – this section explains who is legally responsible for doing what and gives an outline of what the auditors have looked at in the course of the audit.

3. Basis of audit opinion – explains the sources of information on which the auditors' opinion was formulated.

4. Opinion – the auditors give an opinion as to whether the accounts show a true and fair view. The vast majority of sets of accounts you see will have a 'clean' audit report (the auditor saying that the accounts *do* show a true and fair view) as discussions during the audit will probably have led to any necessary amendments to the accounts to make sure that the auditor can say this. But if the auditors find that they do not have enough evidence on which to make their opinion or if they believe that the accounts do not show a true and fair view then they must say so in their report.

Independent auditors' report to the members of Marks and Spencer Group p.l.c.
We have audited the financial statements which comprise the profit and loss account, the balance sheets, the cash flow statement, the note of group historical cost profits and losses, consolidated statement of total recognised gains and losses and the related notes. We have also audited the disclosures required by Part 3 of Schedule 7A to the Companies Act 1985 contained in the directors' remuneration report ('the auditable part').

Respective responsibilities of directors and auditors
The directors' responsibilities for preparing the Annual Report, the directors' remuneration report and the financial statements in accordance with applicable United Kingdom law and accounting standards are set out in the statement of directors' responsibilities.

Our responsibility is to audit the financial statements and the auditable part of the directors' remuneration report in accordance with relevant legal and regulatory requirements and United Kingdom Auditing Standards issued by the Auditing Practices Board. This opinion has been prepared for and only for the Company's members in accordance with Section 235 of the Companies Act 1985 and for no other purpose. We do not, in giving this opinion, accept or assume responsibility for any other purpose or to any other person to whom this report is shown or in to whose hands it may come save where expressly agreed by our prior consent in writing.

We report to you our opinion as to whether the financial statements give a true and fair view and whether the financial statements and the auditable part of the directors' remuneration report have been properly prepared in accordance with the Companies Act 1985. We also report to you if, in our opinion, the directors' report is not consistent with the financial statements, if the Company has not kept proper accounting records, if we have not received all the information and explanations we require for our audit, or if information specified by law regarding directors' remuneration and transactions is not disclosed.

We read the other information contained in the Annual Report and consider the implications for our report if we become aware of any apparent misstatements or material inconsistencies with the financial statements. The other information comprises only the directors' report, the unaudited part of the directors' remuneration report, the chairman's statement, the operating and financial review and the corporate governance statement.

We review whether the corporate governance statement reflects the Company's compliance with the seven provisions of the Combined Code specified for our review by the Listing Rules of the Financial Services Authority, and we report if it does not. We are not required to consider whether the Board's statements on internal control cover all risks and controls, or to form an opinion on the effectiveness of the Company's or Group's corporate governance procedures or its risk and control procedures.

Basis of audit opinion
We conducted our audit in accordance with Auditing Standards issued by the Auditing Practices Board. An audit includes examination, on a test basis, of evidence relevant to the amounts and disclosures in the financial statements and the auditable part of the directors' remuneration report. It also includes an assessment of the significant estimates and judgements made by the directors in the preparation of the financial statements, and of whether the accounting policies are appropriate to the Company's and Group's circumstances, consistently applied and adequately disclosed.

We planned and performed our audit so as to obtain all the information and explanations which we considered necessary in order to provide us with sufficient evidence to give reasonable assurance that the financial statements and the auditable part of the directors' remuneration report are free from material misstatement, whether caused by fraud or other irregularity or error. In forming our opinion we also evaluated the overall adequacy of the presentation of information in the financial statements.

Opinion
In our opinion:

- the financial statements give a true and fair view of the state of affairs of the Company and the Group at 29 March 2003 and of the profit and cash flows of the Group for the year then ended;

- the financial statements have been properly prepared in accordance with the Companies Act 1985; and

- those parts of the directors' remuneration report required by Part 3 of Schedule 7A to the Companies Act 1985 have been properly prepared in accordance with the Companies Act 1985.

PricewaterhouseCoopers LLP
Chartered Accountants and Registered Auditors
London
19 May 2003

Notes to the Accounts

The Notes to the Accounts give more information about particular figures in the financial statements. When you look at the statements you will notice little numbers alongside many items referring you to the notes which typically follow later in the accounts. Many of these are specifically required by law or other regulations (remember Chapter 6) but they can also be used by the directors, who are responsible for the annual accounts, to make sure the users of the accounts have enough detailed information to appreciate how the business has performed over the year. Usually the length of all the notes exceeds the length of the main financial statements (balance sheet, profit and loss account and CSF) by some distance.

Non-financial information

It is becoming increasingly common for users to demand much more non-financial information. Answers to the following questions may be seen as important by various groups of accounts users:

- How 'green' and environmentally friendly are the products of the business?
- What type of company is it to work for?
- Does the company provide
  - training?
  - crèche facilities?
- How many women are there in senior positions within the company?

Published accounts may incorporate some of this type of information at the discretion of the directors. It is often called 'soft' data in that the numbers are much more subjective; they are not hard data in the way that a financial transaction is and so they are not audited in the same way as the main financial statements. They must, therefore, be treated with caution.

Much of this type of information will be found within the notes to the accounts or in the **chairman's statement**, which typically reviews the year, highlights the major achievements and outlines the future prospects. In spite of the fact that it is not audited, this statement is often the most popular with shareholders.

Some accountants are not happy with the move to include more information of a non-financial nature. They see this as undermining the true purpose of a set of accounts and feel there is a danger that the published accounts become no more than a public relations document. Many companies actually employ a PR agency to help make their accounts more 'effective' in promoting the corporate image.

Groups of companies

Many businesses operate as groups of companies. Consequently, at the year end they prepare **consolidated accounts**, which show users the state of affairs and profit or loss for the year for the whole group.

In a typical group situation, the **parent company** (or **holding company**) does not directly own all the factories, shops, etc.: it owns shares in **subsidiary** companies. The manufacturing and marketing work is carried on by the various subsidiary companies. However, the subsidiaries are controlled by the parent company and are therefore deemed in economical terms to be part of the same business.

If you looked at the parent company accounts alone they would show the investments in subsidiary companies as a single asset on the balance sheet. The process of consolidation involves replacing those investments by the actual assets and liabilities controlled in the subsidiaries. Thus the group balance sheet will show the total fixed assets, stocks, cash, creditors, etc. of all the companies in the group. As part of the process of consolidation, the investment by the parent in the subsidiaries' shares and amounts owed to each other by group companies are cancelled out, leaving the group presented as a single business alongside the figures for the holding company itself.

As a result of this process, two extra headings tend to appear in group balance sheets.

- A parent company normally pays more to acquire a going concern subsidiary than the accounting value of the subsidiary's assets, mainly because of items like goodwill and staff loyalty. Consequently, an asset called 'goodwill on consolidation' sometimes appears in the group balance sheet (the difference between the price paid for the company and the balance sheet value of all its tangible assets).

- Some subsidiaries are not owned 100 per cent by the parent, even though the holding company is able to control them. The people who own the remainder of the shares, other than the parent company, in effect own a small share of the total group. This is recognised by including a 'minority interests' figure in the liabilities on the group balance sheet.

Some drawbacks to published accounts

Because published accounts are prepared in retrospect and in money terms, there are some drawbacks to the amount and type of information that users are able to get from them. For example:

- The accounts look backwards, usually over the past year, so they are of limited value to people who want to estimate future performance.

- We have seen that the contents of published financial statements are largely prescribed by the Companies Acts (supplemented by SSAPs and FRSs). Most organisations treat the Companies Acts as the maximum disclosure requirement and do not give much more information than that to outsiders, on grounds of confidentiality and maintaining competitive advantage.

- Some important assets that cannot be easily valued in money terms have to be left out, for example customer goodwill, staff skill and employee loyalty.

- Assets are generally recorded at historical (original) cost which, after a period of inflation, can be quite out of touch with their current values. It is possible to address this problem by revaluing specific assets, if needed, to understand the company's position better.

FINAL COMMENTS

The aim of this chapter has been to build on the examination of the balance sheet and profit and loss account in earlier chapters and to look at the wider picture that the whole set of published financial statements can provide for the informed user. This links with Chapter 11 which discusses the corporate governance information also published in the annual report.

It should be clear that, to get a good understanding of the performance of a business, it is not possible to focus on single indicators such as profit or share price. For example, if the company has made a profit, is it also solvent and able to pay bills as they fall due?

It is necessary to take a much wider view to form a reliable opinion of past performance if you hope to make decisions about the future. In the next chapter we consider the interpretation of accounting reports and the ways in which we can begin to evaluate financial performance.

SUMMARY

In this chapter we have looked at some of the additional information you can find in the financial report. The following concepts and techniques have been covered:

■ The cash-flow cycle and the importance of cash to the business were discussed. Several examples were given of how different business circumstances led to different rates of cash flow.

■ This led on to the worth of having a financial statement, called the cash-flow statement, that reported retrospectively on how cash had been used in the business in the accounting period just ended.

■ We also looked at the other financial statements required by the accounting regulations:

  – the statement of total recognised gains and losses

  – the statement of historical cost profits and losses

  – the notes to the financial statements.

■ In addition we noted that the financial statements often contain other, non-financial information such as the chairman's report and the directors' report.

■ As many companies operate using funds supplied by shareholders who do not take an active part in the day-to-day running of the business, the auditors' report is the shareholders' reassurance that an independent third party has examined the stewardship of the company's assets by the directors.

■ However, there are some drawbacks to relying upon company accounts to understand what has been going on in the business and to using them as a basis for making decisions about future actions.

Please turn to the back of the book for detailed answers to questions marked with a ❓. Answers to the other questions can be found on the companion website at www.thomsonlearning.co.uk/accountingandfinance/hand

REVIEW QUESTIONS

RQ 7.1 Evaluate the major accounting statements in terms of their usefulness to a potential investor by examining the information content of each.

RQ 7.2 Review the CFS in the published accounts of any company. Can you explain the main figures in the CFS by reference to other parts of the accounts?

RQ 7.3 Can you identify any limitations in the CFS as discussed in this chapter?

NUMERICAL PROBLEMS

NP 7.1 **County Brewery revisited** Return to the figures from Task 4.6 on County Brewery. The figures, although not very detailed, should allow you to produce a CFS for the firm.

NP 7.2 **Health and pharmaceutical retailer – cash-flow statements** Consider the CFS for the company below. The company retails health care products, medicines and general beauty products. Some of the products are also manufactured by the firm, while others are bought in. Note down the main points which this statement reveals about the company.

	Year 2 £m	Year 2 £m
Profit before tax	132	117
Depreciation	14	15
	146	132
Working capital		
Stocks (increase) decrease	13	(21)
Debtors (increase) decrease	1	(11)
Creditors increase	19	3
Net cash flow from operating activities	179	103
Returns on investment and servicing of finance		
Dividends paid	(33)	(27)
Taxation paid	(40)	(45)
Cash flows from investing activities		
Fixed assets bought	(58)	(83)
Sale of fixed assets	20	13
Investment in new subsidiaries	(18)	(2)
Net flows before financing activities	50	(41)
Financing activities		
Loan repayments	(6)	—
Shares issued	1	1
Increase/(decrease) in cash balances	45	(40)

NP 7.3 Avago – cash-flow statements Prepare a CFS for Avago plc (an imaginary firm) for Year 2 and Year 3, from the income statements and balance sheets given below.

Income statements

	Year 1 (£m)		Year 2 (£m)		Year 3 (£m)
Sales		500		600		800
Cost of goods sold		300		360		520
Gross profit		200		240		280
Loan interest	2		4		4	
Depreciation	18		18		20	
Other expenses	124	144	158	180	174	198
Net profit before tax		56		60		82
Corporation tax		24		26		36
Net profit after tax		32		34		46
Dividend		12		20		20
Profit retained		20		14		26

Balance sheets

	Year 1 (£m)	Year 2 (£m)	Year 3 (£m)
Fixed assets	180	238	252
Less depreciation	50	68	88
	130	170	164
Current assets:			
Stock	68	72	88
Debtors	56	60	100
Cash	—	—	4
	124	132	192
Current liabilities (payable in less than one year)			
Creditors	38	40	60
Tax	24	26	36
Dividend	12	20	20
Overdraft	—	2	—
	74	88	116
Net current assets	50	44	76
Loans	(30)	(50)	(50)
Net assets	150	164	190

▶

Share capital	100	100	100
Reserves	50	64	90
	150	164	190

NP 7.4 Colours

	Red %	Orange %	Yellow %
Assets			
Land and building	3	0.5	33
Other fixed assets	0.5	5.5	7
Goodwill	—	3	—
Stocks and work in progress	—	25	40
Trade debtors	67	55	8
Other debtors	5	5	2
Cash and investments	24.5	6	10
	100	100	100
Liabilities			
Trade creditors	82	35	38
Other creditors	7	27	16
Bank overdrafts	20	5	—
Loan capital	5	8	17
Share capital and reserves	6	10	24
	100	100	100

The summarised balance sheets of three companies are shown above, expressed in terms of percentage of net assets employed in each kind of asset/ liability.

Each comes from one of the following sectors:

- advertising and public relations
- construction
- high street banking
- retail clothing chain with a large number of shops.

Can you decide which industry each company comes from and explain your choice?

NP 7.5 Comparative balance sheets Below are the activities of eight companies, and information from the companies' balance sheets expressed as percentages of net assets employed. You are required to state, with reasons, which balance sheet you consider belongs to which of the companies.

The respective areas of activity of the companies are:

A general engineering
B investment in properties for rental
C estate development and house builders
D whisky distillers and blenders
E brewers
F retail stores
G conglomerate with various activities
H insurance brokers.

The assets and current liabilities shown as percentage of net assets employed are:

	Company							
	1 (%)	2 (%)	3 (%)	4 (%)	5 (%)	6 (%)	7 (%)	8 (%)
Land and property	83	31	2	32	72	81	11	147
Other fixed assets	13	28	3	22	23	7	9	3
Stock and work in progress	8	43	111	45	—	11	75	—
Trade debtors	11	36	36	56	436	4	18	7
Cash/temporary investments	4	5	1	3	91	7	1	1
	119	143	153	158	622	110	114	158
Trade creditors	(19)	(34)	(35)	(47)	(509)	(10)	(9)	(9)
Bank overdrafts	(—)	(9)	(18)	(11)	(13)	(—)	(5)	(49)
Net assets employed	100	100	100	100	100	100	100	100

WEB RESOURCES

www.thomsonlearning.co.uk/accountingandfinance/hand

The companion website has free additional resources for you to use alongside this book. If you are a student you can access material to help with revision, including practice questions with answers to test how much of the material you have understood. There are also useful hyperlinks to companies and information sources mentioned in the book as well as interactive quizzes. There are additional resources for lecturers using this book on their courses; the details can be found in the preface at the front of this book.

CHAPTER 8

The interpretation of accounting statements

LEARNING OBJECTIVES

After studying this chapter you should be able to:

- understand and apply the full range of accounting ratios
- calculate a range of accounting ratios appropriate to the analysis you are about to undertake
- demonstrate an ability to select the correct data and calculate an appropriate ratio
- understand the strengths and weaknesses of using accounting ratios to perform analysis.

Introduction

Having worked through Chapters 6 and 7 you will now be familiar with the contents of the published financial statements. These reports and the analysis undertaken fall within the domain of financial accounting. The question raised in this chapter is: how can the information contained within the published financial statements be analysed to reveal more about the performance of the business?

We will look at ways in which we can use the basic information presented in the financial statements to glean more information than at first appears, and how we can interpret that information and hence judge the performance of the managers and of the business as a whole. In particular, shareholders may wish to use the accounts as a basis for economic decisions. Should they continue to hold the shares they have, should they purchase some more or should they sell all their holding? Fundamentally the analysis performed is based upon external publicly available information contained within a set of published accounts. Clearly the managers will have access to more detailed accounting information and will be performing their own analysis for monitoring and control purposes.

Methods of evaluating performance

Investors, managers and other groups will attempt to assess the performance of a firm using many different sources of information, non-financial as well as financial. The accounting statements will be the primary source of financial information for those outside the company.

Incidentally, don't forget that there are limitations to accounting data which may reduce the value of the information, such as the fact that it is historical information. In earlier chapters we saw that past performance is no guarantee of future success, and that some of the figures, like depreciation and stocks, are subjective and based on decisions specific to a particular company.

The amounts shown as figures in the statements (profit/asset values, etc.) will tell us something about the business. However, absolute (or actual numerical) values are of little use in interpreting the underlying performance of the business. If the profit was £5000, for example, is this good, bad or mediocre?

We could look at the trend or direction/size of change. For example, if profit goes up from £500 000 in Year 1 to £600 000 in Year 2 we can say that it has increased by 20 per cent. It will often enhance our understanding if we are also able to set these observations in a wider context – either the longer term (by looking for trends in the performances of the single firm over successive years) or in the context of the business sector; for example, what are competitors achieving? What is the average for this business sector?

Increased insights into the firm's financial performance can be gained by looking further and examining relationships between various important values in the accounts using ratio analysis.

Ratio analysis

Accounting ratios are merely the result of bringing together two figures and expressing one as a percentage or ratio of the other.

Thus, the figure of £500 000 profit above, when compared to our sales value of (say) £10m, tells us that we are obtaining a 5 per cent profit on sales. If we have access to information for the previous year we may discover that profit was £450 000 on sales of £7.5m (i.e. 6 per cent). Although sales and profits have increased in absolute terms we are receiving a lower return on our sales than last year.

The ratio calculations will, of course, depend upon the availability and accuracy of basic accounting data. People outside the organisation will have to rely upon the historic data published in the annual report. Within the firm far more detailed information will be available than to outsiders and so it will be possible to produce a far more detailed ratio analysis. It is also common practice to evaluate forecast information using ratios to see what effect the future plans will have on these performance indicators. In this chapter we will examine only some of the ratios that can be calculated from published accounts.

Many different ratios may be calculated from the financial statements of a business. The only limit should be the perceived usefulness to the user. Users may create a particular ratio of value to them that no one has considered before. There is no limit to the number of ratios that could be calculated. However, the more useful ratios are commonly grouped into four categories, which we will examine shortly:

- profitability
- liquidity
- gearing (or borrowing)
- investment.

In practice, you will often see slight variations in the formulae used to calculate many of the ratios. This often depends upon exactly who will be using the information. But for the purposes of consistency within this book we will define the main ratios in the ways that we demonstrate below and at the same time we will use the accounts of Sainsbury's and Tesco to illustrate how the ratios are calculated and interpreted.

Profitability ratios

Not surprisingly profitability ratios are a group of ratios which help to assess the performance of the business in terms of how its profit (or loss) relates to certain other figures in the accounts. You could calculate ratios which relate profit to any other figure in the whole set of accounts, but it would not be very helpful to work out a ratio of profit to, say, the amount that is owed to suppliers, as these are unlikely to be interdependent figures.

However, a shareholder, for example, might be very interested in the ratio of how much profit the business has made given the amount of finance made available by the shareholders.

Return on equity

$$\text{Return on equity} = \frac{\text{Profit before tax} \times 100}{\text{Shareholders' funds}}$$

Return on equity gives an overall measure of the return which the business is achieving upon the funds that shareholders have provided. This ratio is sometimes calculated using the profit after tax, as it is recognised that tax is imposed by the government and has to be paid before the shareholders can hope to get any dividend. A shareholder would want to use this ratio to compare the company's performance with other investment opportunities.

	Ratio 2002	Ratio 2001
Sainsbury's	$\frac{571 \times 100}{4\ 848} = 11.78\%$	$\frac{437 \times 100}{4\ 751} = 9.19\%$
Tesco	$\frac{1201 \times 100}{5\ 530} = 21.71\%$	$\frac{1054 \times 100}{4\ 978} = 21.17\%$

Sainsbury's and Tesco summarised accounts £millions profit and loss accounts

Sainsbury's			Tesco	
2002	2001		2002	2001
17 162	17 244	Turnover excluding VAT	23 653	20 988
15 905	16 082	Cost of sales	21 866	19 400
1 257	1 162	Gross profit	1 787	1 588
(632)	(629)	Administration	(465)	(422)
0	0	Other income	32	13
625	533	Operating/trading profit	1 354	1 179
(5)	(20)	Exceptional items	0	0
(49)	(76)	Net interest payable	(153)	(125)
571	437	Profit before tax	1 201	1 054
(200)	157)	Taxation	(371)	(333)
371	280	Profit after tax	830	721
(7)	(4)	Minority interest	0	1
364	276	Attributable profit	830	722
(285)	(274)	Dividends	(390)	(340)
79	2	Retained profit	440	382

Balance sheets

Sainsbury's			Tesco	
		Fixed assets		
263	278	Intangible assets	154	154
6 906	6 215	Net tangible fixed assets	11 032	9 580
174	164	Long-term investments	317	304
7 343	6 657		11 503	10 038
		Current assets		
2 193	1 914	Sainsbury's Bank		
751	763	Stock	929	838
398	546	Debtors	454	322
16	12	Short-term investments	225	255
370	475	Cash and deposits	445	279
3 728	3 710		2 053	1 694
		Less current liabilities		
(2 060)	(1 796)	Sainsbury's Bank		
(345)	(374)	Short-term borrowings	(1 474)	(1 389)
(140)	(127)	Taxation payable	(259)	(292)
(207)	(197)	Proposed dividend	(283)	(246)
(1 956)	(1 831)	Trade and other creditors	(2 793)	(2 462)
(980)	(615)	Net current liabilities	(2 756)	(2 695)
(1 223)	(1 000)	Long-term borrowings	(2 741)	(1 927)
(231)	(238)	Other long-term liabilities	(440)	(402)
4 909	4 804	Net assets	5 566	5 014
4 848	4 751	Shareholders' funds	5 530	4 978
61	53	Minority interest	36	36
4 909	4 804		5 566	5 014

An investor has a wide range of investment opportunities available. The returns that can be obtained are broadly connected to the degree of risk the investor is prepared to take. A zero risk investment would be to place the funds in a deposit account with a bank or building society which would currently give a return of between 3 and 4.5 per cent. Alternatively you could buy a share in Tesco which is offering 21.71 per cent or Sainsbury's at 11.78 per cent. However, with both Tesco and Sainsbury's you take the risk that you may lose some or all of your original investment. The value of your shares can go down as well as up. On the basis of this one ratio Tesco appears to be a much better performing company than Sainsbury's, with a return on equity nearly double that of Sainsbury's. But how has this been achieved? We need to calculate a broad range of ratios before we are able to come to any firm conclusions about the relative strengths and weaknesses of the two businesses.

Specifically the return on equity ratio is used as a guide to the potential return that a particular company may generate in the future and would be used as a benchmark figure for any investor considering making an investment in either of these two companies.

Return on capital employed

Return on capital employed is often abbreviated as ROCE.

$$\text{Return on capital employed} = \frac{\text{Profit before interest and tax}}{\text{Total long-term capital}}$$

By total long-term capital we mean shareholders' funds together with any long-term debts. This ratio then is very similar to return on equity but, by including the long-term debt, we are looking at the return earned from the total capital employed in the business as opposed to the pure equity.

The profit before interest and tax figure cannot be picked directly from the profit and loss acount. But for this ratio we want a profit figure before the payments to any of the providers of finance are deducted. Therefore we will add back the interest figure to the profit before tax figure.

Sainsbury's			Tesco	
2002	2001		2002	2001
571	437	Profit before tax	1 201	1 054
49	76	Interest payable	153	125
620	513	Profit before interest and tax	1 354	1 179

The long-term capital is found by taking the shareholders' equity plus long-term borrowings.

Sainsbury's			Tesco	
2002	2001		2002	2001
(1 223)	(1 000)	Long-term borrowings	(2 741)	(1 927)
4 848	4 751	Shareholders' funds	5 530	4 978
61	53	Minority interest	36	36
4 909	4 804		5 566	5 014

	Ratio 2002	**Ratio 2001**
Sainsbury's	$\dfrac{620 \times 100}{4\ 909 + 1\ 223} = 10.11\%$	$\dfrac{513 \times 100}{4\ 804 + 1\ 000} = 8.8\%$
Tesco	$\dfrac{1\ 354 \times 100}{5\ 566 + 2\ 741} = 16.30\%$	$\dfrac{1\ 179 \times 100}{5\ 014 + 1\ 927} = 16.99\%$

The ratio represents the return that the total investment in the two businesses is generating. This will be used as a benchmark by managers and investors in ranking the businesses alongside other investment opportunities. Remember, though, that the greater the return the greater degree of risk. One has to be careful and not to risk all of one's investments within high-earning projects as there is a greater risk of losing all one's money.

Note that the return on investment is in each case lower than that shown from the return on equity calculation. This is because both companies have taken on debt and have become more highly geared. This has the consequence of increasing the returns available to shareholders. Essentially both businesses have borrowed funds at a low rate and then invested them in the business and generated the returns we see in the above table. The extra return goes to the shareholders as an extra benefit.

Users interested in the efficiency of the business might look at the next two ratios as a guide to how effectively the business controls the costs of the business. These look at two different levels of profit and compare them to the earnings from sales.

Gross margin

$$\text{Gross margin} = \frac{\text{Gross profit}}{\text{Sales}} \times 100$$

Gross margin indicates the profitability of products sold before any other general costs of the business have been considered. It can be expressed as the number of pence of gross profit in each pound of sales, or as a percentage. In an ideal situation this ratio would, at least, remain constant, if not increasing. This would mean that, as price increases are received from suppliers, the company is able to pass them on directly to their customers. However, the market may be very price sensitive and so the comany may not be able to do this. As a result margins would fall and this would be reflected in the ratio. The ratio can also be affected by the stock holding policy and the levels of stock shrinkage that the business incurs. This ratio then is often used to monitor the efficiency of the warehousing function within the organisation.

	Ratio 2002	Ratio 2001
Sainsbury's	$\dfrac{1\ 257 \times 100}{17\ 162} = 7.32\%$	$\dfrac{1\ 162 \times 100}{17\ 244} = 6.73\%$
Tesco	$\dfrac{1\ 787 \times 100}{23\ 653} = 7.55\%$	$\dfrac{1\ 588 \times 100}{20\ 988} = 7.57\%$

We can see that Tesco has a slightly larger margin than Sainsbury's which, allied to a greater amount of sales (Tesco's £23 billion to Sainsbury's £17 billion), gives Tesco a clear profit advantage as they then make more profit on each £ of sale than Sainsbury's. Groceries do not have large profit margins so the supermarkets must go for large volume in sales. Their other strategy is to move into selling items with higher profit margins and this explains the inclusion of clothing and homeware into their product ranges. The gross profit margins in the UK are significantly higher than the European average of around 2.5 per cent and the US average of only 0.5 per cent. It was these high margins that prompted the Competition Commission to investigate the supermarkets but the final report largely exonerated the UK supermarket business.

Net profit

$$\text{Net profit to sales} = \frac{\text{Profit before tax}}{\text{Sales}} \times 100$$

The **net profit to sales ratio** focuses on profit, after all expenses of the business, compared to sales.

It indicates the profitability of each £1 of sales.

If you spot a variation between one period and the next in the net profit to sales figure you may wish to investigate further by calculating individual expenses as a proportion of sales.

	Ratio 2002	Ratio 2001
Sainsbury's	$\dfrac{571 \times 100}{17\ 162} = 3.33\%$	$\dfrac{437 \times 100}{17\ 244} = 2.53\%$
Tesco	$\dfrac{1\ 201 \times 100}{23\ 653} = 5.08\%$	$\dfrac{1\ 054 \times 100}{20\ 988} = 5.02\%$

Again note Tesco's superior performance: in 2001 their margin is nearly double that of Sainsbury's! This means that for every £ of sales in 2001 Sainsbury's made a net profit of 2.5 pence whilst Tesco made 5.03 pence.

Another way of looking at efficiency is to focus on activity.

Asset turnover

$$\text{Asset turnover} = \frac{\text{Sales}}{\text{Net assets}}$$

The **asset turnover ratio** measures the 'level of activity' of the business – how efficiently the assets of the business have been used to generate sales. This kind of measure might be used by the owners to take a view on how well managers are utilising the assets. A falling ratio may indicate redundant assets, or assets not being fully utilised.

	Ratio 2002	Ratio 2001
Sainsbury's	$\frac{17\,162 \times 100}{4\,909} = 3.5\%$	$\frac{17\,244 \times 100}{4\,804} = 3.59\%$
Tesco	$\frac{23\,653 \times 100}{5\,566} = 4.25\%$	$\frac{20\,988 \times 100}{5\,014} = 4.18\%$

To build a new large supermarket can cost in the region of £3 million to £4 million. It is essential that this investment generates as much revenue as is possible. Two of the measures often used by the retail sector is 'sales per square foot' and 'profit per square foot'. This is their way of monitoring how well they are using the asset of selling space available to them.

Liquidity ratios

Liquidity ratios are designed to help the user take a view of the ability of the business to meet bills as they fall due. So they could be used by anyone who is thinking of lending to a company, or supplying it with goods, or hoping that they may be paid a dividend. But use these ratios with caution, since they are all calculated from the year end accounts and the picture could well have changed if the ratio is being calculated at a date some time after that balance sheet date.

Current ratio

$$\text{Current ratio} = \frac{\text{Current assets}}{\text{Current liabilities}}$$

The **current ratio** indicates the amount of cover for the short-term liabilities: in other words, the number of times the current liabilities can be paid out of the current assets. Take the figures straight from the balance sheet: this calculation is easy and quick to calculate.

Sainsbury's	Ratio 2002	Ratio 2001
	$\dfrac{3\ 728}{4\ 708} = 0.79{:}1$	$\dfrac{3\ 710}{4\ 325} = 0.86{:}1$
Tesco	$\dfrac{2\ 053}{4\ 809} = 0.42{:}1$	$\dfrac{1\ 694}{4\ 389} = 0.38{:}1$

Some textbooks offer a simple yardstick stating that this figure should ideally be around 2:1, and should never approach 1:1 as this will mean that the company is in danger of becoming insolvent. (By this they mean that the company would have insufficient cash to pay any bills or the wages of the workers on a particular date). But, as can be seen from the above, both Tesco and Sainsbury's are operating at much lower figures than this. Their current assets are actually lower than their current liabilities! This is because a supermarket generates lots of cash every day through the tills and so they can afford to have minimum levels of cash on deposit to meet outstanding debts, knowing that they will be receiving more cash through the business every day.

Quick ratio

$$\text{Quick ratio} = \frac{\text{(Current assets less stock)}}{\text{Current liabilities}}$$

The **quick ratio** shows how well short-term liabilities are covered by cash or near-cash assets. This is a particularly useful secondary calculation if the business happens to be one where it can take quite a long time to turn the stocks into cash, for example heavy construction. It is less vital in an industry where you would expect very speedy turnover of stocks, for example, a greengrocer.

Bank overdrafts are sometimes excluded from current liabilities in the calculation of this ratio because, although overdrafts are legally repayable on demand, in practice they are often long-term liabilities.

	Ratio 2002	Ratio 2001
Sainsbury's	$\dfrac{3\ 728 - 751}{4\ 708} = 0.63{:}1$	$\dfrac{3\ 710 - 763}{4\ 325} = 0.68{:}1$
Tesco	$\dfrac{2\ 053 - 929}{4\ 809} = 0.23{:}1$	$\dfrac{1\ 694 - 838}{4\ 389} = 0.195{:}1$

Again, many textbooks state that this ratio should not fall below 1:1. This is too general a statement. It all depends upon the nature of the business. As previously stated, supermarkets can afford to operate on very low figures for this ratio because of their cash generating abilities; for other businesses with long production and delivery times this would not be appropriate and as a result their ratios will be at a much higher level. An ideal figure therefore does not exist; it all depends upon the nature of the particular business.

Interpretation of the ratios

We would not be looking for any 'ideal' answer from these ratios. The appropriate level of liquidity varies from business to business, depending on the kind of sector in which it is operating, which will determine how long the working capital takes to circulate through the business. Working capital is the amount of money needed to finance the current assets and liabilities of the business – for example, if you allow your customers to buy goods from you on credit, you must have enough cash to be able to keep operating until they pay you, say, 30 days later.

Further liquidity ratios

It is often useful to calculate some further ratios which look more closely at the constituent parts of the current assets and current liabilities figures and can help to explain unexpected movements in the current and quick ratios.

Stock turn or stock turnover

You may come across either stock turn or **stock turnover** – the terms are used interchangeably.

$$\text{Stock turnover} = \frac{\text{Cost of sales}}{\text{Stock}}$$

This ratio measures the average speed at which stocks move through the business. It gives you an idea of whether the business is using its working capital efficiently, by moving stocks very quickly (a high stock turnover), or inefficiently – a low stock turnover implies that the stocks spend a long time sitting in the warehouse. There are also non-financial considerations that should be taken into account here though, in that too high a stock turnover may mean that there is not enough stock kept in the warehouse and unlucky customers may find the firm unable to fulfil an order.

The figure of stock in this calculation could either be the year end figure or the arithmetic average using the opening and closing stock figures if available. A word of caution: the levels of stock held at year end may be different from the actual levels throughout the year.

	Ratio 2002	Ratio 2001
Sainsbury's	$15\ 905 \div \dfrac{751 + 763}{2} = 21.01$	$\dfrac{16\ 082}{763} = 21.07$
Tesco	$21\ 866 \div \dfrac{929 + 838}{2} = 24.75$	$\dfrac{19\ 400}{838} = 23.15$

For the year 2002 we were able to use the opening and closing figures of stock from the balance sheet to calculate average stock. Clearly the information is not available to repeat the process for 2001 so we have used the closing stock figure only. This is quite common in this type of analysis and so we need to take this into account when analysing the results.

In each year Tesco are turning their stock over more times than Sainsbury's, which suggests that Tesco have better control of the stock in terms of availability and throughput to the customers and/or a lower level of stock loss than Sainsbury's.

Debtor turn or debtor turnover

$$\text{Debtor turnover} = \frac{\text{Sales}}{\text{Trade debtors}}$$

Debtor turnover measures the average speed of customer payments. In general, the higher this ratio the better, as this means that there is only a small proportion of sales made that have not yet been paid for.

	Ratio 2002	Ratio 2001
Sainsbury's	$\dfrac{17\ 162}{398} = 43.12$	$\dfrac{17\ 244}{546} = 31.58$
Tesco	$\dfrac{23\ 653}{454} = 52.01$	$\dfrac{20\ 988}{322} = 65.18$

Sainsbury's are shortening the length of time they are giving their debtors to pay whereas Tesco's position is slightly deteriorating. For both business this is not a critical ratio as the bulk of their customers pay immediately in cash. For a manufacturing concern selling on credit then this would be a much more important ratio as it would represent a significant investment in working capital.

Creditor turn or creditor turnover

$$\text{Creditor turnover} = \frac{\text{Cost of sales}}{\text{Trade creditors}}$$

Creditor turnover indicates the average speed of payments to suppliers.

	Ratio 2002	**Ratio 2001**
Sainsbury's	$\dfrac{15\ 905}{1\ 956} = 8.13$	$\dfrac{16\ 082}{1\ 831} = 8.78$
Tesco	$\dfrac{21\ 866}{2\ 793} = 7.83$	$\dfrac{19\ 400}{2\ 462} = 7.88$

Creditor, debtor and stock turnover ratios are often adjusted to show the number of days' trading represented by the amount of creditors, debtors or stock held at the year end. To convert, divide your answer into 365:

$$\frac{365}{\text{Debtor turnover ratio}} = \text{the number of days' sales for which customers owe us money}$$

These 'days ratios' can be useful measures to assist a business in achieving performance targets. For example, many businesses say that they will allow their customers 30 days to pay. If you do the debtor days calculation and find that they are actually not collecting debts for an average of 52 days you have immediately identified an area for improvement.

Calculation for stock days

	Ratio 2002	**Ratio 2001**
Sainsbury's	$\dfrac{365}{21.01} = 17.37$ days	$\dfrac{365}{21.07} = 17.32$ days
Tesco	$\dfrac{365}{24.75} = 14.74$ days	$\dfrac{365}{23.15} = 15.77$ days

Calculation for debtor days

	Ratio 2002	**Ratio 2001**
Sainsbury's	$\dfrac{365}{43.12} = 8.46$ days	$\dfrac{365}{31.58} = 11.5$ days
Tesco	$\dfrac{365}{52.01} = 7.02$ days	$\dfrac{365}{65.18} = 5.6$ days

Calculation for creditor days

	Ratio 2002	Ratio 2001
Sainsbury's	$\dfrac{365}{8.13} = 44.9$ days	$\dfrac{365}{8.78} = 41.57$ days
Tesco	$\dfrac{365}{7.83} = 46.62$ days	$\dfrac{365}{7.88} = 46.32$ days

Tesco are managing to take a few more days' credit from their suppliers than Sainsbury's. This means that they are able to manage their working capital more efficiently.

We can demonstrate the full effect of this by calculating the cash conversion cycle. This shows how long it takes for one item of stock to be purchased, stored and sold on to the customer for cash thus allowing the resulting inflow to buy another batch of stock. This issue of cash and stock flows was discussed in Chapter 7.

Days	Sainsbury	Tesco
Stock	17.37	14.74
Debtor	43.12	52.01
	60.49	60.75
Less creditor	44.9	46.62
Equals cash conversion days	15.59	20.13

TASK 8.1

Customer debts

How do you think a business might improve (reduce) the number of days it takes them to collect customer debts?

We will return to the subject of the management of working capital (stocks, debtors, cash and creditors) later in the chapter.

Gearing ratios

Gearing relates to the capital structure of the firm; the extent to which the business is dependent upon external capital (often carrying a fixed rate of interest), compared with shareholder funds. There are two major ways to evaluate gearing: interest cover and balance sheet gearing.

Interest cover

$$\text{Interest cover} = \frac{\text{Profit before interest and tax}}{\text{Interest}}$$

Interest cover shows how well (or badly) the interest costs are covered by profits. Essentially, the higher this ratio the more comfortable the shareholders will feel, because then the more likely it is that there will be some profits left for them to be given as a dividend after the interest and tax have been paid.

The profit before interest and tax is not directly available from the figures so we need to add back the interest figure to the profit before tax figure.

Sainsbury's			Tesco	
2002	2001		2002	2001
571	437	Profit before tax	1 201	1 054
49	76	Interest payable	153	125
620	513	Profit before interest and tax	1 354	1 179

	Ratio 2002	Ratio 2001
Sainsbury's	$\frac{620}{49} = 12.65$	$\frac{513}{76} = 6.75$
Tesco	$\frac{1\ 354}{153} = 8.85$	$\frac{1\ 179}{125} = 9.43$

This shows that Sainsbury's is in a stronger position than Tesco in that they can charge their interest more times to profit before the profit becomes a loss. If Sainsbury's wanted to borrow more money from the banks they would be viewed more favourably than Tesco. It could be that Tesco have more debt; this is reflected in the fact that they have paid out twice as much in interest charge than Sainsbury's. The size of borrowing is addressed in the next ratio.

Balance sheet gearing

$$\text{Balance sheet gearing} = \frac{\text{Loans (over 1 year)} \times 100\%}{\text{Total equity + loans}}$$

Balance sheet gearing indicates the extent to which the firm depends upon borrowing for its long-term finance. This will be a number less than 100 per cent (as all companies have to have some shares) but the higher it gets the more anxious ordinary shareholders will become as that means that there will be many prior claims on the profits and assets of the business.

There are many variations on this ratio in practice as different people have different views on the precise definitions of 'loans'. It usually includes all forms of finance where the business is committed to paying a fixed rate to the provider; so that includes bank loans, debentures, preference shares, loans from friends, etc. Some people argue that bank overdrafts should be included as long-term liabilities in the calculation of this ratio because, although overdrafts are legally repayable on demand, in practice they are often used as long-term finance.

When calculating the figures for Sainsbury's and Tesco the long-term debt is as follows:

Sainsbury's			Tesco	
(1 223)	(1 000)	Long-term borrowings	(2 741)	(1 927)
(231)	(238)	Other long-term liabilities	(440)	(402)
1 454	1 238		3 181	2 329

with shareholders' equity as:

Sainsbury's			Tesco	
4 848	4 751	Shareholders' funds	5 530	4 978
61	53	Minority interest	36	36
4 909	4 804		5 566	5 014

	Ratio 2002	Ratio 2001
Sainsbury's	$\dfrac{1\ 454 \times 100}{4\ 909 + 1\ 454} = 22.85\%$	$\dfrac{1\ 238 \times 100}{4\ 804 + 1\ 238} = 20.49\%$
Tesco	$\dfrac{3\ 181 \times 100}{5\ 566 + 3\ 181} = 36.37\%$	$\dfrac{2329 \times 100}{5\ 014 + 2\ 329} = 31.72\%$

This proves our earlier analysis that Tesco has more debt than Sainsbury's and is therefore more highly geared.

Investment ratios

This group of ratios is of most interest to current and prospective shareholders and their advisers; and also, by implication, the management of the company, who will be concerned about the impression that is being given to these important groups of users.

Earnings per share

$$\text{Earnings per share} = \frac{\text{Profit after tax (after exceptional items) less minority interest}}{\text{Number of ordinary shares issued}}$$

Earnings per share (EPS) is a measure of general profitability for shareholders. It gives them an idea of the maximum payout that the company could give them in dividends if it did not retain any profits within the business. They would then be able to compare this to what dividend they actually get and see if they approve of the policy. It used to be the most popular single measure for evaluating business performance.

From mid-1993 EPS has become a lot more volatile than in the past as the definition of the 'earnings' part of the calculation was amended to include all the activities of the business in the year, even those which might be described as one-off or unusual items. (Previously these were excluded in an attempt to give a fairer picture of the trend in earnings, but this made the calculation more of a subjective exercise, and also – wrongly, perhaps – encouraged users to concentrate on just one measure of performance.)

Number of ordinary shares in issue (million)	2002	2001
Sainsbury's	1 923.5	1 911.4
Tesco	6 887.0	6 792.0

	Ratio 2002	Ratio 2001
Sainsbury's	$\dfrac{364}{1\,923.5} = 18.92$ pence	$\dfrac{276}{1\,911.4} = 14.44$ pence
Tesco	$\dfrac{830}{6\,887.0} = 12.05$ pence	$\dfrac{722}{6\,792.0} = 10.42$ pence

Dividend per share

$$\text{Dividend per share} = \frac{\text{Total dividend}}{\text{Number of shares issued}}$$

The **dividend per share** is the immediate cash return to shareholders – that is, how much dividend each share is entitled to for that accounting period. This is almost always lower than the 'EPS' figure described above.

	Ratio 2002	Ratio 2001
Sainsbury's	$\dfrac{285}{1\,923.5}$ = 14.82 pence	$\dfrac{274}{1\,911.4}$ = 14.34 pence
Tesco	$\dfrac{390}{7\,001.0}$ = 5.57 pence	$\dfrac{340}{6\,926.0}$ = 4.9 pence

Dividend yield

$$\text{Dividend yield} = \frac{\text{Dividend per share}}{\text{Market value of one share}} \times 100\%$$

The **dividend yield** indicates the immediate rate of return for investment in the shares of the firm as it relates, the dividend which will be received to the price that would have to be paid to buy the share. Generally, the higher this figure is, the less confident the market is in these shares, since the price that people are willing to pay bears a close relation to the amount they think they will reliably get back. Investors will calculate a personal yield by using the price that they actually paid as opposed to the current market price. They will then use this personal yield to help them evaluate their investment situation and whether they should sell/hold this particular investment in the context of returns offered by other investment opportunities.

Market price on 29 March	2002	2001
Sainsbury's	£3.99	£3.80
Tesco	£2.41	£2.485

	Ratio 2002	Ratio 2001
Sainsbury's	$\dfrac{0.1482 \times 100}{3.99}$ = 3.7%	$\dfrac{0.1434 \times 100}{3.80}$ = 3.78%
Tesco	$\dfrac{0.557 \times 100}{2.41}$ = 23.0%	$\dfrac{0.48 \times 100}{2.485}$ = 19.71%

Price/earnings ratio

$$\text{Price/earnings ratio} = \frac{\text{Market value of one share}}{\text{EPS}}$$

The **price/earnings (P/E)** *ratio* measures how the Stock Market rates the company and indicates whether shares are relatively expensive or cheap. The higher this ratio the better, as people will be willing to pay a high multiple of earnings if they think that a share is going to perform reliably and well in the future.

Note, at this stage, that users are often interested in the market values of the shares. Nowhere within a set of accounts will this very useful information be available. It is necessary to consult other sources (e.g. newspaper financial pages or recent records of dealings in the company's shares) to be able to calculate these last two ratios.

Market price on 29 March	2002	2001
Sainsbury's	£3.99	£3.800
Tesco	£2.41	£2.485

	Ratio 2002	Ratio 2001
Sainsbury's	$\frac{3.99}{0.1892} = 21.09$	$\frac{3.80}{0.1444} = 26.30$
Tesco	$\frac{2.41}{0.1185} = 20.33$	$\frac{2.485}{0.1042} = 23.84$

The essence of the analysis suggests that at this time the market perception of the relative performances of the two company's was that Sainsbury's was more likely to recover from the effects of the downturn than Tesco. This is shown by Sainsbury's having a higher ratio than Tesco. The market is not omniscient and this is just a perception (at one point in time) of the future which may or may not be correct.

There now follows a worked illustration – Jondoe – to further demonstrate the calculation and interpretation of accounting ratios. In contrast to Sainsbury's and Tesco, Jondoe is an imaginary company and we will assume that Jondoe is a manufacturer.

ILLUSTRATION 8.1

141 INVESTMENT RATIOS

Jondoe – an example of ratio analysis with comments

Balance sheets		Year 1		Year 2
			(£000s)	
Fixed assets		1 600		1 900
Current assets:				
Stock	500		600	
Debtors	450		600	
Cash	100		120	
		1 050		1 320
Trade creditors (under one year)		(280)		(500)
Tax and dividends owing		(220)		(200)
Working capital		550		620
Total assets less current liabilities		2 150		2 520
Loans (over one year)		(600)		(870)
Net assets		1 550		1 650
Share capital (£1 shares)		500		500
Reserves		1 050		1 150
Equity		1 550		1 650

Income statements	Year 1		Year 2
		(£000s)	
Sales	4 100		4 800
Less cost of sales	2 950		3 500
Gross profit	1 150		1 300
Less expenses	600		800
Profit before interest and tax	550		500
Interest	70		100
Profit before tax	480		400
Taxation	140		100
Profit after tax	340		300
Dividends	150		200
Profit retained	190		100
Market value of one share	£6.50		£5.00

Ratios for Jondoe plc

PROFITABILITY	Year 1	Year 2
Return on shareholders' funds: has fallen dramatically (by 21% of the yr 1 figure), reasons appear below	31.0%	24.2%
Gross margin: slightly reduced. More competitive prices? Higher cost levels?	28.1%	27.1%

PROFITABILITY	*Year 1*	*Year 2*
Net profit to sales: large reduction, by 29% of year 1 figure, due to expenses and interest increases	11.7%	8.3%
Asset turnover is slightly improved indicates greater efficiency	2.6	2.9
LIQUIDITY	*Year 1*	*Year 2*
Current ratio: reductions in both ratios reflects a worrying increase in creditors of 78%	2.1	1.9
Quick ratio: although the business is still able to cover all of its liabilities	1.1	1.0
Stock turnover is marginally slower; stocks increasing *faster* than sales	5.9	5.8
Debtor turnover – slower collections from customers, an extra £150 000 tied up in debtors	9.1	8.0
Creditor turnover – much slower, creditor rise is very significant, they have nearly doubled	10.5	7.0
GEARING	*Year 1*	*Year 2*
Interest cover: lower cover because profits have fallen while interest costs have risen (see profit and loss account)	7.9	5.0
Balance sheet gearing: the firm is more dependent on borrowing, note the greater loans over one year	27.9%	34.5%
INVESTMENT		
EPS: down, reflecting profit fall	68p	60p
Dividend per share ⎫ unjustified rise in	30p	40p
Dividend yield ⎬ dividends?	4.6%	8.0%
P/E ratio: fall reflects lower share price; the market does not like developments at Jondoe!	9.6	8.4

We can summarise the performance of Jondoe based on accounts and ratios for two years as follows:

▶

- There are disturbing increases in expenses and creditors, which suggests a lack of firm control over this area of working capital.
- The expansion in sales is not supported by profits and liquidity, there is a decline in performance on collecting debts, and stock and creditors have been allowed to increase. Furthermore, the dividend policy seems odd.
- There is a need for a tighter control of margins, expenses, and working capital.

A note of caution about ratio analysis

Ratio calculation should never be seen as an end in itself, it is merely a way of beginning to look at business performance. Ratios are frequently based on imperfect data and should be viewed cautiously. It is the sensitive interpretation of ratio calculations which is the key to understanding the messages in the accounts.

Often the ratios will raise new questions about the business, such as: Why did the gross profit margin suddenly go up? Why is the rate of stock turnover slowing down? In Jondoe (above) we cannot answer all of our questions about the company's performance from the ratio analysis. But the ratios at least raise questions about areas that require some attention.

The answers to these questions may appear obvious but more information may be needed before conclusions can be reached. You may choose to confirm what you think by getting evidence from a collaborating source, not necessarily financial (you may have a conversation with the production manager for example), or seeking more evidence of a similar type but expanding the basis period.

To start with, if you just have the accounts of one company, you will normally have the figures for this current year and last year (comparatives) available, (although companies listed on the Stock Exchange have to show summaries of the last five or ten years' figures).

Do not place too much emphasis upon the calculations of one year: it is far more important to observe the emergence of trends in the ratios. It is also useful to calculate the percentage changes in ratios from year to year in order to gain a better insight into the company. In addition, it is essential to be aware of general economic developments – a change in the rate of VAT or National Insurance contributions, or leaving the International Exchange Rate Mechanism – which may affect all businesses in the country.

It will be helpful if you can get similar information about other organisations in the same sector, or even averages for all companies in that sector. There are a number of computer packages available which are regularly updated with financial data for hundreds of companies and to which you can refer in order to form a wider picture.

We indicated near the start of the chapter that ratios are not the only way of analysing financial information. We have said before that the efficient management of working capital and liquidity is often the key to the success of a business, at least in the short run. The next section takes a deeper look at this crucial area.

▬ ▬ ▬ ▬ Working capital management

'Time is money!' we are told. In the management of working capital this can be true in the literal sense. The move towards just-in-time management, with the emphasis on rapid throughput and very low inventories, was, in part, a response to the very high costs of maintaining working capital levels. For working capital is a 'dead' investment – each day in which a debt remains unpaid or an item of stock remains unsold carries a real cost, that is the opportunity cost of not converting that working capital into cash. In simple terms this may be thought of as the lost interest on that cash. This next task illustrates this point.

TASK 8.2

Debtor investment

A firm has £1m tied up in debtors on annual sales of £5m and profits before interest of £800 000. Interest paid is at a rate of 20 per cent. Thus the cost of financing the debts (20% $\times$ £1m = £200 000) is eating up one quarter of the pre-interest profits. Debtors represent 73 days of sales ($\frac{1}{5} \times$ 365). A reduction of only 10 days in this ratio would lead to debtors of £863 000 ($\frac{5}{365} \times$ 63): a reduction of £137 000, and an annual saving of (137 000 $\times$ 20%) = £27 400.

What would be the extra cost if the debtor collection period rose from 73 to 80 days?

Recall the early part of Chapter 7 on working capital and cash flows, in which the management of working capital within different types of businesses was examined. We can now take a wider view of the time invested in working capital: we can view the whole cycle in terms of days, relating back to ratio analysis tackled earlier in the text. A further task will demonstrate this point.

TASK 8.3

Cash conversion

A manufacturing firm has annual sales of £1m, purchases of £700 000, and the following ratios:

■ 60 days' sales in debtors
■ 50 days' cost of sales in stock
■ 40 days' purchases in creditors.

Gross profit is 25 per cent of sales.

1. What is the length of the cash conversion cycle in days?
2. What is the value of the firm's investment in working capital (excluding cash)?

The costs of cash

The costs of not having enough cash are considerable and include high interest payments, poor relationships with suppliers, an inability to obtain resources, lost opportunities for development and, ultimately, **insolvency**. Occasionally firms have the reverse problem: too much cash! This may seem odd, but if a business builds up a cash mountain and cannot devise good investment opportunities it may find that predator firms (i.e. firms looking to acquire other 'cash-rich' firms) will begin to consider takeover plans to get their hands on the cash surplus of the 'victim' firm.

Takeover jargon is full of emotive and physical language including' 'victims' (the firms subject to takeover), 'predators' (the firms making the bid) and 'white knights' (companies who make friendly bids to rescue victims from the clutches of unfriendly predators!).

Some firms in a cash-rich situation will decide to repay the cash direct to shareholders to allow the individual investors to reinvest the surplus funds at an appropriate rate.

Expansion and cash flows

Business planning needs to consider the effect of growth on cash flows. However, many firms have failed to cope with success through a poor understanding of cash-flow management when expanding. When prospects are good and customers are queuing up for your products it is easy to forget that expansion actually costs money in the short term. This next illustration makes the point.

ILLUSTRATION 8.2

Overtrading

A firm begins trading on 1 May with the following balance sheet:

	£
Stocks (100 units @ £1 each)	100
Cash	50
Equity (i.e. total owners' investment)	150

During May all stocks are sold for cash at a price of £1.20 each. The stock is replaced and an increase in stock of 50 units is also taken on to cope with expected extra demand.

The May income statement looks like this:

	£
Sales	120
Cost of goods sold	100
Profit	20

and the balance sheet at the end of May shows: ▶

	£
Stocks	150
Cash (50 + 120 − 150)	20
Equity	170

A reconciliation of the profit with the change in cash would show:

	£
Profits	20
Increase in stocks	−50
Reduction in cash	−30

Although the business reports a profit of £20, we can see that the cash resources are reduced by £30 due to the expansion of working capital.

This kind of expansion is fine, provided that there are adequate resources to cope with the short-/medium-term drain on cash resources. If the activity becomes excessive, however, the firm may find that it cannot finance the expansion. In extreme cases success will, paradoxically, bring disaster through a liquidity crisis. This is known as 'overtrading'.

Profits and cash

From an early age, we learn the importance of cash management; frequently this is a painful lesson! At a personal level, our cash flows can have a major effect on the quality of our lives. Similar concerns for cash flow exist within a business organisation where the ultimate disaster of inadequate cash flow is insolvency! Despite the crucial nature of cash for business survival and expansion, the development of accounting has tended to emphasise profit rather than cash. It is only since the early 1970s that what are now known as cash-flow statements were introduced into the reporting package, and then as something of an afterthought.

FINAL COMMENTS

In this chapter we have given an introduction to the important area of the interpretation of accounts, getting the most out of published data by calculating and evaluating ratios. We have also looked at the related topic of the cash-flow cycle which examines how much working capital is tied up in the business and helps to evaluate how much or how little is needed.

Having completed this chapter you should now understand the following key points:

- The calculation of ratios and trends for accounting analysis.
- The limitations of ratio analysis and the need to bring into the analysis non-accounting data.
- Working capital investment and management.

Please turn to the back of the book for detailed answers to questions marked with a 🕐 . Answers to the other questions can be found on the companion website at www.thomsonlearning.co.uk/accountingandfinance/hand

REVIEW QUESTIONS

RQ 8.1 Review the completed illustration on Jondoe plc within the chapter, and comment upon the limitations of the analysis.

RQ 8.2 Assume you were the lending officer at a bank. Which ratios would you be particularly interested in and why?

RQ 8.3 Your Aunt Agatha wishes to invest £30 000 into the Stock Market and she has come to you for advice. She always shops at Sainsbury's and wondered if they might make a good investment.

1. What ratios should a private investor calculate?
2. Advise Aunt Agatha.

RQ 8.4 Given that by the time the accounts of a company are actually published the information is out of date, why do you think it is that users perform this basic ratio analysis?

NUMERICAL PROBLEMS

NP 8.1 Trenton plc – missing numbers and ratios Below is given:

- the completed balance sheet and income statement for the year 2001
- the partly completed balance sheet, income statement and cash-flow statement for 2002.

You are required to:

1. Complete all missing information (figures to nearest £m).
2. Calculate ratios for the year ending 2002.

Balance sheets at the end of	2001		2002	
		(£m)		
Fixed assets				
Factories	50		20	
Less depreciation	10	40	5	15
Retail outlets	70		130	
Less depreciation	10	60	20	110
		100		125
Current assets				
Stocks		50		
Debtors		40		
Cash				2
		90		
Current liabilities				
Trade creditors		20		
Taxation		1		
Dividends		1		
Bank overdrafts		30		0
		52		
Working capital		38		
Loans		10		
Net assets		128		134
Share capital (£1 shares)		40		40
Reserves		88		
Equity		128		134
Market value of one £1 share		£1.00		

Income statements	2001		2002
		(£m)	
Sales	200		
Cost of sales	150		—
Gross profit	50		
Depreciation	4		
Cash-based expenses	40		45
Profit before interest	6		
Interest	3		
Profit before tax	3		
Taxation	1		
Profit after tax	2		—
Dividends	1		
Profit retained	1		—

▶

Cash-flow statement	2001	2002
Profit before tax		
Depreciation (all on retail outlets)		<u>10</u>
Reduction in stocks		
Reduction in debtors		
Increase in creditors		
Operating funds		
Dividends paid		
Taxation paid		
Factories sold		
Purchase of retail outlets		
Loans repaid		—
Increase in cash	(30 + 2)	<u>32</u>

Profitability

Return on shareholders' funds
Gross margin
Net profit to sales
Asset turnover

Liquidity

Current ratio
Quick ratio
Stock turnover
Debtor turnover
Creditor turnover

Gearing

Interest Cover
Balance sheet gearing

Investment

EPS
Dividend per share
Dividend yield
P/E

NP 8.2 NKG plc – ratio analysis Read the information about NKG plc which follows and write a report on the performance of NKG as revealed by the financial statements. This gives practice in interpretation of ratios.

NKG plc is a large firm which supplies components for the construction industry. Balance sheets, income statements and cash-flow statements for NKG covering three recent years are set out below.

You may assume that there have been *no* significant changes in cost and price levels during this period, thus inflationary factors can be ignored.

Balance sheets

	Year 1	Year 2 (£m)	Year 3
Fixed assets (building, plant and machinery)	1 200	1 400	1 600
Less depreciation	500	650	820
	700	750	780
Current assets			
Stocks	400	400	350
Debtors	300	300	250
Cash	100	—	35
	800	700	635
Current liabilities			
Trade creditors	470	430	400
Taxation	20	—	20
Dividends	10	—	10
Bank overdraft	—	50	
	500	480	430
Working capital	300	220	205
Long-term loans	(200)	(200)	(200)
Net assets	800	770	785
Share capital (£1 shares)	100	100	100
Reserves	700	670	685
Shareholders' funds	800	770	785
Market value of one share	£1.20	£0.70	£0.90

Income statements

	Year 1	Year 2 (£m)	Year 3
Sales	1 800	1 600	1 600
Production costs of goods sold	1 440	1 300	1 280
Gross profit	360	300	320
Administration expenses	300	300	250
Interest charges	20	30	25

▶

Net profit/(loss) before tax	40	(30)	45
Less taxation	20	—	20
Profit (loss) after tax	20	(30)	25
Less dividends	10	—	10
Retained profits	10	(30)	15

Cash-flow statements

	Year 2	Year 3
		(£m)
Net profit (loss) before tax	(30)	45
Depreciation	150	170
	120	215
Reduction in:		
Stocks	—	50
Debtors	—	50
Creditors	(40)	(30)
Cash flow from operating activities	80	285
Dividends paid	(10)	—
Tax paid	(20)	—
Fixed assets bought	(200)	(200)
(Reduction)/increase in cash	(150)	85

Ratio analysis

	Year 1		Year 2		Year 3	
			(£m)			
Profitability						
Return on shareholders' funds	$\frac{40}{800}$	5%	$\frac{(30)}{770}$	—	$\frac{45}{785}$	5.7%
Gross margin	$\frac{360}{1\,800}$	20%	$\frac{300}{1\,600}$	19%	$\frac{320}{1600}$	20%
Net profit/sales	$\frac{40}{1\,800}$	2.2%	$\frac{(30)}{1\,600}$	—	$\frac{45}{1\,600}$	2.8%
Asset turnover	$\frac{1\,800}{800}$	2.3	$\frac{1\,600}{770}$	2.1	$\frac{1\,600}{785}$	2.0
Liquidity						
Current ratio	$\frac{800}{500}$	1.6	$\frac{700}{480}$	1.5	$\frac{635}{430}$	1.5
Quick ratio	$\frac{400}{500}$	0.8	$\frac{300}{480}$	0.6	$\frac{285}{430}$	0.7

▶

	Year 1		Year 2 (£m)		Year 3	
Stock turnover	$\dfrac{1\,440}{400}$	3.6	$\dfrac{1\,300}{400}$	3.3	$\dfrac{1\,280}{350}$	3.7
Debtor turnover	$\dfrac{1\,800}{300}$	6.0	$\dfrac{1\,600}{300}$	5.3	$\dfrac{1\,600}{250}$	6.4
Creditor turnover	$\dfrac{1\,440}{470}$	3.1	$\dfrac{1\,300}{430}$	3.0	$\dfrac{1\,280}{400}$	3.2
Gearing						
Interest cover	$\dfrac{60}{20}$	3.0	$\dfrac{0}{30}$	0	$\dfrac{70}{25}$	2.8
Balance sheet gearing	$\dfrac{200}{1\,000}$	20%	$\dfrac{200}{970}$	21%	$\dfrac{200}{985}$	20%
Investment ratios						
EPS	$\dfrac{20}{100}$	20p	$\dfrac{(30)}{100}$	(30p)	$\dfrac{20}{100}$	25p
Dividend per share	$\dfrac{10}{100}$	10p	$\dfrac{0}{100}$	0	$\dfrac{10}{100}$	10p
Dividend yield	$\dfrac{10}{120}$	10%	$\dfrac{0}{70}$	0	$\dfrac{10}{90}$	11%
P/E	$\dfrac{120}{20}$	6.0	$\dfrac{70}{(30)}$	—	$\dfrac{90}{25}$	3.6

NP 8.3 Little and Large The following is a summary of some of the accounting ratios of two companies in the same industry and of a comparable size for the year ended 30 June 19X5.

	Little plc	Large plc
Dividend yield	4%	7%
Dividend cover	3.6	2.1
Earnings per share	17p	23p
P/E ratio	14	8
Return on equity	22%	27%
Return on capital employed	18%	15%
Profit margin	20%	25%
Asset turnover ratio	0.9	0.6
Gearing ratio	28%	76%

Write a report for a prospective investor on the comparative return on investment, risk and performance of these two companies.

NP 8.4 Hayfor and Caxton Hayfor Limited is a small firm manufacturing high-quality paper. The bulk of its output has traditionally been purchased by Caxton plc, a large printing firm. The management of Hayfor are becoming increasingly concerned over the financial statements for Caxton plc and have begun to monitor the financial viability of their major customer. These statements, together with information from Inter Company Comparisons Limited, are presented below:

Balance sheet as at 31 December	20–4 (£000s)	20–5 (£000s)
Assets		
Fixed assets at cost	11 516	15 050
Depreciation	4 398	5 031
	7 118	10 019
Goodwill	1 000	500
Current assets		
Stocks	2 775	2 003
Debtors	8 294	7 098
Cash	353	72
	19 540	19 692
Liabilities and shareholders' equity		
£1 Ordinary Shares	1 963	1 963
Redeemable Preference Shares	420	—
Share Premium	332	332
Retained Earnings	4 780	1 721
Loans	2 931	4 608
	10 426	8 624
Current liabilities		
Creditors	6 589	6 692
Overdraft	2 174	4 361
Tax	108	7
Dividend	243	8
	9 114	11 068
	19 540	19 692

Income statement for the year ended 31 December

	20–4 (£000s)	20–5 (£000s)
Sales	28 846	27 663
Profit before interest and tax	730	(2 311)
Interest	377	712
Tax	103	11
Profit after interest and tax	250	(3 034)
Dividend	130	25

▶

Average ratios for the printing industry	20–4	20–5
Return on capital employed	13.0%	13.5%
Return on sales	4.8%	5.2%
Asset turnover	2.7%	2.6%
Current ratio	1.4%	1.5%
Sales/stocks	7.6%	7.7%
Average collection period	86 days	79 days

Prepare a ratio analysis report for the management of Hayfor Limited evaluating the financial performance of Caxton plc. In your report draw particular attention to any areas of weakness you identify and detail any further information you might require in making your analysis.

WEB RESOURCES www

www.thomsonlearning.co.uk/accountingandfinance/hand

The companion website has free additional resources for you to use alongside this book. If you are a student you can access material to help with revision, including practice questions with answers to test how much of the material you have understood. There are also useful hyperlinks to companies and information sources mentioned in the book as well as interactive quizzes. There are additional resources for lecturers using this book on their courses; the details can be found in the preface at the front of this book.

CHAPTER 9

Accounting for the future: planning and control through budgets

After studying this chapter you should be able to:

- understand the values of budgeting as an accounting support for management
- describe and analyse the various stages in the budget process
- appreciate the techniques and assumptions that accountants use in producing budgets
- appreciate how budgets may be used for managing an organisation
- describe some of the difficulties that are inherent within any budgeting system
- prepare basic budget reports for profits, balance sheets and cash flows
- analyse and explain the major causes of differences between budget and actual performance, including basic standard costs and variances.

Introduction

Before studying this chapter on budgets, we suggest that you remind yourself about the management accounting ideas outlined in Chapters 2 (products and services) and 3 (managers' decisions), as some of the techniques and concepts from these earlier chapters (for example, fixed and variable cost and contribution) are used again here.

Accounting statements, as we have seen, often report the past. Indeed, the roots of the accounting profession were in 'scorekeeping', for profit and cash-flow statements are financial accounting reports on the recent history of the firm in financial terms. However, we have already shown in Chapters 2 and 3 that managers make decisions about the future, and that management accounting reports can provide some estimate of the impact of their decisions on future costs, revenues, profits and cash flows. In those earlier chapters, however, we were working at the micro-level of the business (that is to say that we focused on specific decisions). There is also a need for macro-level management accounting reports (those which take an overall view of the firm) that look ahead. Most organisations produce both historic and forward-looking accounting reports, but notice the key differences:

1. The obvious differences is that they cover different time periods – historic reports may be for the previous year, month or week; typically firms will have forward-looking statements covering next year, next month, or even five years ahead.

2. Only historic reports are legally required (by company law) and publicly available to stakeholders outside the management group; for a small fee anyone may access the accounting reports for any limited company. By contrast, managers can have as much or as little forward-looking information as they want (and are prepared to pay for!), and they do not have to disclose it to outsiders. **Budgets, business plans** and other forward-looking statements are often closely guarded secrets within organisations.

3. The information in forward-looking statements is qualitatively different from that in historic reports. Although there may be some questions about the correctness and truth of some historic statements (and in extreme cases, such as Enron, the questions may have very uncomfortable answers). Given that such statements will be subject to audit, they should be credible and provable. Forward-looking statements are not like this. By their very nature they are influenced by:

    (a) the subjective judgments of the managers who produce the estimates

    (b) the inherent risk and uncertainty that is a natural part of business life.

In this chapter we are entering a different world of accounting. As we have seen in previous chapters it is the world of financial accounting that deals with matters of historic, legally regulated reports. The world of management accounting, which includes budgeting, is a different world: a world full of 'what-ifs' and possible outcomes, but with few certainties. It is worth stressing this point now to avoid the temptation to regard projected figures (of which we will see a lot in this chapter) as facts. They are not facts but views of the future, and should always be treated with healthy scepticism.

Personal budgets

Consider this: do you ever make plans, and do those plans ever have financial consequences? We are guessing you have answered 'yes' to both these questions, for few of us have lives that are completely unplanned and devoid of financial consequences. It is likely then that you have already carried out what accountants would call 'budgeting'. Maybe you have to review the week (or month, or year) ahead? For your chosen time period, do you consider what income you may expect, and how you may be likely to spend it? This is budgeting at the personal level. The undergraduate away from home for the first time faces the problem of living on what may be a very tight budget. But all of us take some view about future income and expenses, whether that is a very organised (planned in great detail) view, or whether we take a relaxed, or 'hope-for-the-best' approach.

The need for forward-looking financial information is fairly natural, and probably relates to our fear of an uncertain future. Individuals, governments and organisations often try to map out the future in financial terms. Ask yourself: have you ever made financial predictions, perhaps when planning a holiday? Or when spending a large amount on (say) a car? Or just to see if you can make ends meet for the next few months? If you have never done this kind of exercise, now is your chance!

TASK 9.1

A personal financial prediction

First, draw up approximate personal cash-flow predictions covering the next week or month (or some other period that makes sense to you), identifying the major cash inflows and outlays that you expect. Now answer the following questions about your predictions:

1. Which were the easiest and most difficult cash flows to predict?
2. How confident are you about the accuracy of your predictions?
3. Take the total level of expense which you are predicting – given that this can't be completely accurate, what would you estimate as the highest and lowest possible totals which you might spend?
4. This part may be more difficult, but try it. Can you separate out expenses which are relatively fixed (will not change despite your level of activity) from those which are variable (will tend to rise or fall depending on your activity level)? What 'measure' of personal activity did you use to make these judgements (e.g. miles travelled would be a suitable measure of activity for your travel costs, numbers of meals eaten could be an activity measure for your food costs)?

Financial predictions in a business

In a business organisation the major forward-looking accounting reports are called budgets, and the activity called **budgeting** is a technique widely used in business that involves all levels of management. Production, marketing, sales, research, design and, indeed, all departments should be represented (along with finance people) in the budgeting process. Budgeting is a particularly important area for managers in business – for, whatever your special interest or area of work, you will probably be touched by a budget system at some time during your working life. The budgeting process covers many aspects of managers' work, and involves three main stages:

1. setting of budgets (or financial plans)
2. monitoring of actual performances against those targets
3. taking action based on the comparison of actual and budget outcomes.

Clearly these budgets do not emerge spontaneously, for most firms have plans of some kind that are continuously under review. Such plans relate to products, markets, people, investments and the changing nature of the business and its environment – the budget merely provides a financial framework for the future.

Budgeting, then, may be described as: periodic financial planning which reflects the impact of strategic and project plans over the short-term (usually a period of one year). This financial planning should be closely linked to the overall strategic plan for the organisation, and will normally include financial projections for revenues, expenses, assets, liabilities and sources of finance (i.e. the same elements that we have seen within the accounting models used for historic financial reports). The second element of budgeting is that the financial plans (budgets) are then used as a means of monitoring and controlling the activities of the organisation (hence the related term **budgetary control**).

Although the description of budgeting above is focused upon financial elements, it is important to realise that budgeting is far more than an accounting technique. Budgets, to have real value, should involve an evaluation of the entire organisation and the impact that plans will have on the allocation of resources within the firm. Thus budgeting and budgetary control are major management activities which raise many issues about the organisation and the people within it. For our purposes in this accounting text, however, we are primarily concerned with the financial aspects of the **budget process**.

From our description of budgeting above we can see:

■ that budgeting implies monetary values – managers may have general ideas about the shape of the future, but such plans do not become a budget until they are quantified in financial terms

■ that the accounting model is used when reviewing future plans – just as revenues, expenses, assets, etc. are recorded historically, so they may also be stated as future targets.

Having introduced the ideas behind budgeting in a general sense, we will now look at an illustration (Illustration 9.1) that will help you to understand the key elements in a budget prediction. One thing to notice as you look at Babington's figures is that costs are described as either variable (V) or fixed (F). This way of looking at costs was introduced in Chapters 2 and 3, where we wrote that:

■ **Variable costs** are those costs which tend to change in line with activity levels – for example, if output goes up by 10 per cent then the total variable cost will also increase by 10 per cent. Put another way, the variable cost per unit remains the same at any level of activity.

■ **Fixed costs** are those costs which tend to remain the same in total despite changes to activity levels. An implication is that the fixed cost per unit will decline as output rises because we are spreading the same total fixed costs over more units.

	Type of cost	Total costs	Unit costs
Exhibit 9.1 Features of variable and fixed costs	Fixed	Remain unchanged despite changes to activity levels	Decrease as activity rises, increase as activity falls
	Variable	Increase in line with activity	Remain unchanged despite changes to activity levels

Clearly, they are simplifications, and we explored some of the variations on cost behaviour in Chapter 2. But for now the simple fixed/variable distinction will allow us to consider Illustration 9.1 in some detail.

ILLUSTRATION 9.1

159 FINANCIAL PREDICTIONS IN A BUSINESS

Babington

Babington Ltd is a company that has only recently started up, and which makes and sells a single specialised component for the motor industry. Babington has reached the end of its first trading year and the management accountant is in the middle of producing information about the first year (historic) and the second year (budgeted).

The accountant has begun with estimates of the quantities of components made and sold as these quantities will affect many of the costs and revenues.

	Units	
	Year 1 (Historic)	Year 2 (Budget)
Components produced	100 000	105 000
Components sold	91 000	102 000
Stock of finished components		
at the beginning of the year	0	9 000
at the end of the year	9 000	12 000

We immediately notice that Babington is expecting some fluctuations in production, sales and stock levels – building up stock in the first year to 9000 units and then by a further 3000 units in Year Two, taking final stock up to 12 000. The way in which these completed (but unsold) stocks are valued is discussed below.

The actual income statement (or profit and loss account) is also available to the accountant for Year One and this will form the basis for the second year's budget figures. At this stage just the historic numbers are given – the budgets are to be calculated later. In these statements some costs are marked (V) for variable and others (F) for fixed.

Income statements (or profit and loss accounts)

	Year 1 – Historic (£)	
Raw material used (V)	100 000	
Direct labour (V)	70 000	
Power (V)	5 000	
Factory overheads (V)	18 000	
Variable production costs (V)		193 000
Indirect labour (F)	20 000	
Factory overhead (F)	20 000	
Fixed production costs (F)		40 000
Total of all production costs (note 1)		233 000

▶

Add the cost of finished goods at start	0
Less the cost of finished goods at the end (note 1)	(20 970)
Cost of components sold (note 1)	212 030
Sales revenues (all of the 91 000 units were sold for £3.50)	318 500
Profit on manufacturing (i.e. before selling and administration costs)	106 470
Less selling and administration costs (F)	100 000
Net profit	6 470

Note 1 We see that the 100 000 units produced in Year One have cost £233 000 to make – i.e. each unit has cost £2.33. This figure can then be used to estimate the value (at least for accounting purposes) of the completed, but unsold, items. Nine thousand units are unsold and are therefore valued at 9000 × £2.33 = 20 970. Put another way, the number of units actually sold is 91 000 which have cost (2.33 × 91 000) = £212 030 to make. Using the matching concept that we discussed in Chapter 6 we therefore match these costs (of components sold) against the revenues of £318 500.

The accountant therefore has a pretty accurate set of figures for the year just ended, and now needs to produce figures for the year ahead. For this illustration we are assuming that only the quantities of components to be sold and produced are changing for the year ahead, and that other cost factors such as the levels of fixed costs remain unchanged. Production is set to rise by 5 per cent (from 100 000 to 105 000 units) while demand is stronger and sales are set to rise by around 12 per cent (from 91 000 up to 102 000).

When establishing budget figures for Year Two we must look closely at variable costs. Those variable costs that relate to production we can expect to also rise by 5 per cent in that they should fluctuate in line with production levels. All of the selling costs are fixed (as are some of the production costs) and these we will assume will not change. For simplicity we assume that Babington operates in an 'inflation-free' world and the only factor that will change costs is the activity level (measured here by production).

We can now see how the accountant would put together a budget profit and loss account, and could compare the budget against the previous year's actual figures thus:

Income statements (or profit and loss accounts)

	Year 1 Historic (£)	Year 2 Budget (£)
Raw material used (V)	100 000	105 000
Direct labour (V)	70 000	73 500
Power (V)	5 000	5 250

Factory overheads (V)	<u>18 000</u>	<u>18 900</u>
Variable production costs (V)	193 000	202 650
Indirect labour (F)	20 000	20 000
Factory overhead (F)	<u>20 000</u>	<u>20 000</u>
Total production costs	233 000	242 650
Finished goods at start (add)	0	20 970
at end (deduct)	<u>(20 970)</u>	<u>(27 720)</u> (note 2)
Cost of goods sold	212 030	235 900
Sales revenues	<u>318 500</u>	<u>357 000</u>
Profit from manufacturing	106 470	121 100
Less selling and administration costs (F)	<u>100 000</u>	<u>100 000</u>
Net income (or profit)	<u>£6 470</u>	<u>£21 100</u>

Note 2 The stock value at the end of Year Two is made up as follows:

105 000 units made for £242 650 or £2.31 each
12 000 units left in stock are therefore valued at (12 000 × £2.31) = £27 720.

In unit costs terms this shows a slight reduction in unit value. The first year's stocks were valued at £2.33, but in the second year this falls to £2.31. This is because the fixed production costs of £40 000 are spread over 105 000 units of production instead of 100 000 units. Fixed costs carried in each unit of stock were therefore 40p in the first year (£40 000/100 000) and in the budget year 38p (£40 000/105 000).

Explaining the profit differences

How can we explain the significant increase in profits? After all sales have only increased by around 11 per cent yet profits have risen by over 300 per cent!

The simplest way of showing this is to revert to our use of contribution that has been used thoughout the text. Each unit sells at £3.50 and has variable costs of £1.93, hence a contribution of £1.57.

	Year 1	Year 2
Units sold	91 000	102 000
Contribution per unit	£1.57	£1.57
	(£)	(£)
Giving an overall contribution of	142 870	160 140
Less fixed costs (unchanged)	<u>140 000</u>	<u>140 000</u>
Which leaves	2 870	20 140

▶

Increase in fixed costs that have been spent and are carried forward in stock values (note 3)	3 600	960
Total profit	6 470	21 100

Note 3 Because Babington values stocks at full cost (i.e. to include a fixed cost element) we are carrying forward some of our fixed costs in the stock values. In the first year this amounts to (40p per unit × increase in stock of 9000 units) = £3600; in the budget year the new element of fixed costs in stock is (38p × 12 000 units) = £4560, an increase of £960 on the year.

Final comments

The Babington illustration has been used to demonstrate how a basic budget may look based on simply projecting the year ahead from previous figures and allowing for the effect of volume changes. In reality more would change – for example, inflation may impact on costs, and the way in which Babington organises and structures itself may change with consequent impact on cost and revenue levels. As an introduction, however, Babington serves to show that budget profit statements are very like the historic reports we have seen in earlier chapters, but that they carry a 'health warning' concerning their predictive and uncertain nature.

Budgeting for assets and liabilities

Illustration 9.1 was about profit budgets. Equally important may be the impact of plans upon the balance sheet and cash balances. Your next task brings in the working capital and liquidity aspect of budget plans.

TASK 9.2

A balance sheet budget

A small manufacturing business has just started up and at the beginning of its first year of trading the balance sheet contained the following items:

	Assets (£)	Liabilities (£)
Fixed assets	9 000	
Stocks	8 000	
Debtors	0	
Cash in the bank	2 000	
Short-term creditors		3 000
Long-term bank loan		6 000

Owners' capital invested		10 000
Totals	19 000	19 000

The firm expects to expand quite rapidly in the first full year, and wants to negotiate a further loan with the bank. The bank asked for a prediction of changes to fixed assets and working capital levels over the next twelve months as part of a business plan. The following predictions regarding the first year of trading were made:

- additional investment in fixed assets would be £6000
- depreciation on all fixed assets would be £2000
- expansion would take stocks up by 25 per cent on top of the opening figure
- by the end of the first year debtors would be approximately 20 per cent of sales turnover (which was expected to be around £150 000)
- short-term creditors would be approximately equal to half of the total of (debtors + stocks)
- retained profits (after deducting depreciation and interest charges) were expected to be 4 per cent of sales.

1. Use this information to draw up a budgeted balance sheet at the end of the first year (ignore tax and dividends).
2. Comment on these predictions from the viewpoint of the bank manager.

The budget process

We now have a general picture of what budget statements look like. But where do the figures actually come from? And how can managers know the likely levels of expense and revenues for the future? The **master budgets** (profit and loss, balance sheet and cash flow) are supported by a range of other subsidiary detailed budgets (sales, production, etc.). Each of the budgets should interlink to form part of a cohesive business and financial plan. To gain a better understanding of the way in which the final budgets come together we need to think a little more about the budget process for an organisation. We will use Exhibit 9.2 below to examine the various stages in this process.

We can see from this model that the process tends to follow these main steps:

1. An external review of the economic environment.
2. An internal review of the firm's key problems and opportunities.
3. Identification of general targets and any principal budget factors or constraints.
4. A sales budget and –
5. – a linked **capital expenditure budget**

Exhibit 9.2

A model of the
budget process

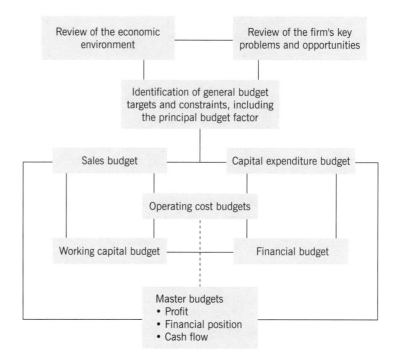

6. Detailed **operating budgets**.

7. A budget for working capital and finance.

And these seven steps lead on to the construction of

8. master budgets for profit, financial position and cash flow.

We now consider each of these stages in turn.

1. Review of the environment

The firm's environment will include customers, competitors, suppliers and government policies. This external review should be about developments that may bring about opportunities or threats for the business, and could include the following questions:

- Will new markets open or old ones close?
- Are customers likely to have more, or less, spending power?
- What government policies are likely to affect the firm (e.g. interest rates, public sector spending, credit restrictions)?
- What will be the rate of inflation in the short and medium term?
- How will price level changes affect costs, revenues and demand?
- What new developments amongst competitors are likely to affect the firm?

2. Review of problems and opportunities

Just as we look outside into the environment so we need to look inside at problems and opportunities within the business. This assessment of strengths and weaknesses will largely determine problems and challenges which the organisation may tackle in the near future. The kinds of questions to examine here include:

- Is the firm in strong financial shape?
- Are there any liquidity difficulties?
- Are borrowings excessively high?
- Have recent profit levels been acceptable?
- Are there any new product opportunities on the horizon?
- Can the firm take advantage of improved technology?
- Does the firm have sufficient levels of skilled labour?
- Are production facilities adequate and as good as the best in the sector?
- Do customers appear to be satisfied with our products?

3. Principal budget factors

From the internal and external review should emerge the most important issues for the firm during the coming period and hence the main constraints and opportunities which will affect the budget. It may be that one major constraint will emerge which will operate on the firm during the budget period (sometimes called the **principal budget factor** (PBF), and similar in principle to the 'limiting factor' that we discussed in Chapter 3).

For many firms the PBF will be demand for product and services, while the second most common PBF is finance or cash flow. For example, a growing internet company may have no problem in generating new business yet may be constrained by limited finance for expansion if it is seen as a high-risk venture. All organisations are constrained by some key factor, and other possible PBFs we can suggest are skilled labour (in textiles or the IT sector), raw materials (for oil refining) and management skills (premier league soccer).

After the general review stage and identification of any PBF we move to the 'nitty-gritty' detailed budget statements, the most important of which are:

- sales
- capital expenditure
- operating costs
- working capital and finance.

We will now have a closer look at each of these critical areas in turn.

4. Sales budget

For most businesses, demand is the PBF. It makes sense, therefore, for the sales budget to be constructed before other predictions are made. This budget should provide an analysis of the sales revenue for the budget period, broken down in a way that is appropriate for the type of business. The analysis could, for example, be between geographical regions, main customers, products, months of the year, retail outlets or salespeople.

The sales budget will normally give details of volumes, selling prices and total revenues for all main product lines. The process of constructing the sales budget will vary between firms, and the two extreme approaches are sometimes referred to as **top down** and **bottom up**.

Top-down budgets A sales budget may be produced by considering forecasts of industry-wide demand levels, existing levels of sales for the firm, potential for changes to that market share and the financial and physical capacity of the firm to increase sales. A view may then be formed, by marketing managers, of the likely level of sales for the budget period. The 'top' management group then decides on feasible sales budgets for the whole organisation, and these are communicated 'down' the organisation to those who will have to carry out the plans.

Bottom-up budgets At the other extreme, a sales budget may be constructed by combining the individual, local predictions of salespeople. Under this approach the managers who are closest to the customers produce sales expectations based on their specific knowledge of likely customer demands. These predictions are then taken 'up' to managers for building into the organisation's budgets.

The budget approach chosen will largely be determined by the industry and the type of firm. For example, a national house-builder may use a broad top-down approach, while a company selling specialist engineering equipment to relatively few customers may be more bottom-up. In government departments, for example education, where resources are largely determined centrally, a top-down approach is evident. Thus a large comprehensive school will be informed of its budget allocation 'from above' based upon the expected number of pupils.

In reality, of course, organisations use a combination of both methods. The purpose, whatever the approach taken, is to arrive at a sales revenue budget which is realistic, but which encourages the firm towards improved performance. There may have to be a series of iterations (involving discussions at all levels of the organisation) before the final budget targets can be agreed.

5. Capital expenditure budget

Along with the sales budget, the capital expenditure budget is possibly the most critical budget statement. Plans for expenditure on such things as buildings, machinery, vehicles and computers, or even the acquisition of other firms, commit the firm to large outlays of cash, and are not easily changed. The capital expenditure budget will be determined during the review stage discussed earlier and will normally be a list of capital projects which are likely to incur expenditure during the budget period. Chapter 10 will look at such long-term decisions in more detail. The timing of the capital expenditure should also be estimated, as the amounts are likely to be large and will therefore have a dramatic effect on the cash flows of the firm at particular times during the budget year.

The sales and capital expenditure budgets are likely to be closely related. For example, the sales potential of Next plc will, in part, depend on the firm's ability to buy and develop new retail outlets in good locations. The sales targets of the house-builder Barratts may require capital expenditure for the purchase of new land.

6. Detailed operating cost budgets

After sales and capital expenditure budgets have been agreed, detailed cost budgets can be prepared for each of the departments in the firm – production, sales, design, research, administration, finance and so on.

In this book we have already noted (Chapter 2) the distinction that management accountants make between fixed and variable costs. We return to this again now – and also extend the simple two-way split a little further (taking it closer to reality) by looking again at stepped and semi-variable costs. We will use an illustration relating to a printing and publishing business.

ILLUSTRATION 9.2

Printing and publishing

A small printing division of Taylor Publishing carries out the specialist printing of academic texts in low volumes. The division requires £5 of paper and other materials to produce one book and pays £3 author's royalty on each book sold. Thus variable costs of one book are £8 in total. Whether the publisher sells ten or ten thousand books, the £8 per book variable cost should (in theory at least) remain the same.

Stepped costs, while rising with output, do not show constant increases. The stepped costs remain constant over certain ranges of output. Thus, in this case, the academic publishing division employs ten production workers and pays £400 per week to each one. The team of ten can produce up to 5000 books in one week. But above that volume one extra person must be employed for each extra 1000 books. The stepped labour cost budget would appear as follows:

Output range (books)	Numbers of workers	Stepped labour cost per week (£)
1–5000	10	4000
5001–6000	11	4400
6001–7000	12	4800
7001–8000	13	5200
and so on . . .		

Stepped costs, we can see, behave like fixed costs, but within a limited range of activity. Other examples include:

1. Sainsbury's need for warehouse space to service their retail outlets. If expansion of stores hits a certain level then extra warehouse space is needed.

2. Nottingham Business School's student admissions staff can cope with student numbers up to a certain point beyond which an extra member of staff must be employed.

These are not variable costs as they do not rise directly in line with sales or student numbers or some other measure of activity, but rather they 'jump' suddenly in steps.

Fixed costs are costs that remain unchanged despite quite large changes to levels of activity. Examples for a printer or publisher could include rent costs, administrative and management salaries, and depreciation and maintenance of computers and printing equipment. Assume that Taylor's printing division has fixed costs of £50 000 each week.

Semi-variable costs are those costs that have a fixed and a variable part. Perhaps our publisher pays £100 per week plus £2 per copy sold to the agent who sells the books. Semi-variable costs would then be £200 if 50 were sold in a week (i.e. £100 + (50 × £2)), and £400 if 150 were sold (£100 + (150 × £2)).

TASK 9.3 **The printer's costs**

1. From the illustration above, calculate the printer's budget total weekly costs if the number of books published and sold is:
   - 1000
   - 3000
   - 7000.
2. Analyse the total weekly costs, between variable cost per book and total weekly fixed costs.
3. If each book sells for £40, what would you expect the budgeted profit to be at each of the levels of output?

Of course, any attempt to classify the variety of costs in a typical business into broad categories is bound to be a simplification. For example, fixed costs will vary in their degree of fixedness (rent may be totally fixed unless the firm shuts down; depreciation, on the other hand, is only fixed until we decide to sell off the fixed asset to which it relates).

The main learning point here is that managers will aim to budget for costs under their control in a way which makes sense to them. Clearly, cost budgeting is full of practical problems (uncertain levels of inflation and efficiency, for example) and here we are only touching upon the activity because it is part of the overall budget process. The next task is to get you thinking about the practical difficulties of producing cost budgets.

TASK 9.4

Cost budgeting

Imagine that you are a sales manager for a toys and games firm, and you are controlling a team of twenty salespeople who travel the country talking to retailers and getting orders for toys and games. Your cost budget is an important measure of your ability to manage your department.

What cost headings do you think would be in your budget?

How would you (as manager) go about estimating what the costs under these headings would be for next year?

7. Working capital, cash flows and finance budget

As the sales, capital expenditure and cost budgets are constructed, decisions will be made which will affect the working capital and sources of finance in the firm. A plan by Comet (the electrical retailer) to open new retail outlets, for example, has implications for amounts of stock held. A sales budget by Orange (mobile phones) that includes sales to new, untried, overseas markets would be certain to raise the level of debtors and possibly bad debts. And a motor manufacturer's plans (e.g. Peugeot or Nissan) to build a new factory may require additional borrowing facilities.

In the working capital section of the budget the following questions and issues are important:

- What changes are likely to occur in stock values, debtors and creditors? Consideration of stock policies and credit periods (both with debtors and creditors) will be necessary. The objective here is to attempt a prediction of the values that will be tied up in working capital both during, and at the end of, the budget period.

- The detailed cash flows, borrowings and gearing of the firm should also be reviewed at this stage. Needs for the repayment of loan finance should be evaluated and the implications for interest costs considered. Plans to raise new funds from shareholders, taxation charges and the firm's dividend policy should also be evaluated in this part of the budget.

- Working capital changes ultimately affect the cash flows of the business. Detailed cash budgets are designed to address potential liquidity problems in some detail, showing specific receipts and payments of cash during the month (or week or even day) in which the cash actually flows. Thus the cash budget tends to be a prediction (or budget or forecast) of what is likely to happen to cash flows. Used in this way the cash budget allows managers to foresee liquidity problems before they arise, and possibly to take action to overcome them.

ILLUSTRATION 9.3

Cyclops – cash budget

Cyclops is a small business that makes and sells specialist cross-country cycles to retailers. Cyclops' business is seasonal and cash flow is particularly critical around Christmas time, as large quantities of bicycles have been produced and sold to shops, but the cash for these sales will not be received until the New Year. Cyclops' cash budget for the period November to January is shown below:

Cyclops – Cash Budget (£000s)	November	December	January
Receipts from customers			
Paying in month of delivery (taking discounts)	10	8	4
Paying two months after delivery	20	30	60
Total receipts	30	38	64

▶

Payments			
Materials	20	15	11
Labour costs	20	15	11
Cash expenses	5	5	5
Fixed assets	10	—	10
Interest payments	—	3	—
Total payments	55	38	37
Cash surplus/(deficit) for the month	(25)	—	27
Cash balance or (overdraft) at the beginning of the month	10	(15)	(15)
Cash balance or (overdraft) at the end of the month	(15)	(15)	12

The scale of Cyclops' cash-flow difficulties become clear from the cash budget. Many customers take two months to pay and this causes the firm problems of liquidity because payments for materials and labour are paid out before cash is received from customers. Cyclops needs, perhaps, to set up temporary overdraft facilities during the Christmas period.

8. Master budgets

The information from the detailed budgets can now be summarised in the master budgets (i.e. profit, financial position (balance sheet) and cash budgets). The accounting model which we encountered in earlier chapters is normally used to indicate the overall performance of the firm that may be expected during the budget period.

- The profit budget is a forward-looking income statement showing sales revenues, costs of sales, overhead costs, interest, profit before and after tax and expected dividend payments.
- The budget of financial position is a projected balance sheet indicating the assets, liabilities and equity expected at the end of the budget period.
- The cash budget is (as with Cyclops above) a prediction of how cash will move into and out of the bank account throughout the budget period, while the cash-flow budget takes a more holistic view and brings together the major sources of cash (e.g. profits, share issues, loans, reductions in stocks, etc.) and shows how that cash will be used (e.g. for capital expenditure, taxation, dividends, increases in debtors or stocks, etc.). This budget indicates the total anticipated change to working capital and cash balances during the budget period.

In order to 'put some flesh on the bones' of this general discussion about the budget process and to provide tangible material about what a budget may look like, we include at the end of this chapter a detailed case study (Blackthorn) to demonstrate how budget statements could appear for a multiproduct manufacturing firm. Please refer to this case after you have reviewed the remainder of this chapter.

Getting the budget right

Although the preparation of the master budgets concludes the budget preparation, it is quite possible that the results as shown in these budgets will be unacceptable and fail to meet shareholder or managerial expectations. Perhaps profits are too low, or perhaps the budgets appear to overstretch the firm's liquid resources or borrowing capacity. The budget targets may need to be reviewed and changed until an agreement can be reached on an acceptable budget. Even if major changes appear unnecessary it is certain that fine-tuning will occur between the submission of original budgets and final agreement. You should see budgeting as a continuous process of negotiation rather than an isolated task which only occurs at particular times.

Typically, a firm with a financial year ending in December may:

- begin provisional reviews of the environment and of internal strengths/weaknesses in June – issue 'top-down' guidance to middle managers
- ask for 'bottom-up' forecasts from operating managers in July/August
- determine priorities for the approaching year in August/September
- produce draft budget statements by the end of October
- allow discussion/negotiation on the draft budgets with a view to finalising by the end of November.

Having explained in some detail how an organisation may go about producing budget statements, we will now examine 'why' budgets are used.

Why produce budgets?

The budget process takes up a lot of management time, and firms are not compelled by law to budget. Why then is it common practice? Several reasons why managers go to the trouble of producing detailed budgets can be advanced, and mainly revolve around notions of planning, decision-making, coordination and control.

Focus on planning

The process of compiling a budget focuses attention on planning within the firm. Managers are compelled to think ahead, and to anticipate problems and opportunities within their own area of responsibility.

Decision-making

As the budget is constructed, hard decisions will have to be faced by management. The budget is likely to throw up questions about, for example, the allocation of scarce resources, levels of employment, investment in fixed assets, the development of new products and the exploitation of markets. Although such questions would arise even without a formal budget system, the budgeting process should focus the management's attention on these crucial issues at an early stage, allowing the decisions to be taken in a considered manner within a logical framework (represented by the budget) rather than in an *ad hoc* fashion.

Coordination

Ideally, budgeting should involve all managers in the firm, and should definitely not be left only with the accountants! If the various key areas of the firm are involved in the setting of budget targets this should lead to a closer coordination between managers and the early identification of uncoordinated activities. For example:

1. The original budget targets may show that sales are predicted to be well above production capacity – decisions will have to be taken and incorporated into the budget regarding either obtaining additional capacity or reducing sales targets.
2. If a firm faces depressed demand for its products, then its production targets may only require (say) 500 production personnel, while the original labour budget shows 600 people. Difficult decisions – concerning ways of increasing demand, alternative use of personnel or job losses – must be made.

Setting targets and control

The entire budget process rests upon the idea that targets can be set for revenues and expenses in the firm. These targets should provide a framework for judging future performance. The problem is: what is a fair target? Budgets which are too 'tight' and are perceived as not achievable may be disregarded. Budgets which are very generous will be easily achieved and provide no incentive for improved performance. Somewhere between these extremes is a fair budget that, while achievable, stretches the manager towards better performance. Budget targets must be set with care if they are to be effective benchmarks.

Budgets provide measures of performance that can be compared with later actual results. Individual managers or groups of people may be monitored by budgets. Failure to achieve targets may result in corrective action to bring actual performance back into line or a revision of budgets if experience has shown them to be unrealistic.

The control aspect of budgeting requires careful management. If targets are set at unrealistic levels managers may be demotivated. If, however, targets are too easily achieved then the budgets may serve no useful purpose.

Variances from budget

Your personal financial predictions: how did they turn out?

Return to your own personal financial predictions earlier in the chapter (Task 9.1), and ask yourself these questions:

■ How accurate were the predictions?
■ What were the causes of differences between your predictions and what actually happened?
■ What extra information would have helped you to produce a more accurate picture in advance?

We assume that, in some parts, your predictions in Task 9.1 proved to be inaccurate. When setting a budget, one thing we can be very sure about is that it will be incorrect! Unless we have perfect foresight there are certain to be predictions that, in the event, prove to be wrong. The management accountant can help by explaining the causes of **variances** between budgets and actual performance. In turn, such **variance analysis** can lead towards managerial actions to improve performance and to bring the company back 'on track'.

ILLUSTRATION 9.4

Toys

A sales manager for a toy business budgets to sell 1000 toys each week at a price of £10 each, giving a weekly sales revenue budget of £10 000. Last week his sales were 900 toys and the total revenue from these sales was £9500. We can see that the total difference (or variance) for his sales is (£10 000 − £9500) = £500.

A closer look at the figures, however, shows that two factors played a part in this reduced sales figure.

First, there was a price increase that provided more sales revenue. Selling only 900 toys at budget price would have given £9000 revenue. The extra £500 is due to price increases. Second, the manager sold 100 fewer toys which caused a drop in revenues of (100 × £10) = £1000. To summarise:

Price factor	£500 (favourable)
Volume factor	£1000 (unfavourable)
Explains the overall variance of (£10 000 − £9500)	£500 (unfavourable)

The accountant's task is to unpick and explain the variance from budget in as much detail as possible. For the sales manager the questions coming out of this analysis are:

- Will the price increases be sustainable?
- Can we expect that trend to continue?
- Why did volumes drop?
- What can be done to improve sales volumes?

TASK 9.6

Explaining cost variances – furniture

A timber furniture business makes special wooden chairs, and expects to spend £10 on good quality timber for each chair. Last month 120 chairs were made, and the timber used in making them cost £1300 – i.e. just £100 more than expected.

One of the managers is puzzled as he knows: 'that prices of timber reduced by 10 per cent in this period – I would have expected to save money, not spend more!'. It appears that a new employee had been making the chairs and, because of inexperience, had wasted a lot more timber than usual.

How much did the extra waste cost?

From these illustrations and tasks we see that even relatively straightforward differences from budget may often have more than one cause, and that sometimes (as with the chair-making task) these factors work in opposite directions.

Your next task is a little more complex and brings together several aspects of budgeting and areas of accounting covered in previous chapters.

TASK 9.7

Jane Roser – when plans go wrong

Budgets and plans rarely work out exactly as planned. This task considers the financial impact on a business that, for various reasons, drifts away from its initial budgets.

Jane Roser runs a market stall, selling men's casual shirts. She expects to sell 30 shirts in one day, buying them at an average cost of £10 and selling for an average of £15. She budgets to pay her part-time assistant £20 for a day's work and £30 rental per day on the stall. All of Jane's transactions are cash. From these budgets Jane expects to make a profit of £100 a day – all in cash.

On Friday Jane had a cash float of £400; she then bought 30 shirts for a good price (£9 each), and had hopes that she would make good profits on the following day. But Saturday was a very bad day! To begin with, when she arrived at 7.30am to set up the stall the market manager reminded Jane that the rental had gone up to £40 per day. To make matters worse her part-time assistant had a hangover, did not arrive until 11am, and so only received half a day's pay.

And the weather was terrible. Jane was only able to sell 20 of the 30 shirts at £15 each. As Jane was packing away at the end of the day she wondered whether it was worth the effort. She had done a rough calculation and worked out that she:

▶

- had 10 unsold shirts that cost £9 each
- had made a profit of only £70
- had cash left of £380 – i.e. a fall of £20.

Your tasks are to:

1. Show a detailed calculation of Jane's budget profit (£100) and actual profit (£70).
2. Explain, in as much detail as possible, the difference between the two profits.
3. Show why her cash balance has reduced by £20.
4. Explain the difference between Jane's actual profit (£70) and cash reduction (£20).

Standard costing and variance analysis

In the 'variances' section above we touched upon the differences between budgets and actual performance. In some sectors, particularly the manufacturing sector, where there is large volume production, this type of analysis may come under the management accounting technique called **standard costing** and variance analysis. Depending on the course that you are following you may be required to consider this area in more detail, and this next section therefore takes the ideas a little further.

Standard costs and variance analysis are normally employed in businesses where there is a great deal of repetition about the manufacturing process (e.g. beer or textiles) or service provision (e.g. hospital beds or school meals).

A **standard cost** may be described as a budget for a single unit of the product or service, and the aims of standard costing systems are to:

- set standards as performance targets for product cost and profit
- compare actual performance with standards
- investigate reasons for the variances
- reset standards if necessary
- take action where necessary to achieve greater levels of efficiency.

Linearity – the basis of variance analysis

Standard costing and variance analysis both use an underlying assumption of linearity concerning the behaviour of costs and revenues in relation to levels of activity. This **linearity assumption** implies that the majority of items that make up the product cost and profit calculation respond in a directly linear manner to changes in activity, i.e. they are strictly variable. Graphically, the implications can be shown as in Exhibit 9.3.

At activity level A, the cost and revenue elements should (if they are strictly variable) be at levels C and R respectively. If, however, activity falls to level B then costs should (if they are strictly variable) fall to CC, while we would expect revenues to be at level RR.

The level of expected costs and revenues given by the graph is called the **flexed budget**; that is to say, it is changed or *flexed* to reflect the actual level of output achieved. Thus, although we are dealing here with standard costing, the key figure, upon which the variance calculations are based, is the *actual* level of output. This follows from the variable nature of the costs and revenues, and means that we will be comparing 'like with like' within the variance analysis. Put another way, if we originally budgeted to make and sell 100 units, but actually only made and sold 90, then (for variable costs and revenues) we should be comparing actual performance against 'what we would have expected to be the revenues and costs at 90 units' – comparing like with like. The process of restating the budget at actual level of output (here restating to 90 from 100) is called **flexing the budget**, and Illustration 9.5 demonstrates this.

Exhibit 9.3

Assumed relationships between costs, revenues and activity in a standard costing system

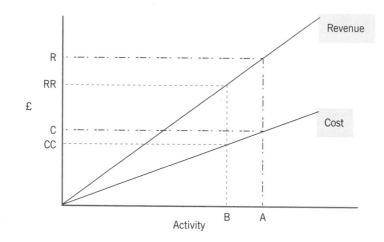

ILLUSTRATION 9.5

Adam: flexing the budget

Adam Manufacturing has set standard costs for one of its products as follows:
For each unit produced, 12kg of material at £9 per kg and 1 hour of labour at £20 per hour are expected to be used.

	£
Standard costs per unit are thus:	12 @ £9 = 108 materials
	1 @ £20 = 20 labour
	128

Given the linearity assumption, the flexed budgets for materials and labour can be set for any level of output. For example:

Output in units	Materials kgs	Materials £	Labour Hours	Labour £
1	12	108	1	20
10	120	1 080	10	200
20	240	2 160	20	400
30	360	3 240	30	600

Flexed budgets

and so on . . .

Let us assume that, in one week, Adam's actual output achieved is 240 units. Let us further assume that the actual costs incurred in making the output were:

Materials	2 640kg	costing	£26 400
Labour	252 hours	costing	£5 544

We are now in a position to set up a framework for analysis.

Variance summary

	Standard quantity	Standard cost (£)	Cost per unit (£)	Flexed budget (£)	Actual costs (£)	Total variances (£)
Material	12kg	9	108	25 920	26 400	(480)
Labour	1 hour	20	20	4 800	5 544	(744)
			128	30 720	31 944	1 224)

The flexed budget column here is a result of multiplying the actual output (240 units) by the standard cost of one unit. The actual costs, of course, relate to that same level of output. Flexed budget and actual costs have been compared to derive a 'total variance'.

Variance notation We have used a convention of showing adverse, or unfavourable, variances in brackets here. Bracketed variances (as in this example) represent reductions in profit. If variances are favourable (i.e. not bracketed) then actual profit is higher than expected.

At this stage, you will see that no detailed analysis of the variances is identified – this will be the next stage. Clearly, both labour and materials show adverse variances. Now we will attempt to calculate the breakdown of these total figures.

▶

Adam's material variances

	kg	£	£
1. Actual costs	2 640	10	26 400
2. Price variance	2 640	(1)	(2 640)
3. Actual material inputs at standard cost	2 640	9	23 760
4. Usage variance	240	9	2 160
5. Flexed budget (i.e. standard inputs for actual output)	2 880	9	25 920

Comments on the above variance analysis:

Line 1 Actual costs are given.

Line 3 The quantity used is left at actual level, but is repriced at standard cost. The only difference between lines 1 and 3 is the price variance of the inputs (in this case kg of material).

Line 2 The price variance emerges naturally from lines 1 and 3. In this illustration each kg has cost £1 more than the standard cost.

Line 5 The flexed budget for materials. Notice that this line is concerned with *output*. Two hundred and forty units were produced and it is the standard cost of that output which appears on the bottom line.

Line 4 The usage variance emerges from lines 3 and 5. Although 2640kg were actually used, 2880 was the standard usage. The 240kg represents a saving of material, and is evaluated at standard price (£9).

Adam's labour variances

	Hours	£	£
1. Actual costs	252	22	5 554
2. Rate variance	252	(2)	(504)
3. Actual hours at standard cost	252	20	5 040
4. Efficiency variance	(12)	20	(240)
5. Flexed budget (i.e. standard for actual output)	240	20	4 800

Notice the similarity between the labour and material analyses. They are almost identical in form and content. Terminology differs because of the different resources being discussed. Thus:

Material		**Labour**
Price variance	is equivalent to	rate variance
Usage variance	is equivalent to	efficiency variance

Although the terminology differs, the principles used are exactly the same.

Our next illustration includes revenue and profit as well as costs. This illustration (Cain) will provide an opportunity to deal with standard and actual profits, and also the idea of an original (as opposed to a flexed) budget.

ILLUSTRATION 9.6

Cain

Cain makes and sells a cleaning compound called Spot. Standard costs and revenues for one cylinder of Spot are:

Selling price:	£100
Materials	100kg @ 20p per kg
Labour	10 hours @ £6 per hour

Cain has budgeted to produce and sell 500 cylinders in each month. Actual costs and revenues for this month are as follows:

Sales revenue	530 cylinders @ £95 each
Materials	55 000kg @ 18p per kg
Labour	5 000 hrs @ £7 per hour

From this information we can produce the frameworks for variance analysis as we did for Adam earlier.

Variance analysis

	Standard quantity	Standard cost/ revenue (£)	Cost/ revenue per unit (£)	Flexed budget (£)	Actual costs/ revenues (£)	Total variances (£)
Materials	100kg	0.2	20	10 600	9 900	700
Labour	10 hours	6	60	31 800	35 000	(3 200)
Total cost			80	42 400	44 900	(2 500)
Revenue	1 unit	100	100	53 000	50 350	(2 650)
Profit			20	10 600	5 450	(5 150)

This framework is similar to that for Adam, with the addition of sales revenue information.

▶

Detailed variance analysis

Materials

	kg	£	£
Actual costs	55 000	0.18	9 900
Price variance	55 000	0.02	1 100
Actual quantity @ standard cost	55 000	0.20	11 000
Usage variance	(2 000)	0.20	(400)
Flexed budget	53 000	0.20	10 600

Cain has gained £1100 by buying cheaper material, but has lost £400 through excess usage. It is possible that these variances are connected. Maybe cheaper material leads to greater wastage? The point to notice is that variances should never be viewed in isolation, and managers should think about the overall position and possible linkages between variances before commenting on them or before taking action.

Labour

	Hours	£	£
Actual costs	5 000	7	35 000
Rate variance	5 000	(1)	(5 000)
Actual hours @ standard rate	5 000	6	30 000
Efficiency variance	300	6	1 800
Flexed budget	5 300	6	31 800

As far as labour costs go, Cain has had to pay greater than standard rate, but has gained 300 hours over standard. The variances provide a series of questions: Is the labour standard too loose? Does the labour rate standard need revising? Answers to such questions require a fuller knowledge of the business in question.

In all of the discussion above notice that the detailed variances sum to the total variance. For example, Cain's labour variances are:

Rate (−£5 000) + efficiency (+ £1 800) = total (−£3 200)

Cain's sales variances appear as follows:

	Units	£	£
1. Actual sales revenue	530	95	50 350
2. Sales price variance	530	5	2 650 (unfavourable)
3. Flexed budget i.e. actual quantity sold @ standard price	530	100	53 000

Sales quantities

The sales quantity variance lies outside the framework that we have used up to now. Notice that the sales price variance (£2650) on line 2 above has already dropped out of the total variance calculation for Cain. Remember that we are reconciling actual performance against flexed budget.

The quantity aspect of sales relates to a comparison between the flexed budget (530 units for Cain) and the original budget (500 units).

Variance analysis should always show impact on profit, and thus for the sales quantity (or volume) variance we will use the profit per unit and *not* the selling price of the product. If Cain sells one extra unit then the effect on profit is an extra £20 – i.e. standard profit per unit. Sales revenue *will* increase by £100 but material and labour costs would also increase, leaving only the £20 profit. (To be strictly accurate we should describe this not as profit but as contribution, as we are not considering fixed costs.)

Thus, if we wish to explain the movement away from original budget, we can produce the following analysis:

	Units	£	£
Original budget profit	500	20	10 000
Sales volume variance	30	20	600
Flexed budget profit	530	20	10 600
Sales price variance			(2 650)
Material variances			700
Labour variances			(3 200)
Actual profit	530		5 450

Recapping variance analysis

1. All variances relate to the difference between flexed budget and actual performance except the sales volume variance which reconciles the original budget to the flexed budget.
2. Flexed budget is the performance we would expect given the actual level of activity or output.
3. For cost variances it is helpful to take out the price variance first; other variances may then be calculated using standard prices.
4. In flexing the budget we assume that linearity exists, i.e. that the items which we are flexing behave in a strictly variable manner in relation to output.

FINAL COMMENTS

This chapter has aimed to provide an introduction to the budgeting process. This is an area which is important to anyone who is involved in organisational life, for budgeting is probably the aspect of accounting which touches most people in business in some way.

Although the text has concentrated on the 'numbers' aspects of budgets, we should conclude by emphasising that budgets are a part of the wider organisational framework for control and planning – you will almost certainly encounter the topic again whatever your career path or course of study.

SUMMARY

Having completed this chapter you should now understand the following key points:

- The process of producing budgets, and time scales for compiling budgets.
- The main budget statements, including profit, balance sheet and cash flow.
- Why budgets are used, and some of the problems that exist within budget systems.
- Variances from budget and how they may be analysed.

Please turn to the back of the book for detailed answers to questions marked with a ❓. Answers to the other questions can be found on the companion website at www.thomsonlearning.co.uk/accountingandfinance/hand

REVIEW QUESTIONS

❓ **RQ 9.1** If the future is, by definition, uncertain, what is the point in preparing detailed plans and budgets that you know are bound to be wrong?

RQ 9.2 The budget system is a very formal way of controlling people in a organisation. Can you think of other controls which operate on people at work?

RQ 9.3 Taking an industry of your own choice, discuss the most important challenges and problems likely to face a firm operating within this sector of the economy as its budgets are prepared for the approaching year.

❓ **RQ 9.4** Imagine that you are the accountant with a construction company which is facing a heavy increase in demand for houses over the next 12 months. As you help to draw up the budgets, what are likely to be the major aspects of your budget reports which will show evidence of the planned expansion, and what are the likely major financial issues to be faced?

NUMERICAL PROBLEMS

❓ **NP 9.1 Magic Lantern – cash budget** Magic Lantern sells a single product, a children's novelty. From the following information prepare a monthly cash budget for the period from July to December.

Each lantern sells for £40 and has a variable cost (all materials) of £26. Suppliers of materials are paid two months after the material is used in production. Customers are expected to settle their debts two months after the date of sale.

Sales and production quantities are expected to be as follows:

	May	June	July	Aug	Sept	Oct	Nov	Dec
Production	1 200	1 400	1 600	2 000	2 400	2 600	2 400	2 200
Sales	1 000	1 200	1 400	1 600	1 800	2 000	2 200	2 600

Fixed costs are £6000 per month, paid at the end of the month. Tax of £18 000 is to be paid in October. A motor vehicle, costing £8000, will be paid for in August. The company expects to have an overdraft of £3000 on 30 June.

NP 9.2 Brickup – cash budgets in the building industry Brickup is a house-building firm in the Midlands, building affordable homes for first-time buyers. The accountant of Brickup is gathering information to enable cash budgets to be prepared for the four-month period November to February. Relevant facts and predictions regarding Brickup's activities for recent and future periods are as follows:

	July	Aug	Sept	Oct	Nov	Dec	Jan	Feb
Plots of land acquired	0	0	0	0	1	1	2	1
Houses started	400	300	250	150	100	100	200	300
Houses completed	550	500	400	400	300	250	150	100

Each plot of land is large enough for 200 houses and costs £1m which is paid in the month of acquisition. The costs and revenues associated with house building are as follows:

- Materials cost £10 000 per house, 50 per cent of which is delivered to the site in the month in which the house is started. The remaining materials are delivered in two equal amounts in the two months following commencement. Suppliers are paid in the month following delivery.
- Labour costs £16 000 per house which is incurred equally over the four months taken for construction. The labour force is paid during the month that the work takes place.
- Plant hire costs incurred in any month are usually around 20 per cent of labour costs for that month and are paid one month after plant use.
- Fixed overheads are expected to be £500 000 per month until and including November, after which they will rise to £550 000. Twenty per cent of fixed overheads are paid during the month in which they are incurred, and the remainder in the following month.
- Variable overheads of £3000 per house are paid in the month in which the house is completed.

■ Each house sells for £70 000, of which £25 000 is paid to Brickup in the month of completion and the remainder three months later.

Prepare the four-month cash budget for Brickup.

NP 9.3 Gunners – an exercise in budget presentation Gunners Ltd imports three electrical products known as Vizi, Ordi and Funi, and sells them to retailing firms in the UK. Results for the last year and budgets for next year are as follows:

| | Last year | | | Budget year | | |
	Vizi	Ordi	Funi	Vizi	Ordi	Funi
Sales (000 units)	250	100	150	237.5	95.0	142.5
Sales revenue (£000)	25 000	8 000	18 000	26 125	8 360	18 810
Expenses (£000)						
Cost of imported goods sold	12 500	4 000	9 000	15 675	5 016	11 286
Separable fixed costs (i.e. those directly associated with the specific product)	4 500	1 000	5 000	4 950	1 100	5 500
General fixed costs	5 000	2 000	3 000	5 500	2 200	3 300
Profit or (−) loss	3 000	1 000	1 000	0	44	−1 276

1. You are asked to redraft the information for both years in a form which will assist management in both the interpretation of the information and in the use of the information for decision-making purposes.

2. The general manager of Gunners is disturbed by the budget information in 1. above. You are further required to calculate the effect on budgeted profit of the following revised assumptions which are to be considered separately and independently:

   (a) that separable fixed costs for the budget year could be cut back to 90 per cent of last year's level

   (b) that the company ceases to import the Funi product

   (c) that selling prices for budget year are increased by 25 per cent on last year's prices resulting in a demand level at 90 per cent of last year.

3. Comment briefly upon the state of the business as revealed by the information that you have.

NP 9.4 D Ltd – preparation of budgets It is mid-October and the management accounting team of D Ltd is preparing annual budgets for the year to the following 31 December. D Ltd manufactures and sells only one product, with a current selling price of £150, but the marketing director believes that the price can be increased to £160 with effect from 1 July of the budget year and that, if that price increase were to happen (i.e. for the third and fourth quarters), then sales volumes for each quarter will be as follows:

	Sales volume
Quarter 1 – January/March	40 000
Quarter 2 – April/June	50 000
Quarter 3 – July/September	30 000
Quarter 4 – October/December	45 000
Sales for each quarter of the year *following* the budget year are expected to be	40 000
Sales for each quarter of the current year (the year *preceding* the budget year) can also be assumed to be	40 000

Each unit of the finished product which is manufactured requires four units of component R and three units of component T, together with a body shell S. These items are purchased from an outside supplier. Currently prices are:

	£
Component R	8.00 each
Component T	5.00 each
Shell S	30.00 each

The components are expected to increase in price by 10 per cent with effect from 1 April of the budget year, but no change is expected in the price of the shell.

Assembly of the shell and components into the finished product requires six labour hours and labour is currently paid at £5.00 per hour. A 4 per cent increase in wage costs is anticipated to take effect from 1 October of the budget year.

Variable overhead costs are expected to be £10 per unit for the whole of the period under review. Fixed production overhead costs are expected to be £240 000 for the year, and are absorbed on a per unit basis.

Stocks at the end of the current year (i.e. immediately prior to the budget year) are expected to be as follows:

Finished units	9 000 units
Component R	3 000 units
Component T	5 500 units
Shell S	500 units

Closing stocks at the end of each quarter in the budget year are to be as follows:

Finished units	10% of next quarter's sales
Component R	20% of next quarter's production requirements
Component T	15% of next quarter's production requirements
Shell S	10% of next quarter's production requirements

You are required to:

Prepare the following budgets of D Ltd for the budget year, showing values for each quarter and the year in total:

1. sales budget (£s and units)
2. production budget (units)
3. material usage budget (units)
4. material purchases budget (£s)
5. production cost budget (£s).

NP 9.5 Genesis – variances from standard costs Genesis makes a product which has the following standards and budgets:

Materials	15 square metres @ £3 per square metre
Labour	5 hours @ £4 per hour
Production budget	1 000 units per month
Sales budget	1 000 units per month
Selling price	£100 per unit

Actual performance for the month just ended is as follows:

Materials	22 000 square metres @ £4 per square metre
Labour	6 800 hours @ £5 per hour
Production	1 400 units
Sales	1 400 units
Selling price	£102 per unit

Produce a variance summary and detailed variance calculations for Genesis including labour, materials and sales variances.

CASE STUDY: BLACKTHORN

Blackthorn produces components for the electronics industry. In the approaching budget year:

- product P will be phased out, and will only be sold in the first four months
- product Q will be sold throughout the year
- product R will be introduced and will be sold in the last six months of the year.

In addition to P, Q and R, which are manufactured, Blackthorn imports component X, and sells it without incurring any further production costs.

Variable cost, selling prices and product contributions during the budget year are expected to be:

| | Product (£000) | | | |
	P	Q	R	X
Raw materials				
A	5	7	10	0
B	1	3	5	0
Bought in parts	0	0	0	3
Unit variable cost	6	10	15	3
Selling price	11	18	28	7
Unit contribution	5	8	13	4

Demand is the principal budget factor for the firm, and the sales budget has been set as in Exhibit 9.4.

As far as capital expenditure is concerned, Blackthorn's plant and equipment are in need of updating and a major replacement programme is planned during the budget year. Installation and expenditure will take place in the following months:

	£000
February	5 000
April	5 000
June	300
August	5 000
Total	15 300

Exhibit 9.4

Monthly sales
budget

			JAN	FEB	MAR	APR	MAY	JUN	JUL	AUG	SEP	OCT	NOV	DEC	TOTAL
Volumes	P		575	575	575	575	—	—	—	—	—	—	—	—	2 300
(000 units)	Q		105	105	105	105	105	105	105	105	105	105	105	105	1 260
	R		—	—	—	—	—	—	100	100	100	100	100	100	600
	X		130	130	130	130	130	130	130	130	130	130	130	130	1 560
		Selling price													
Values (£000)	P	£11	6 325	6 325	6 325	6 325	—	—	—	—	—	—	—	—	25 300
	Q	£18	1 890	1 890	1 890	1 890	1 890	1 890	1 890	1 890	1 890	1 890	1 890	1 890	22 680
	R	£28	—	—	—	—	—	—	2 800	2 800	2 800	2 800	2 800	2 800	16 800
	X	£7	910	910	910	910	910	910	910	910	910	910	910	910	10 920
			9 125	9 125	9 125	9 125	2 800	2 800	5 600	5 600	5 600	5 600	5 600	5 600	75 700

Blackthorn's cost budgets

Variable costs are confined to the raw materials costs for products P, Q and R, and the imported cost of product X. The monthly variable costs related to budgeted sales are given in Exhibit 9.5.

Direct labour is the only stepped cost in Blackthorn's budget, and costs are expected to be incurred as follows:

Product P		Product Q		Product R	
Output (000 units)	Labour (£000)	Output (000 units)	Labour (£000)	Output (000 units)	Labour (£000)
1 500–1 999	1 000	700–999	2 000	400–599	1 500
2 000–2 499*	1 200	1 000–1 299*	2 500	600–799*	2 000
2 500–2 999	1 300	1 300–1 599	2 700	800–999	2 300

*This is the budgeted range of activity for each product, as shown in the sales budget.

Fixed costs

Departmental managers calculated their overhead costs, all of which are fixed within wide ranges of activity. These costs are expected to spread equally over the 12-month period, and are of two types: cash costs, which will paid out in the month they are incurred, and depreciation on fixed assets used by the departments.

A summary of the fixed cost budget appears below.

Department	Cash	£000 Depreciation	Total
Production	6 000	1 000	7 000
Design	3 000	500	3 500
Sales	5 000	200	5 200
Finance	2 000	0	2 000
Administration	2 000	0	2 000
Annual total	18 000	1 700	19 700
Monthly total	1 500	142	1 642

Blackthorn's working capital, finance, tax and dividends

The following additional assumptions have been made by Blackthorn's managers:

■ Debtors will pay for goods two months after the month of sale. (Note that sales for the last two months of the current year, which will bring cash into the budget year, are November £8m; December £8m.)

■ Raw materials and bought-in parts will be purchased in the month preceding sale. Production and sales will take place in the same month. Creditors will be paid one month after purchase. This means that material and parts stocks will always be equal to creditors at the end of any month (represented by the cost of sales for the following month).

Exhibit 9.5

Variable cost of
sales

		JAN	FEB	MAR	APR	MAY	JUN	JUL	AUG	SEP	OCT	NOV	DEC	TOTAL
£000														
Material A	P (£5)	2 875	2 875	2 875	2 875	—	—	—	—	—	—	—	—	11 500
	Q (£7)	735	735	735	735	735	735	735	735	735	735	735	735	8 820
	R (£10)	—	—	—	—	—	—	1 000	1 000	1 000	1 000	1 000	1 000	6 000
	Total	3 610	3 610	3 610	3 610	735	735	1 735	1 735	1 735	1 735	1 735	1 735	26 320
Material B	P (£1)	575	575	575	575	—	—	—	—	—	—	—	—	2 300
	Q (£3)	315	315	315	315	315	315	315	315	315	315	315	315	3 780
	R (£5)	—	—	—	—	—	—	500	500	500	500	500	500	3 000
	Total	890	890	890	890	315	315	815	815	815	815	815	815	9 080
Bought in parts X(£3)		390	390	390	390	390	390	390	390	390	390	390	390	4 680
Total variable cost of sales		4 890	4 890	4 890	4 890	1 440	1 440	2 940	2 940	2 940	2 940	2 940	2 940	40 080

Diagrammatically, the relationship between sales and purchases can be shown as follows:

	Month			
	1	**2**	**3**	**4**
Materials received	O			
Creditors paid		O		
Goods produced and sold		O		
Debtors pay				O

Blackthorn will begin the budget year with a strong cash balance, and does not expect to require additional long-term loans, or overdrafts during the budget year. The sums of £1200 of interest and £4000 of dividend are expected to be taken from profits. Tax will be 30 per cent of pre-tax profit.

Master budgets

Exhibits 9.4, 9.5 and 9.6 (see below) show detailed analysis of sales, costs, and cash flows for Blackthorn. You should follow through the figures in these detailed tables before examining the master budgets which follow.

Bringing all of this information together we can now construct profit, balance sheet, cash and cash-flow budgets.

Blackthorn's budget income statement (or profit and loss account)

	P	Q	R	X	Total
Price per unit (£)	11	18	28	7	
Contribution per unit (£)	5	8	13	4	
Budget volume (000 units)	2 300	1 260	600	1 560	5 720
Sales revenue (£000)	25 300	22 680	16 800	10 920	75 700
Product contribution (£)	11 500	10 080	7 800	6 240	35 620
Direct labour costs (£)	1 200	2 500	2 000	0	5 700
Product profit (£)	10 300	7 580	5 800	6 240	29 920

	(£)
Fixed overheads	19 700
Interest paid	1 200
Profit before tax	9 020
Taxation	2 706
Profit after tax	6 314
Dividend	4 000
Retained profit	2 314

Exhibit 9.6

Cash budget

	JAN	FEB	MAR	APR	MAY	JUN	JUL	AUG	SEP	OCT	NOV	DEC	TOTAL
Receipts – Debtors	8 000	8 000	9 125	9 125	9 125	9 125	2 800	2 800	5 600	5 600	5 600	5 600	80 500
Payments													
Materials and BIP	4 890	4 890	4 890	4 890	1 440	1 440	2 940	2 940	2 940	2 940	2 940	2 940	40 080
Direct Labour P	300	300	300	300	—	—	—	—	—	—	—	—	1 200
Q	208	208	208	208	208	208	209	209	209	209	208	208	2 500
R	—	—	—	—	—	—	333	333	333	333	334	334	2 000
TOTAL direct labour	508	508	508	508	208	208	542	542	542	542	542	542	5 700
Fixed overheads	1 500	1 500	1 500	1 500	1 500	1 500	1 500	1 500	1 500	1 500	1 500	1 500	18 000
Interest	—	—	—	—	—	600	—	—	—	—	—	600	1 200
Plant and equipment	—	5 000	—	5 000	—	300	—	5 000	—	—	—	—	15 300
Taxation	—	—	—	—	—	—	—	—	3 700	—	—	—	3 700
Dividends	—	—	2 500	—	—	—	—	—	2 000	—	—	—	4 500
Total payments	6 898	11 898	9 398	11 898	3 148	4 048	4 982	9 982	10 682	4 982	4 982	5 582	88 480
Surplus (– deficit)	1 102	–3 898	–273	–2 773	5 977	5 077	–2 182	–7 182	–5 082	618	618	18	–7 980
Opening balance (o/draft)	9 185	10 287	6 388	6 115	3 342	9 318	14 395	12 213	5 032	–50	568	1 187	9 185
Closing balance (o/draft)	10 287	6 388	6 115	3 342	9 318	14 395	12 213	5 032	–50	568	1 187	1 205	1 205

Blackthorn's financial position and cash flow

Finally, budgets can be produced showing the overall effect of budget plans on Blackthorn's financial position.

A balance sheet at the beginning of the year is also given for comparison.

	Beginning of year (£)	End of year (£)	Comments
Fixed assets			
Plant and equipment	41 350	56 650	Reflects new capital expenditure
Less depreciation	14 160	15 860	
	27 190	40 790	
Current assets			
Stocks	4 890	3 000	January's cost of sales (assumed at £3 000 for first month of following year)
Debtors	16 000	11 200	November and December sales
Cash	9 185	1 205	From cash budget
Total current assets	30 075	15 405	
Current liabilities			
Creditors (material and bought-in parts)	4 890	3 000	= to stock figure
Taxation	3 700	2 706	From income statement
Dividend	2 500	2 000	= £4 000 − £2 000 paid
Total current liabilities	11 090	7 706	
Net current assets	18 985	7 699	
Net assets	46 175	48 489	
Share capital	10 500	10 500	
Retained profits	25 675	27 989	
Equity	36 175	38 489	
Long-term loans	10 000	10 000	
Net capital employed	46 175	48 489	

Cash-flow budget

	(£000)	Comments
Profit before tax	9 020	From income statement
Depreciation	1 700	
	10 720	
Working capital reduction	4 800	Debtors −4 800 Stocks −1 890 Creditors +1 890

▶

Total sources of cash		15 520
Capital expenditure	15 300	
Taxation	3 700	
Dividends	4 500	
Total applications		23 500
Deficit		7 980
Reduction in cash balance		7 980 (9 185 − 1 205; cash budget)

Your brief

Blackthorn's budgets as shown here have served to quantify all of the factors likely to affect the financial performance of the firm during the budget period. It is now up to the managers to consider whether that performance is acceptable and, if not, what steps can be taken to ensure that it becomes so.

Imagine that you are the management accountant of Blackthorn. Write a report to the board of directors that comments upon the major issues raised by the budgets. Your report should consider

1. the difficulties, challenges and opportunities that are revealed by the budget statements
2. possible actions that may be needed.

WEB RESOURCES   www

www.thomsonlearning.co.uk/accountingandfinance/hand

The companion website has free additional resources for you to use alongside this book. If you are a student you can access material to help with revision, including practice questions with answers to test how much of the material you have understood. There are also useful hyperlinks to companies and information sources mentioned in the book as well as interactive quizzes. There are additional resources for lecturers using this book on their courses; the details can be found in the preface at the front of this book.

CHAPTER 10

Accounting for long-term decisions

LEARNING OBJECTIVES

After studying this chapter you should be able to:

■ have an appreciation of the relationship between long-run and short-run decisions

■ understand the key features of long-term investment decisions: their long time scale, links to strategic direction and inherent uncertainty, and the significance of cash flows

■ be able to place the financial analysis of investment decisions within the context of the overall investment decision process

■ be able to draw up a relevant cash-flow analysis for long-term decisions

■ appreciate the significance of the time value of money and the cost of capital

■ apply the techniques of NPV, payback and IRR for the financial evaluation of long-term decisions

■ appreciate how uncertainty may be dealt with in the financial analysis

■ be aware of the reported practices of businesses in their evaluation of long-term decisions

■ understand the way in which product costs are viewed from a long-term, strategic perspective.

Introduction

In the first chapter of this book we distinguished between management and financial accounting (see Exhibit 1.1). This chapter, like Chapter 9, is located firmly within the management accounting area, and extends the ideas developed in Chapter 3 about decision-making and financial analysis. But here we are focusing upon decisions that have long-term implications for the organisation, that will typically involve the investment of significant amounts of money, and that commit the organisation to a course of action that will not be easy to reverse.

In Chapter 3 we looked at ways in which financial information may influence managers' decisions, and we focused on short-term decisions – for accounting reports that usually means those that can be analysed within a one-year time frame. The current chapter takes the decision analysis a step further and asks the question: 'How can financial analysis take account of the longer-term aspects of decisions?' The more significant decisions in a business will impact on profits and cash flows for far more than one year, and may commit the organisation to changes in its financial position for many years to come.

But first you should review Chapter 3 – in particular, have another look at the concepts of opportunity cost, contribution and relevant cash flows that were discussed in that chapter. Those ideas crop up again in the current chapter and are very important for an understanding of the ways in which financial analysis can be used within business decision-making.

TASK 10.1

A personal long-term decision

Before we look at business decisions we want you to think about personal financial decisions and their time frames. Most readers of this textbook will be studying finance as part of an educational course or development programme – so we will use that experience as an example. Courses of study carry the key aspects of long-term decisions in that they involve you in investing some time (and often cash as well) in the expectation of an improvement in your skill levels that will bring benefits in later time periods. The undergraduate, for example, may well invest cash and time over three years in expectation of gaining better job prospects over 20 years or more. A marketing manager who is taking a short course in financial awareness may invest time and cash for six months in expectation of improved job prospects within their organisation over (say) the next five years.

List the costs and benefits (cash and non-cash) of taking your current course of study or development programme. Try to put the costs and benefits into three time periods: immediate, over the next year and more than one year ahead.

Long term and short term – a continuum

A common feature of the examples in Chapter 3 was that the time scale was short – often less than one year. A short time horizon is very limited and unrealistic for many decisions; indeed, the decisions that really make a difference (e.g. Dyson's decision to close its manufacturing facility in Wales, Wetherspoon's decision to expand its pub chain, BT's decision to re-enter the mobile phone market) all have a time horizon that extends well beyond one year.

As we have discussed in Chapter 3, to label some decisions 'short-run' and others 'long-run' is to oversimplify the world of business, and it is probably more helpful to think of a continuum. In Exhibit 10.1 we see that at one end of the continuum are those decisions which have very short-term implications and which can be altered without too much pain. The other end of the scale contains those decisions which involve much time, commitment, and probably cash. These latter, very long-run decisions may only be altered at considerable expense.

Exhibit 10.1 shows the artificiality of any distinction between long and short-run decisions. Long-run decisions tend to set frameworks within which later short-run decisions take place. An organisation is a dynamic location for a continuous stream of decisions, and none of these decisions can be isolated. Each must be seen in the context of other decisions previously taken or yet to be considered.

Tensions often exist between the short- and long-term priorities of a business. Pharmaceutical companies, for example, expect to invest millions of pounds in new drug development to ensure a strong long-term future, but such investment may damage profits and returns to shareholders in the short term. Railway networks also face choices between, on the one hand, increasing short-term returns for shareholders and keeping prices low for customers and, on the other, investing in new track and technology to ensure a safe and modern network for future years.

Exhibit 10.1

Continuum – short and long-term decisions

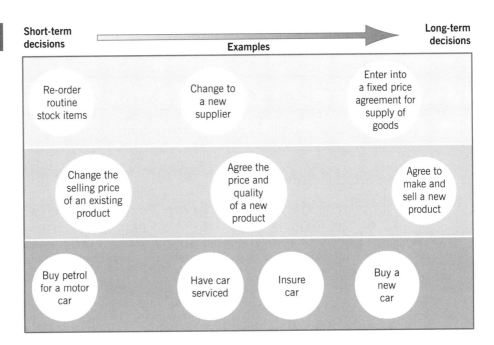

Short- and long-term tensions in the rail networks

Railways require very long-term investment in expensive assets of tracks and rolling stock. At the same time, if privatised, a rail operator has to make short-term returns to shareholders.

Network Rail, the not-for-profit body that took over the running of the UK's rail network, promised that passengers would see real improvements within two years. The company was handed responsibility for the UK's track, signals and stations in what many greeted as a fresh start for the railways after the troubled history of Railtrack.

'It is difficult to just turn around and say, "Yep, in a year's time I can assure you it is all going to be at 90 per cent,"' said John Armitt, Network Rail's chief executive. '[But] by all working together I am sure we will see some real

ILLUSTRATION 10.1

improvements in the next 12 to 24 months.' And he insisted that the company would not put profit before safety.

Mr Armitt and Network Rail were faced with the huge task of restoring public confidence in train travel and upgrading the rail infrastructure. The task of the company was to oversee the running of 23 000 miles of track and 2500 stations. Because Network Rail was set up as a not-for-profit body, any profits it made were to be ploughed back into rail maintenance (long-term goals) rather than being used to pay dividends to shareholders (short-term). The contrast with a Stock-Market-quoted plc, where short-term returns are paramount, is stark.

Key features of long-term decisions

The following five aspects of long-term decisions make them qualitatively different from shorter term decisions.

Time scale

The time period affected by the decision may stretch into a few years (replacement of computer technology by an insurance company's call centre), or may be over decades (Rolls Royce's investment in new-generation aero engines).

Strategic direction

During the 1980s, when Bass Brewers declared that it was set on a diversification strategy away from its core brewing and pubs, the long-term decision to buy into the Holiday Inn chain was a specific investment decision that began to put the general strategy into place. Long-term decisions often are overt signs of the firm's strategic intentions.

Inherent uncertainty

The longer the time scale, of course, the greater will be the uncertainty surrounding the outcomes of any decision. Long-term decisions, by their very nature, contain high levels of uncertainty. This feature is important for the financial analysis – for managers may want the cash-flow analysis to indicate a range of possible outcomes, rather than a single point estimate. Managers will also be interested to know how sensitive the projected outcome of a decision is to changes in the key variables (e.g. demand or cost levels).

Large cash flows

Long-term decisions frequently involve large amounts of cash. Examples are not hard to find: Boots plc's investment in the Children's World chain and later withdrawal from that market; any airline's investment in new aircraft. Indeed the amounts are sometimes so large that the whole future of the business may be affected by the outcome. When, for example, mobile phone operators bid for new licences from the UK government at the start of the twenty-first century, many billions of pounds were involved and these investments would have knock-on effects for the companies for years to come.

Difficulty of reversing the decision

Had the US supermarket Walmart decided that their investment in the UK grocer Asda was incorrect, it would have cost millions of pounds to reverse, while ITV Digital's abortive investment in the English Football League proved to be irreversible and caused the company to collapse. This, then, is the final key feature of the long-term decision: that the cost of going into reverse is very high and could be crippling.

We can see then that – for reasons of time scale, strategic significance, uncertainty, high cash flows, and the difficulty of changing the decision – long-term decisions are critical for the future of a business. These special features help to explain the detailed attention that is paid to the analysis and evaluation of such decisions.

The stages of a long-term decision

Although we are mainly concerned in this chapter with the financial evaluation of long-term decisions, you will find it helpful to have a context within which to place such decisions. Exhibit 10.2 links the main stages for an investment decision: the search for opportunities, the evaluation of choices, the implementation and the control and monitoring stage.

Let us now take a closer look at each stage.

Exhibit 10.2

Stages in a long-term decision

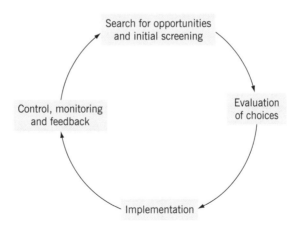

Search for opportunities and initial screening

Some decisions may be reactive, in response to developments by competitors. Food retailers in the UK, for example, played a kind of 'catch-up' for several years – as one became larger so others would seek to invest in new stores and to buy up independent retailers in order to maintain market share. The proposed takeover of Safeway in 2003 was one more example of investment decisions as a reaction to market forces, as Morrisons (the favourite to buy Safeway) sought to increase its size. Other long-term decisions will be proactive, as a result of constant searching for available investments. House-building companies conduct continuous searches for land-buying opportunities, such that as land becomes available they are set to make bids. The point is that decisions of significance rarely appear without warning, but are the result of looking for ways of putting into practice the declared strategy of the business. At this early stage, informal 'screening' will take place before formal evaluation. Next plc, the clothing retailer, is likely to be presented with many possible new locations, each of which will be screened for size, location, condition, etc. in an informal manner. Scottish & Newcastle, or other pub owners, seek locations where there is likely to be a high level of spending power in the vicinity. Only those initial ideas that pass through the initial screening process will be subject to formal financial evaluation at the next stage.

Evaluation of choices

Projects that pass the initial screening test are likely to be subject to formal financial evaluation, which is the main focus of this chapter. At this stage, there will have to be an analysis of likely relevant cash flows, which will then be used to establish the viability of the proposed investment opportunity using techniques such as **net present value** (NPV) and **payback**. These techniques are discussed more fully later in the chapter.

Implementation

Investment opportunities that satisfy the financial criteria are likely to be accepted, subject to there being enough cash to fund the investment. The project then enters the implementation stage – that is to say that it has to be made to work! This may be the toughest aspect of any long-term decision, for many ideas that appear viable at the planning stage may prove difficult to carry out, or may be dogged by weak management. Think, for example, of the Millennium Dome, Wembley Stadium and the Scottish Parliament building, three public investments in the UK that went well over budget and that proved to be nightmares of implementation.

Control, monitoring and feedback

The final stage in this process is concerned with monitoring the project against predictions and providing

1. feedback about the particular project
2. general feedback that may help with investments in the future.

Some organisations will formalise this stage through a post-completion audit when a full analysis of the project's outcomes will be reviewed. Such an audit has some potential for learning within the organisation although there are some difficulties: given the long time scale, it may be several years before a full view of the decision can be taken.

Relevant cash-flow analysis for long-term decisions

The accounting input into this process is mainly focused upon the evaluation stage, although financial managers may also be involved at other stages. The central aspect of the financial analysis is the relevant cash-flow predictions – the assessment of the cash flows that will stem from the long-term decision.

The declared aim of companies is the maximisation of shareholder wealth, and this is achieved through adopting investments that maximise future cash flows, thus providing both strong dividend streams and growth in share price. Relevant cash flows therefore form the basis of any formal financial evaluation for long-term decisions. The focus is on what difference this proposal will make to our future cash flows. There may, of course, be non-quantifiable aspects of a decision that will also require recognition (e.g. its impact on the company's public image), and non-monetary factors may play an important part in the final choice. However, relevant cash flows are a useful starting point.

A moment's thought will tell us that it is not possible to predict future cash flows with precision – what is being aimed for is reasonable accuracy in that the resultant forecasts will assist the decision-makers to choose between alternatives.

TASK 10.2

Predicting cash flows

A retailer of books and stationery is planning to rent a vacant site within a large shopping mall, and wants to gain an idea of the cash flows involved over the next five years. What do you think are likely to be the main cash flows (both expenditure and income) that must form part of the cash-flow predictions for the venture? Two examples would be:

1. sales income from customers
2. staff wages.

What others can you identify? Rank the cash flows in terms of predictability – with the most predictable at the top of your list, and the most uncertain ones at the bottom.

When the cash-flow predictions have finally been arrived at – what then? How do decision-makers decide whether these cash flows are satisfactory for the decision to go ahead? The answers to these questions depend entirely on what criteria the organisation chooses to use to identify worthwhile investments. We now look at the main criteria used within business organisations, but before we do that there is a need to consider an important concept upon which evaluations often rest: the **time value of money**.

The time value of money

Few decisions have all relevant cash flows in the same time period and there needs to be some way in which we can acknowledge the different time periods involved in long-term decisions. For this we need an appreciation of the time value of money (TVoM).

The concept of opportunity cost was introduced in Chapter 3. We can recall that opportunity cost relates to 'benefits foregone' by taking a particular course of action. An intriguing question to ask then is: can money itself have an opportunity cost? A little reflection will show that this must be so. Imagine that you spend £100 tomorrow on an asset which will last for a considerable time (a piece of furniture, for example). The full relevant cost of this asset is not only the £100 cost, but also the interest on that money. If you have taken the cash from your hard-earned savings then you are giving up the interest that those savings could be earning. If, on the other hand, you increased your bank overdraft to buy the asset then the overdraft interest represents the opportunity cost of your money.

The link which we need in order to make sense of decisions covering different time periods is the **opportunity cost of money** (sometimes referred to as the time value of money). To make life even more confusing, the description (**cost of capital**) is frequently used to describe this opportunity cost for businesses, particularly those that are limited companies.

The argument runs along these lines: in a developed, money-based economy, money itself has a price (sometimes called interest). Interest rates represent the costs or benefits of transferring money from one period to another – anyone who has ever borrowed money will know this instinctively – while the borrower can take advantage of the house, car or holiday immediately, they accept that cash in the future will be have to be paid out, including an interest payment (the opportunity cost of the money) that compensates the lender for providing the cash to the borrower. Professional investors will seek out investment opportunities which show a surplus after covering their opportunity cost of money – in other words, they will borrow as long as they can earn a return on the money that exceeds the cost of borrowing.

Mathematically we can demonstrate the idea of the opportunity cost of money through Illustration 10.2.

ILLUSTRATION 10.2

The opportunity cost of money

If I invest £100 for one year at a 10 per cent rate of interest it will be worth:

$$£100 \times (1 + 0.10)^1 = £110 \text{ at the end of the first year}$$

Left for a second year, the sum becomes:

$$£100 \times (1 + 0.10)^2 = £121$$

▶

And for a third year:

$$£100 \times (1 + 0.10)^3 = £133.1 \ldots \text{ and so on.}$$

One significant implication of these calculations is that someone who can borrow and lend money at 10 per cent (assuming that the future returns are certain and without risk) would be indifferent between receiving £100 now and £121 in two years' time. This is because (assuming there is no urgent need to actually have the cash in hand) the amounts are equivalent to each other given the possibility for investing at the given rate of interest.

In general form this relationship between a present value (P), a future value (F), the opportunity cost of money (i) and time periods (n) can be written as:

$$F = P (1 + i)^n$$

This is sometimes referred to as the 'compound interest formula', and can be used to project forward the future value of current wealth. By dividing each side of this equation by $(1 + i)^n$ we get:

$$P = \frac{F}{(1 + i)^n}$$

This final formula is known as the 'present value formula', and it allows us to equate cash flows for different time periods. The formula literally provides (given certain important assumptions) a way of bringing a cash flow in any future time period to a **present value**.

We will now examine the present value concept and calculations (see Illustration 10.3).

ILLUSTRATION 10.3

Boulton

Boulton has been very successful over the past few years and has increased turnover by a considerable amount. Due to this high rate of expansion the firm now has a problem with storage space for its finished products. The managers of Boulton have decided to erect a cheap prefabricated building which will last for five years and will then be removed. The loss of heat from this type of building is high, yet Boulton's products need to be kept in warm conditions. The key choice is whether to insulate the building or to have higher heating costs. If the building is not insulated then heating costs are expected to be £9000 in the first full year (Year One), rising by 5 per cent inflation each year. Insulation will cost £22 000 immediately, and heating costs will be reduced to £3000 in Year One, rising by 5 per cent inflation each year.

How can Boulton's analysis handle the fact that relevant cash flows cover a period of five years? Let us first examine these predicted cash flows.

▶

Boulton's predicted cash flows

Year	Outflows (£)	Savings (i.e. net savings in cash flows) (£)	Net relevant cash flow (£)
0	22 000		(22 000)
1		6 000 (9 000 − 3 000)	6 000
2		6 300 (6 000 × 1.05)	6 300
3		6 615 (6 300 × 1.05)	6 615
4		6 946 (6 615 × 1.05)	6 946
5		7 293 (6 946 × 1.05)	7 293
		Overall cash surplus	11 154

At first glance it may appear that the insulation is viable, giving a cash surplus of £11 154. This figure is quite important as it does indicate the overall saving over the life of the building. However, on reflection it seems that we cannot merely add up the various flows without some prior adjustment for *time*. There is a fundamental difference between the money received in Year One, for example, from those received in Year Three. The difference is that we have to wait longer for the Year Three saving and therefore also lose the opportunity cost – the returns that we could be earning on that cash if we had saved it earlier.

We therefore need to find a way of adjusting the cash flows for this TVoM.

Assume for the moment that Boulton's cost of borrowing and lending is 10 per cent. This is quite a big assumption and later we will consider the source of the figure in more detail. The relevant cash flows can then be discounted using the present value formula as shown below:

Discounting Boulton's cash flows

Year	Factor $£1 / (1 + i)^n$ (taken to three decimal places)	Relevant cash flows (£)	Discounted cash flows (£)
0	1.000	(22 000)	(22 000)
1	0.909	6 000	5 454
2	0.826	6 300	5 204
3	0.751	6 615	4 968
4	0.683	6 946	4 744
5	0.621	7 293	4 529

Total of all **discounted cash flows** = Net Present Value (NPV) =   2 899

Let's have a closer look at the factors in the second column. Recall that the general formula for calculating a present value of a £1 received in (n) years time at (i) opportunity cost was $£1/(1 + i)^n$ and that this is derived from the compound interest formula. Working that through for £1 received in one year's time at 10 per cent gives:

▶

$$£1/(1.1)^1$$
$$= £1 / 1.1$$
$$= £0.909$$

(The answer is actually £0.909090909 recurring, but it will make sense to work to three places of decimals here hence there are some rounding approximations.)

You can also refer to the present value table in the Appendix (see p.294). Reading across the first row of the table for 1 year and 10% finds the same value, 0.9091.

In other words, £1 received in one year's time (assuming 10 per cent opportunity cost) has a present value of £0.909. In one sense, £1 received in one year's time is the same as £0.909 in hand now (because we could invest it for one year at 10 per cent and it would become £1 (£0.909 × 1.1 = £1 (allowing for rounding)).

If we take the idea on one more year we get the calculation:

$$£1/(1.1)^2$$
$$= \frac{£1}{1.21}$$
$$= £0.826$$

Thus £1 received in two years' time has a present value of £0.826. Try this out by assuming an investment of £0.826 compounded at 10 per cent for two years – this will be worth:

£0.826 × 1.10 = £0.9086 after one year
£0.9086 × 1.10 = £0.99946 or £1 (allowing for rounding) after two years

Each of Boulton's annual cash flows has been discounted using the present value formula, and the resultant NPV number of £2899 is the surplus generated by the decision after covering all costs, including the opportunity cost of money. More significantly, the NPV is the increase in the value of the business brought about by this decision. If the decision is undertaken today, then the present worth of the firm should (theoretically) increase by the NPV.

In practice a number of factors may prevent this value increase actually taking place, such as imperfect information in the capital markets and uncertainty surrounding the predictions. Nevertheless, the theoretical meaning of NPV (increase in value of the firm) is important. By this reasoning, decisions that maximise NPV will, so the argument goes, also maximise the wealth of the shareholder group (the assumed goal of the organisation). Simply stated – any decision with a positive NPV is economically worthwhile as it will increase the value of the firm, while a negative NPV decision should be rejected as it will be destroying the value of the firm.

The theoretical nature of the NPV technique may account for its apparent slow acceptance by decision-makers and simpler techniques are sometimes used in practice. One such technique is *payback*.

Payback

'Payback' is, as the term suggests, concerned with the question: 'How quickly do the savings cover (or payback) the initial investment?' If we return to the Boulton example we can work out a payback as follows:

ILLUSTRATION 10.3

Boulton (continued)

The initial investment pays back like this:

Boulton's payback

Initial investment	£22 000		
First year pays back	£6 000	leaving	£16 000
Second year pays back	£6 300	leaving	£9 700
Third year pays back	£6 615	leaving	£3 085
Fourth year pays back	£6 946	which more than covers the outstanding amount of £3 085.	

Some time during the fourth year, therefore, the initial investment is fully covered, and we could say that the payback period is somewhere between three and four years. If we wanted to be more precise we could express the payback period as:

$$\text{three years} + \frac{(3085}{6946)}$$

or approximately 3.44 years – the investment takes just under three and a half years to be paid back.

The payback calculation is relatively simple and focuses upon the speed of cash flowing back to the business, which is clearly a crucial element of business success. The simplicity and cash flow focus of payback possibly explains its popularity, despite its conceptual limitations (for example, payback ignores any cash flows occurring after the payback period, and makes no attempt to discount the cash flows).

Simpler techniques such as payback have traditionally been more popular with decision-makers than NPV, although many firms use NPV and payback together. NPV does provide clear signals about the value of decisions that span a number of time periods. Provided the decision-taker remains aware of the assumptions within the technique it can provide a useful focus for the analysis of decisions with longer horizons.

Internal rate of return

We have seen that when we discount cash flows by applying a given cost of capital we obtain an NPV for the decision. The NPV, we have seen, represents a projected increase in worth of the business as a result of taking that decision. Conversely, a negative NPV would suggest that the decision is likely to result in a reduction in value and so should not be taken. The **internal rate of return** (IRR) criteria is effectively the flip side of NPV. For IRR we try to calculate the cost of capital that would give a zero NPV, effectively a break-even rate. The firm would then set some hurdle rate and would accept any projects that appeared to provide a return that was greater than that rate. Here is an illustration:

ILLUSTRATION 10.4

IRR

A company proposes to invest £1000 and expects returns of £430 each year for three years. The company's cost of capital is around 12 per cent and therefore only accepts investment decisions that offer a greater IRR than 12 per cent. This rate is known as the 'hurdle rate' in that projects must clear that hurdle in order to be accepted.

A simple way of discovering the IRR (or at least a close approximation to it) is first to discount the cash flows at two rates (selecting one above and one below the hurdle rate). So here we will discount at 10 per cent and 15 per cent. The results are as follows:

Year	Cash flow	—10%— Factor	NPV	—15%— Factor	NPV
0	(1000)	1.000	(1000)	1.000	(1000)
1	430	0.909	391	0.870	374
2	430	0.826	355	0.756	325
3	430	0.751	323	0.658	283
Net present values			+69		−18

An increase of five percentage points on the cost of capital has given a reduction of £87 (from + 69 to − 18) on the NPV. Clearly, then, the cost of capital that would give zero NPV (i.e. the IRR) must lie somewhere between 10 per cent and 15 per cent. We can get to an approximation of what the IRR is by considering that:

- five percentage points creates a reduction of NPV of £87
- therefore each percentage point has reduced the NPV by $\frac{87}{5}$ = £17.40
- if we have an NPV of £69 at 10 per cent then it would take $\frac{69}{17.4}$ points to take the NPV down to zero. i.e. $\frac{69}{17.4}$ = 3.97 percentage points (rounded)
- the IRR is therefore approximately 10% + 3.97% = 13.97%.

This is an approximate calculation as the reduction in NPV (if we were to examine the maths a little more closely) would not be a strictly linear relationship as we have assumed in our calculations here. For our purposes, however, it will be close enough to guide the decision-maker.

▶

An IRR of 13.97 per cent is above the company's hurdle rate of 12 per cent and so, on that basis, the project would be accepted. If all the predictions are proved to be correct the investment would yield enough return to more than cover the company's opportunity cost of money.

There is clearly a very close connection between IRR and NPV and they may be seen as the 'opposite side of the same coin' (see Exhibit 10.3, which is a graphic representation of Illustration 10.4). Although not drawn to scale, the graph clearly shows that, as the cost of capital is raised, so the NPV falls until it reaches zero (neither positive nor negative). At that point (called the IRR) the value created by the project is just sufficient to cover the costs of financing it.

Exhibit 10.3

Net present values and IRR

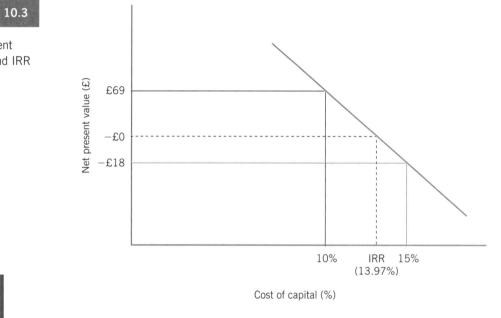

Exhibit 10.4 draws together the two related ideas: NPV and IRR.

Exhibit 10.4

Net present value and internal rate of return compared and contrasted

Concept	What it means	Calculation	Comments
Net Present Value	The increase in value created by accepting an investment opportunity.	NPV is the surplus left after discounting all cash flows from a project over its life span.	The discount rate that provides a zero NPV is the IRR.
Internal Rate of Return	The cost of capital that gives a zero NPV.	Discount the project at various rates until we discover (or extrapolate) the rate that gives zero NPV.	Firms often set a hurdle rate based on their expected returns from projects. Projects, to be accepted, must have an IRR above this rate.

The cost of capital – the discount rate

One of the key numbers in the illustrations above is the cost of capital, for this is the rate at which the company discounts its future cash flows. An important question is: Where does this number come from?

To understand this number it is necessary to view both sides of the funding equation. With few exceptions, a company that is funded by investors is expected to provide these investors with a monetary return. In order to provide these returns, the company must in turn be investing in projects and activities that bring funds into the business. In order for investors to be satisfied with their level of returns the company has to receive from its investments a level of return that is at least equal to the expected returns for investors.

Diagrammatically we can show this connection in Exhibit 10.5.

Exhibit 10.5

The links between project returns, the company and investor returns

Investors (shareholders and other lenders)	The company
Expect a return from the company	In order to satisfy investors' expectations for returns, must invest in projects
The expected return will take account of the perceived riskiness of the company, and of returns that can be obtained elsewhere	Will seek out projects that bring a return at least equal to the returns expected by investors
The cost of capital is a way of expressing the required return for shareholders	The cost of capital is used by the company to discount all projects. If a positive NPV results then the project is expected to increase the value of the business

TASK 10.3

Your own personal cost of capital?

Imagine that you are about to invest a significant amount of money in a new asset, for example property, a vehicle or a computer. In addition to the actual cost of the asset, what are you going to be sacrificing in terms of the cost of the money? If you have large savings and are therefore financing the investment yourself, the cost of capital may be the interest that you will lose on the money that you are taking from your savings. If, on the other hand, you have few savings and use a loan, then the cost of capital for this investment will be the rate of interest that you will be paying on the loan. What would be your own cost of capital for that investment? In other words, what is your own opportunity cost of money?

The cost of capital for a company

In the illustrations so far used we have assumed that the cost of capital is given. In reality, establishing exactly what cost of capital to use is not easy, and some complex models have been established that allow for the calculation to be carried out. For our purposes, however, we merely want you to understand the basic principles at work, which relate to the expected returns of investors, and the extent to which the company is reliant on each investor group for its finances.

ILLUSTRATION 10.5

Cost of capital and finance sources

For this illustration we consider three imaginary companies that are financed by various mixtures of shareholder capital and lending.

Company	Proportion of finance provided by share-holders	Rate of return expected by share-holders	Proportion of finance provided by bank lending	Rate of return expected by banks	Weighted average cost of capital
A	100%	15%	0%	10%	$(1 \times 15) + (0 \times 10) = 15\%$
B	70%	15%	30%	10%	$(0.7 \times 15) + (0.3 \times 10) = 10.5 + 3 = 13.5\%$
C	40%	15%	60%	10%	$(0.4 \times 15) + (0.6 \times 10) = 6 + 6 = 12\%$

Relating this back to our previous long-term decision calculations and NPV company A would be using 15% for discounting purposes, company B 13.5%, and company C 12%.

There are a number of assumptions within the table above, the most significant of which is that we can establish what the required return is from shareholders. For lenders this is not so difficult, as the rate of interest is stated and agreed between lender and borrower. Even here, however, the company may have a mixture of loans and hence there may be some averaging to do to arrive at the required return given in the fourth column. When it comes to estimating the return required by shareholders the calculation is fraught with difficulties, the most significant being that shareholder returns are normally expected to be partly dividend returns (which may be fairly easily stated) and partly from capital returns. Capital returns, as any examination of stock markets in the period 1980 to 2000 would show, are variable (to say the least!). It is not the purpose of this book to examine the detailed complexities of establishing shareholder return calculations – other more detailed financial management texts do that. We only wish to establish that:

■ the cost of capital that is used in discounting calculations should be based on the returns expected by those with an investment in the organisation

■ calculation of that return should take account of the mix of investors.

Uncertainty in long-term decision analysis

We noted in Chapter 3 that uncertainty is a given within decisions, and this is especially true for long-term decisions with very long time horizons. How, then, can the inherent uncertainty be handled within the financial analysis? To recap from Chapter 3, the introduction of uncertainty into the calculations should leave the decision-maker better informed about the range and riskiness of possible outcomes. In effect, the analysis should encourage the decision-makers to review their confidence in predictions and also their attitudes towards risk.

Best and worst

A first step towards incorporating uncertainty could be to ask for more than one set of predictions: pessimistic, optimistic, and most likely. A single-point decision analysis may inform the decision-maker that 'NPV will be £1200 if all assumptions hold up'. But it will be more useful for a decision-maker to be told 'your NPV (from this decision) may be £1000, £1200, or £1500 depending on [for example] levels of market demand or on levels of savings made'.

By providing a worst/most likely/best range of predictions the accountant is encouraging discussion about the decision and about the important variables which will determine the outcome.

What if?

The widespread availability of spreadsheet software opens up the dimensions of uncertainty analysis. Spreadsheets are widely used because they allow managers and accountants to alter the key variables with the decision model and to observe the effect on the outcome (measured in long-term decisions through cash flows, payback or NPV). 'What if?' questions can be asked and multiple solutions generated. A dynamic view of the decision replaces the static 'single-point' estimate. Although clearly an improvement, the spreadsheet model may leave managers feeling uncomfortable, for the decision outcome cannot be summarised as a single NPV outcome.

What do we know about how real companies carry out long-term decision analysis?

The ideas within this chapter (NPV, cost of capital, IRR, etc.) have been developed over time, often from an economics perspective. Some of the concepts may seem very abstract for practical business decision-makers and it is worth considering whether the concepts are used in practice, or whether they are merely textbook ideas. There has been some research into the ways in which organisations actually go about analysing long-term decisions, and we provide a very brief overview of that research here.

Like all management activities it is quite hard to access actual managerial practice; most firms prefer to keep their activities confidential. Within that broad caveat, it appears that there has been a trend over the past 20 or 30 years towards the use of more sophisticated techniques (e.g. NPV) rather than simple payback.

This trend may be explained by a variety of factors: a greater awareness of the techniques, the increased availability of spreadsheets and a more hostile business environment that encourages more analysis prior to the taking of decisions.

Larger companies appear to spend more effort on the more sophisticated techniques than smaller ones. However, the ubiquitous use of spreadsheets and modelling software allows even quite small companies to carry out detailed analysis and to build uncertainty into the process by incorporating 'What if?' questions into the analysis. Payback remains very popular, even though it ignores the TVoM. However, many organisations do not rely upon single criteria when judging long-term decisions. Rather, they utilise a mix of measures including payback and NPV.

Studies certainly suggest an upward trend in 'sophisticated' analysis techniques – i.e. more number-bashing by more firms in more detail. However, it is far from clear what this analysis actually achieves. Few firms seem to reject projects merely because of the numbers (strategic issues for instance are more important) and the screening of projects takes place before numbers are crunched. Furthermore, some studies have raised the question: 'Does analysis improve performance?' – the so-called **paralysis-by-analysis** debate. In brief, there is little evidence of better performance by companies that go in for more extensive financial analysis. The possibility is raised that an overemphasis on the numbers may prevent the exercising of managerial judgement.

A broader context for long-term decision-making

As we have pointed out above, the trend over the past few decades (certainly since the 1960s) has been towards a more 'scientific' analysis of decisions. Some would argue that this trend is merely part of a more scientific (and less spiritual) approach to life in general. The trend (towards deeper financial analysis) fits with the wider social notion of scientific discovery and rational scientific thinking (which, put very simply, suggests that there is an answer and we need only apply the correct research methods and resources to find it!). Within such a culture NPV and the discounting of cash flows appear to be rational approaches, and are therefore to be encouraged. The financial analysis of long-term decisions, as we have seen, places emphasis on the rational and analytical aspects of the decision.

It would, however, be naive to suggest that financial considerations are all that matter. Financial analysis is viewed by many managers as only part of the decision, and not always the most important element at that. Successful investment decisions may rely more on the ability to generate innovative ideas, the desire to follow up on the firm's general strategic direction with specific investments and managerial determination to make ideas work, as well as on the less easily quantified aspects. Let's put this first into a personal context.

TASK 10.4

Retail therapy

The term 'retail therapy' entered the language some time ago to describe shopping as a way of making us feel better (as opposed to buying just what we need). Can you think of any spending decision that you have taken in the past 12 months where other personal and emotional factors played a part in your decision to spend?

A broader view of long-term decisions therefore places the financial aspects in their behavioural and strategic contexts. Two of the issues raised by this perspective follow.

- Investment decisions are taken as part of a negotiation process, and as such the outcome recognises the power position of people within the organisation. For example, a powerful chief executive may insist on decisions that fit with his/her own personal agenda even though the numbers may not strictly 'stack up'.

- At an organisational level, decisions are rarely taken in isolation. Most decisions only make sense in the context of the firm's overall strategy, and these strategic considerations are often paramount in setting the goals for specific investments. Bass Brewers' decision to buy the Holiday Inn chain during the late 1980s was not an isolated decision, but part of a declared strategy of diversification away from its core brewing business. This strategy was taken to its conclusion when Bass (later renamed as Six Continents) divested itself of its brewing operations to InterBrew in 2001.

Goals, decisions and shareholders

A discussion of long-term decisions is incomplete without recognising the importance of goals. It is often argued that business organisations have a goal of maximising the wealth of the ownership group (normally shareholders for a company). Accounting analysis helps to provide guidance for the decision-maker based upon this goal of wealth maximisation.

It is certainly appealing to suggest that shareholder wealth is the driving force behind decisions in the firm. After all, shareholders do own the firm, and they probably have clear economic objectives concerning their own wealth and current consumption (presumably to increase both!). Shareholders' wealth is embodied within the share price while consumption is represented by the dividend. Both share price and dividend are best served by higher profits. Thus, the argument concludes that the firm's goal is to maximise profits (and thereby increase shareholder wealth and consumption).

What is the justification for this (apparently) simple view of business goals?

- This approach allows for clear, unambiguous, analysis. The best choice will normally be clear and will favour one course of action over all others (because it appears to maximise wealth better than other choices).

- We can observe empirically that economic objectives are clearly very influential in any business decision, even though they may not be the only consideration. Wealth maximisation (in accounting terms) is all about maximising the value of all future cash flows and decisions will be judged on their likelihood of achieving this aim.

Without some understanding of goals, our discussion of decisions is incomplete. For any decision presupposes a direction, or aim in view. What, for example, were your personal goals (aims) behind the decision to enrol on your current course of study or to apply for a job? Individuals clearly have goals – but what of organisations? Can they have goals? If so, what are they?

The wealth-maximising view of goals is criticised as being oversimplified. The divorce of ownership from control separates the managing group (directors) from the ownership group (shareholders). Directors are in control of the decision process, and there is no obvious reason (at least in the short-term) why they should take decisions which accord with the aims of the separate shareholder group. Managers will clearly have to recognise the 'wealth needs' of shareholders. However, such needs are probably more in the nature of a constraint on management action rather than a primary goal. A number of research studies have suggested that managers aim to maximise other targets (for example growth, sales or managerial perks) subject to a profit constraint. In Chapter 11 we discuss these issues of accountability more fully.

The very idea of maximising anything has been challenged by some theorists, who would argue that there are inherent limits to the rational pursuit of goals. For instance, how does the organisation know when it has achieved a maximum? Presumably there are other actions which could be taken to increase profit or sales beyond the existing position. Maximising is only a theoretical possibility which depends on perfect knowledge of marginal costs and marginal revenues – for most firms this knowledge is unobtainable and thus maximising is a myth.

Perhaps the most fundamental question is this: 'Can organisations actually have goals?' Surely only people can have goals? The concepts of goal conflict and of negotiation between competing groups and individuals then become important. Chapter 11, which deals with questions of governance, returns to this difficult question.

Perhaps it is more helpful (if also more complex!) to see organisational goals as multiple, changing, ambiguous and negotiated. But how does this leave our unambiguous financial analysis that appears to rest upon the simple wealth-maximising goal? Perhaps we can reconcile the two views by recognising that financial criteria are important for the majority of business decisions, but that many other factors play a part in the decision-making process. Factors influencing the final decision include the political aims of managers, personality types of the managers, previous experiences with similar decisions and differing levels of power between groups or individuals. The financial analysis will provide a particular view of the decision. Whether that view prevails will depend on how those other factors outlined above coincide or are in conflict with the numbers.

Long-term decisions and product costs

In Chapters 2 and 3 we considered the ways in which products and services were costed and priced, and placed particular emphasis on the variable costs of the products and on the contribution (the difference between selling price of the product or service and the variable costs). Fixed overheads, in the short term, are assumed to be difficult to change, and are therefore left out of the product cost equation.

When we take a long-term perspective, however, all costs need to be factored in, for companies need to cover all costs eventually in order to survive and grow. We can illustrate the point by looking at a low-cost airline (similar to EasyJet or bmibaby, although we do not suggest that these figures are the actual numbers relating to those companies).

ILLUSTRATION 10.6

Short-run and long-run costs of an airline operation

FlyCheap incurs variable costs of £5 for each passenger that flies on its aircraft, while the fixed costs for one day of running an aircraft is £18 000. Clearly, in the short run, FlyCheap can charge any price above £5 and gain a contribution. At certain times of the month prices are therefore set at very low levels, between £10 and £20. However, in the long run FlyCheap must cover all of its costs. Let's assume that, in one day, the aircraft makes four journeys, has 200 seats and expects to fill 90 per cent of all seats. The total number of passenger flights are therefore:

$$(4 \times 200 \times 90\%) = 720$$

and the prices that are charged on average must cover all of the costs (i.e. £5 variable and £18 000 fixed). In the long term, therefore, FlyCheap should set average prices above the level of:

Variable costs per passenger flight		£5
Fixed costs per passenger flight	$\frac{(£18\,000}{720)}$	£25
Total costs to recover		£30

Let's assume that the expected profit margin set by the managers is 20 per cent on cost. The average long-term price would then be £36. However, if the airline expects to sell some tickets at rock bottom prices (for promotion purposes and to fill empty seats) then the 'normal' price will also have to take account of the low price tickets.

TASK 10.5 **FlyCheap**

Assuming that FlyCheap sell 20 per cent of all tickets at £10, what should be the price of other tickets?

The low-cost airline example shows quite clearly how there can be two quite different views of product cost: short-term (the cost of one extra passenger is only £5) and long-term (the long-term cost of operating the airline is £21 600 (i.e. £18 000 + (720 × £5)) for each plane per day) and all of these costs must be covered. The management accountant therefore needs to produce both types of information depending on the questions being asked by managers.

Long-term costs also become important if the company is reviewing its overall portfolio of products and services, as shown in this next illustration.

ILLUSTRATION 10.7

Profitable courses?

The Business Faculty of the University of Middle England (UME) offers three types of courses – undergraduate, postgraduate, and in-company courses. Managers of the Business Faculty are reviewing their long-term strategy, and are concerned that the revenues from in-company courses are not covering their long-run costs and should be closed. An initial analysis of revenues and costs is shown in Exhibit 10.6.

On the face of it, the in-company courses are certainly losing money for the faculty, and closure may improve profitability by £130k. The analysis neatly demonstrates the contrast between:

- the short-run view where there is a positive contribution towards fixed costs of £170k, and
- the longer view, taking account of all costs, that shows a loss of £130k.

The faculty managers therefore ask for a more detailed analysis of the general fixed costs that have been allocated to the in-company courses. This deeper analysis reveals that, should the in-company courses be closed, and assuming that no other courses came along to replace them, then the general faculty fixed costs would fall from £2200k to £2010k through staff savings and other cost reductions. Thus closure would save £190k of costs but would, of course, reduce

Exhibit 10.6		Total	Under-graduate	Post-graduate	In-company
UME – financial analysis	Number of students	1 000	500	300	200
	Revenue per student		£5 000	£8 000	£2 000
		£000	£000	£000	£000
	Total revenues	*5 300*	*2 500*	*2 400*	*400*
	Variable costs (e.g. teaching materials) that vary according to the number of students	450	200	220	30
	Separable fixed costs (e.g. staff teaching on the courses and administrators who only work on a particular type of course)	2 400	1 000	1 200	200
	Contribution after deducting variable and separable costs	*2 450*	*1 300*	*980*	*170*
	General Business Faculty fixed costs (e.g. property costs, computing facilities, library, general management and administration)	2 200	1100	800	300
	Profit (loss)	*250*	*200*	*180*	*(130)*

contribution by £170k. Overall profit would therefore be improved by £20k; not a huge amount but still 8 per cent of the present profit of £250k.

Of course the decision to withdraw from in-company courses is more than merely a financial one. The long-term strategy of UME Business School is also at stake. This final task draws out some of the strategic and financial questions that would be raised by such a move.

TASK 10.6   Strategy and profit analysis

At the University of Middle England a faculty strategy meeting has been called within the Business Faculty. There is only one item on the agenda – should the Business School withdraw from the in-company course market? The numbers from Illustration 10.7 are tabled along with the following predictions for the next five-year period:

- The in-company market is expected to expand nationally.

- Two other universities within the geographical area covered by UME are expected to be providing in-company courses. Trentside University has been a competitor in this field for many years, but Merewold University is expected to be a new entrant to the market.

- The amount of funding per student for undergraduates is expected to fall.

- The postgraduate market is expected to be fairly static, though UME has plans (not yet fully developed) to market all postgraduate courses more aggressively to international markets.

1. Given this information, and making whatever assumptions appear to be reasonable, what would be your advice to the faculty?

2. What other information would be helpful for informing the decision?

3. How significant do you believe the accounting numbers would be in reaching the decision?

Taken together FlyCheap and UME demonstrate that views of product costs and profitability are influenced by the time frame of the decisions. If the decision is short term and takes place within a given strategic portfolio of products or services, the short-term contribution may be a useful guide.

However, once we begin to question the strategic balance of the services or products that are provided, then all costs must be factored in and a long-term view taken. Although fixed costs are assumed to be difficult to change in the short term, when a long-term view is taken, then all costs should be considered; for in the long-term, all costs (not just variable ones) can be managed and changed.

SUMMARY

In this chapter we have focused upon long-term aspects of financial analysis. The following concepts and techniques have been covered:

- Connections between short- and long-term decisions.
- Key features and stages for long-term decisions.
- Financial analysis for long-term decisions, including the time value of money.
- Payback, net present value and internal rate of return.
- The cost of capital.
- Uncertainty in long-term decision analysis.
- Goals and decision-making.
- Long-term views of product costs.

Please turn to the back of the book for detailed answers to questions marked with a ❓ . Answers to the other questions can be found on the companion website at www.thomsonlearning.co.uk/accountingandfinance/hand

REVIEW QUESTIONS

❓ **RQ 10.1**   Financial implications are an important factor for any long-term decision. Can you name others?

❓ **RQ 10.2**   Contrast the NPV and payback approaches to the financial analysis of decisions.

RQ 10.3   Think about an actual long-term decision for any organisation. How significant do you think would be the financial aspects of the decision compared with strategic and behavioural issues?

RQ 10.4   Consider a house-building company – what would be some of the differences between the short-term and long-term views of product costs?

NUMERICAL PROBLEMS

❓ **NP 10.1 JRC Cars**   The investment committee of JRC Cars, a manufacturer of luxury cars, is considering the investment programme for the coming year. Before the committee are two very different projects. You are the management accountant for the committee, and have been asked to provide information to assist the committee in reviewing the two projects.

The first project is a modification programme to an existing car – the XR9. In this highly competitive luxury market manufacturers are expected to maintain a competitive position by updating models on a regular basis, but this is an expensive investment. The net cash inflows over a five-year period (shown below) represent extra contributions from the sales which JRC would hope to achieve if the modifications are made.

The second project is an investment in labour-saving robotic equipment. JRC has undertaken similar projects in the past and is fairly certain about the savings which can be achieved (see below).

The relevant cash inflows and outflows (shown in brackets) for each project are estimated as follows (all figures are in £000):

Year	XR9	Robotics	
0	(200)	(70)	(*Note*: Year 0 means at the present time)
1	50	++	
2	90	++	
3	90	++	
4	60		
5	60		

++: The robotics project has a life of three years and the relevant cash savings relate to labour and materials costs. Labour is paid at £10 per hour and the firm works a 50-week year. The project will save a total of 80 hours per week for Year One and 100 hours per week for Years Two and Three. For materials, there will be a saving because of less scrap material. This will amount to £200 per week in each of the three years. JRC's cost of capital is 20 per cent. From this information, you are required to do the following:

1. Undertake an appropriate financial analysis based on the above information (including relevant cash flows, payback periods and NPVs).
2. Calculate the effect on the NPV of the XR9 project if cash inflows cease in Year Three.
3. Comment on your financial analysis.

NP 10.2 Ripton Building Society You are a freelance financial journalist writing for specialist magazines particularly in the IT and finance fields. Your eye is caught by a piece in your local newspaper:

RIPTON BUILDING SOCIETY AT THE LEADING EDGE

Ripton Building Society (RBS) rejected the idea of floating as a company in the 1990s and since then has fiercely protected its independence. After many years as a staid and (some would say) boring building society, Ripton's dynamic, chief executive Helen Van Slyke (who had previously turned round the ailing retailer Zips) now wants to take the next step, taking RBS into the twenty-first century by adopting 'leading edge IT technology' at the Ripton head office and all 30 of the branches throughout the region.

You sense a specialist story and arrange an interview with Helen Van Slyke. The chief executive (HVS) is quite open with you at the interview – indeed she sees the interview as a 'free' opportunity for some positive PR for her proposals. Your interview notes show the following additional information.

The Ripton Building Society is a medium-sized, northern building society with a large base of regular savers and mortgage borrowers. Following the general opening up of financial services in recent years, RBS is now offering more financial products to customers, the most significant of which is insurance. The IT policy of RBS has been on a 'catch-up' basis up to now. Once systems are tried and proven elsewhere, RBS has adopted them, normally two or three years after the industry leaders. This tends to provide 'safe' systems but leaves RBS with a competitive disadvantage regarding information flows and new market opportunities. RBS currently spends around £1m each year on upgrading and maintaining computing facilities. If there is no change to policies this figure is expected to rise at a rate of 20 per cent cumulative into the foreseeable future to keep up with competition.

The proposed approach (which HVS refers to as 'leading edge') would provide a link-up with a renowned UK computer firm, UKIT, who will offer special prices on hardware and software plus free staff development and training if RBS will use new software and hardware at an early stage of development. Despite the favourable terms offered by UKIT, overall IT costs will rise due to the extra investment. Annual IT costs are expected to total £3m in Years One and Two (i.e. an *extra* £2m per year); and £2.5 for Years Three, Four and Five (a five-year horizon is regarded as acceptable by HVS given the pace of change in the industry).

Cost savings which are expected to come from the investment relate to tracking of mortgage payments and flagging up of problems with payments, fewer bad debts and lower interest costs and fewer fraudulent mortgage applications. The value of these benefits over the five-year period are expected to range as follows (all figures are in £m):

Year	Best	Worst
1	0.5	0.4
2	1.5	1.0
3	2.5	1.8
4	3.0	2.0
5	3.0	2.0

The cost of capital for RBS during this time is expected to be around 15 per cent.

Other benefits (although very significant) are difficult to evaluate and are thought to include an improved database for communications with savers and borrowers, more accurate and effective mailshots, an improved customer image and, ultimately, extra customers in the long term.

Your brief is to write an article for *IT in Business* (a business-related computing journal) explaining and evaluating the important issues surrounding Ripton's investment plans. Your piece should be supported by estimated financial analysis, as your readers are familiar with NPV and payback.

NP 10.3 Exotic Holidays Exotic Holidays plc is a fast-expanding holiday firm specialising in unusual holidays. Its success has stretched its booking system to its limits, so the company is considering the expansion of its computing facilities. Two options have been presented, one by the computing services department, the other by the booking department itself. Both projects are expected to have a life of five years, given the rapid rate of development in computing systems.

Computing services This option involves upgrading the existing mainframe facilities at a cost of £2m. The system in use at present has been very reliable and the department is skilled in its maintenance. The department's estimates are that additional cash maintenance costs with the new system will be a constant £5000 per annum over the next five years. They would, however, need to employ an extra systems analyst at a cost of £18 000 per annum. Anticipated salary increases in the sector are in the order of £1000 per annum. Additional annual running costs (disks and other consumables) are estimated at a constant £2000.

Booking department Whilst computing services might be happy with the technical performance of the existing system, the booking department finds it slow and unfriendly. They propose an entirely new system based on networked PCs. This would offer exactly the same benefits (detailed below) as the mainframe option but, at an initial cost of £1.5m, would be considerably less expensive. However, a specialised maintenance contract would have to be taken out, with charges set at £25 000 a year for the first two years and £30 000 a year in following years. (This is instead of the £5000 each year under the computing services' alternative.) Running costs would be as for the mainframe project, as would analyst costs; but specialised network support would be required. Initial talks with a network support firm have indicated that a five-year contract would start at a base price of £45 000 rising by £5000 each year.

Common savings and benefits Significant staff savings are anticipated from the enhanced system. After the first year of operation six clerical staff posts will be saved, rising to seven in Year Two and nine in Year Four. Clerical staff are paid £12 000 per annum at present: this is anticipated to rise to £13 000 in Year Three and £14 000 in Year Five. The remaining staff will be able to deal with orders much more efficiently, handling an extra 1000 holidays in the first year, rising in each of the following years by 500 a year. Anticipated prices per holiday for the next five years are £200, £210, £220, £230 and £240. In addition, considerable efficiency savings are expected following the results of a quality audit which foresees annual savings as follows: Year One, £5000; Year Two, £10 000; Year Three, £15 000; Year Four, £20 000; Year Five, £20 000.

The company's cost of capital is 8 per cent.

The two proposals are to be submitted to the company's capital authorisation committee for approval, but first they must be financially assessed by the management accountant. Provide a financial evaluation of these proposals, including any inadequacies you feel are present in the data, or any further data you might require.

The case is set in the later part of the twentieth century in the period after the collapse of Communist control in Eastern Europe.

The following article has recently appeared in both UK and Polish newspapers:

Polish tourist markets set to expand

NOW THAT Eastern European markets are opening up, and that the recession in the Western economies appears to be receding, things look set fair for companies who are well placed to exploit the expected upturn in both business and private trade. Poland, in particular, looks a good bet for investment. The cheaper zloty should mean more tourists, particularly from the USA and the UK. Short breaks and longer holidays are set to take off again as people take the chance to make up for the last few years of gloom and despondency. Prospects look good for the Polish hotel trade – particularly those who can target well-off tourists and business class customers.

A Polish government minister said that 'business comes first, politics comes second' when discussing new developments for investing in Polish industry. The government is advancing the privatisation policy as fast as possible. Overseas companies are being offered incentives and cheap finance to invest in particular sectors of the economy (including tourism). Meanwhile the new Polish Finance Corporation (PFC) has been established as an independent company, owned by the banks, to 'pump-prime' new investment opportunities. Interest rates are (by Western standards) very high in Poland – but PFC offers finance to new ventures at a rate of 15 per cent – well below existing rates.

An exciting example of new investment is Milestone plc's venture into the Polish hotel trade. Milestone, the UK company controlled by James Silversmith (whose recent acquisitions include the UK Castle Hotels group), is considering expanding its hotel operations by buying into Poland's Zorbis chain. Since the announcement that 12 of the Zorbis hotels, located in tourist and business centres such as Poznan and Warsaw, were to be privatised by the Polish government, Milestone has been hotly tipped to be the successful bidder. The deal will include a three-part consortium of Milestone (providing 70 per cent of the finance), the Polish government (15 per cent) and the Central Polish Bank (15 per cent). Part of the deal will ensure that the Central Polish Bank will gain access to some hard currencies, and be able to offer and develop financial services such as credit cards and insurance. Milestone/Zorbis may face competition in the near future as the US Hilton chain moves in to form partnerships with other hotels, and time will tell whether this kind of venture will succeed – but Silversmith's camp appears to be optimistic. Milestone's share price has certainly not been harmed by the persistent rumours of the Zorbis acquisition.

Milestone

The history of Milestone plc is largely the history of James Silversmith. Silversmith is an entrepreneur who saw the opportunity some 15 years ago for buying out ailing companies (particularly in the hotel, leisure and property sectors), selling off unprofitable parts and turning round the performance of the remainder. Milestone plc is now a large, well-established company with a market capitalisation of £2.5bn – although the Silversmith family retains a controlling interest. Investments by Milestone, in the recent past, have largely consisted of buying out other companies, plus a smaller amount of reinvestment costs in the new operations. Milestone is organised and managed through three divisions: hotels, leisure and property.

Silversmith's reputation as a 'short-term moneymaker' has been tempered recently. His new strategies appear to take a longer-term view of investments. Clearly the Polish venture is in this category – the economic environment in Eastern Europe is highly uncertain and significant returns cannot be expected for several years. The Zorbis acquisition will differ from others in two resepcts. First, Milestone, while having a controlling interest, will share ownership with the Polish government and banks and, second, this is Milestone's first venture into Eastern Europe.

Major new investments within the Milestone Group have to be approved by the New Investment Committee; and the most influential people on this committee are James Silversmith and his accountant, Matthew King.

James Silversmith

Silversmith is a natural entrepreneur who has a proven track record for spotting opportunities for company development. His preferred approach is to buy into a business at a low price, sell off parts of the business which do not fit Milestone's business strategy and improve efficiency and cut costs in the remainder of the business. His philosophy for business was neatly caught in a radio interview of some years ago: when asked how he balanced the short-term and long-term aims of the business, he replied: 'well, as I see it, in the long run we are all dead!' However, since reading the ideas of the new management guru Ral Ipofski, he has been taking a much longer-term view of his investments. Silversmith aims to plan and control the performance of his divisions through a series of quantitative measures, the most important of which are:

1. for historic performance – return on assets and profit to sales
2. for future investments – NPV, IRR and payback.

Matthew King

King comes from a long line of traditional, cautious accountants. Strong on analysis but short on imagination, Matthew has worked for Milestone for three years after experience in a merchant bank. He has introduced NPV and IRR calculations into Milestone's investment procedures to supplement the payback measure that has been used traditionally. All acquisitions and investments now go through a rigorous NPV, IRR and payback analysis. King also likes to stress the effect of investments upon the earnings per share (EPS) of the group, as he believes it is important to maintain a strong share price for Milestone for future acquisitions that are often financed by the issue of Milestone shares.

Zorbis Hotels

The Zorbis chain consists of 50 hotels scattered around Poland, mainly in large centres of population and tourist areas. The hotels are of a good standard (although not exceptional by international standards). They have been used by business people and government and political officials in recent times and have not seen significant changes for many years. Policy (such as it is) has been determined in Warsaw by an over-manager (a government appointment). Operational decisions are taken by the local manager in each hotel. Twelve of the Zorbis hotels may be sold to the Milestone consortium – the remainder may be developed by different partnerships, bought out by the local managers or closed if not viable.

> 1. As a member of Milestone's Investment Committee, how would you go about evaluating the proposed investment in Zorbis? What would be the key variables which would need to be predicted? What techniques of financial analysis may be helpful and feasible? To what extent would quantitative, strategic, and financial criteria be important? How might you go about establishing a maximum acceptable price for the acquisition? For this part, specific numbers are not required (nor possible!) – restrict yourself to general issues and principles.

It is now six months later, and Milestone's takeover of Zorbis has gone through. Milestone is now considering further inward investment in the Zorbis group, to take advantage of the expected upturn in the Polish economy.

Two investment proposals are being considered. Milestone's overall cash forecasts suggest that none, one or both of the investments can be accepted in the present budget year – depending on how their predicted appraisals turn out.

Investment proposal – refurbishments

It is proposed that the 12 hotels be refurbished to take them into a higher classification and therefore to attract higher prices and more affluent customers, particularly prestigious business conferences and the overseas tourist trade. Projections for the refurbishment are:

- total immediate investment outlays = £5m (i.e. in Year Zero)
- time horizon for the investment = four years (i.e. until the next refurbishment would be needed)
- Milestone's cost of capital for UK investments = 15 per cent.

Milestone expects relevant cash flows from this investment to be:

Year	Extra running costs	Extra revenues
1	0.1	1.0
2	0.2	2.5
3	0.3	3.0
4	0.4	2.0

(£m)

The pro-business governments of recent years plus tax breaks for foreign investments means that tax charges will be minimal and can be ignored.

> 2. For the refurbishments investment calculate: payback, NPV – and an approximate IRR. Discuss the proposal in terms of: risk, return and strategic fit.

Investment proposal – information technology

A second proposal is to install more sophisticated computing facilities within the Zorbis hotels, to match those in other Milestone outlets. In the centrally controlled Zorbis chain (including the 12 hotels taken over by Milestone) there existed a very old system which offered payroll, invoicing, financial accounting and monthly budget reports, but not customer billing, which is done at the hotels on very old PCs.

Current proposals are to enhance the existing system by installing networked PCs in each of the 12 hotels alongside a new custom-built reservations and customer billing system. Each of these machines will be linked to the head office machine by use of the links now available thanks to the digitalisation of the local telephone network. This will not only allow inter-hotel reservations but also create a central client database that will be used for targeted mailshots. This solution will involve the following initial costs for *each* of the 12 hotels:

New PC	£2 000
Printer	£500
Network adaptors	£200
Network connection	£1 000

There will also be annual running costs per terminal of £3000.

The new software will cost £100 000 in total to write. A feasibility study has already been undertaken at a cost of £25 000. As with other investments, the pro-business governments of recent years, plus tax breaks for foreign investments, means that tax charges will be minimal and can be ignored.

The expected benefits of the computing investment fall into three categories, all of which are thought to apply to the same time scale of the refurbishment investment:

- The ability to use the central client list to generate new business. Zorbis estimates that this will generate an additional £40 000 annually of contribution in total.
- Improved customer service, thanks to swifter reservation, reception and invoicing. In addition, the use of a state-of-the-art system is expected to enhance the company's image in the eyes of its new target market. While important, this benefit is seen as intangible and difficult to quantify.
- The freeing up of the existing old PCs will allow them to be used by hotel managers for financial planning and labour scheduling. The limited use by one manager of a spreadsheet for the latter has already indicated a potential gain of £4000 a year per hotel through better matching of resources to demand.

3. For the IT investment proposal (without including any intangible benefits) calculate: all relevant cash flows, NPV, payback and (approximate) IRR.

   Discuss, in general terms (i.e. without calculations), the uncertainties surrounding the IT investment, and also ways in which the value of intangible benefits could be calculated

4. Consider any interrelationships between the IT and refurbishment proposals.

   Discuss any other strategic, behavioural, process or cultural issues which you believe are raised by the case.

WEB RESOURCES www

www.thomsonlearning.co.uk/accountingandfinance/hand

The companion website has free additional resources for you to use alongside this book. If you are a student you can access material to help with revision, including practice questions with answers to test how much of the material you have understood. There are also useful hyperlinks to companies and information sources mentioned in the book as well as interactive quizzes. There are additional resources for lecturers using this book on their courses; the details can be found in the preface at the front of this book.

Corporate governance: the UK experience

After studying this chapter you should be able to:

- why corporate governance is an important part of the regulatory framework within which business operates
- the factors which brought about the need for corporate governance systems
- which are the key reports in the development of the UK's system of corporate governance.

Introduction

We have hinted throughout this book that accounting is not a precise science. Accounting statements are produced utilising UK accounting standards which are a vital element of the self-regulatory framework created and organised by the accountancy profession. In spite of this users have expressed dissatisfaction with the quality of the information contained therein. Users are particularly sceptical when companies have been reporting steady and increasing profits and then an unexpected 'black hole' emerges in the accounts and suddenly the fortunes of the company have changed overnight. In 2003 the travel company 'MY Travel', after issuing profit warnings, suddenly announced it had various accounting problems which would wipe £30 million from forecast profits and that it was going to need to make further significant increases to its levels of borrowing. The shares in MY Travel fell from 75p to 13p in one day: six months earlier the shares had been worth £1.50, and two years earlier, over £3.

A further difficulty is the relationship between the owners of the business (shareholders) and the managers of the business (directors). The problem appears to be that the managers are not always working to the full benefit of the owners. This is not a new phenomenon and was first noted by Adam Smith in the eighteenth century when he wrote in his seminal work *The Wealth of Nations*:

> *managers who are watching over other peoples money cannot be expected to use the same anxious vigilance if it were their own. Negligence and profusion, therefore, must always prevail.*

The directors are in a unique position in that they are able to set their own terms of employment and conditions, particularly with regard to remuneration.

Background to the emergence of corporate governance

A number of financial scandals have hit the press over the last few years. Take the case of Greg Hutchings, chief executive of Tompkins plc. Greg Hutchings was an aggressive dealmaker and successful businessman who had helped to build the fortunes of the company. However, it emerged that in the process he had awarded himself excessive perks. It has been claimed that both his wife and gardener were on the company payroll, and that he had three London flats for private use, had authorised corporate donations to a political fund to help make Lord Archer mayor of London and, most controversially of all, had used company jets for private holidays. It was rumoured that one trip was to take a hockey team with which he was connected to a competition in the south of France. At the time, October 2000, his salary was £1.5m, which included an annual bonus of £456,000. He also had share options for more than 5m shares. This meant he would be able to buy shares at some future date at a price less than the market value, sell them on at market value and make an instant profit.

This would appear to be a classic case of a chief executive who has misused company assets for his own use. He had in effect treated the business as if he were the sole owner. Cases like this are not uncommon but are generally of a lesser scale. Ultimately, it is the shareholders who own the business, but the executive directors are in such powerful positions that it is difficult for an individual shareholder to monitor the directors' actions and to call them to account.

Director remuneration

One of the ways in which this inability to make the directors more accountable manifests itself is in the area of remuneration. The directors are in a unique position in that they are able to set their own terms of employment and conditions, particularly with regard to remuneration. How much an executive should be paid is a vexed question. As a general rule of thumb, company executives used to be paid in the region of 20 to 30 times the salary of an average worker. By the 1970s this figure had risen to 39 times and, by the end of the 1990s, to 1000 times. How has this happened? Particularly during the 1980s and 1990s we have had periods of stock market booms. During such times it is difficult to distinguish how much of a company's share price increase is due to the efforts of the directors and how much to general movements within the market. Directors have aligned their remuneration to performance measures which are not always clear but usually have a stock market component. When the market was booming shareholders were reaping benefits (as well as the directors) and no one seemed to mind. The problem emerged during 2000–2003 when share prices collapsed, workers' increases in earnings were in the order of between 3 per cent and 5 per cent, yet directors' pay continued to soar. According to all the latest surveys in the financial year (2002/03) directors received an average 24 per cent pay rise. One of the aims of corporate governance is to make the directors of the company more accountable to the owners (shareholders) of the business; another is to make the directors' actions more transparent to owners and stakeholders in the business.

Definition of corporate governance

What is **corporate governance**? A number of definitions have been produced. One by the Overseas Economic Council for Development (OECD) states:

> *Corporate governance involves a set of relationships between a company's management, its board, its shareholders and other stakeholders. Corporate governance also provides the structure through which the objectives of the company are set, and the means of attaining those objectives and monitoring performance are determined. Good corporate governance should provide proper incentives for the board and management to pursue objectives that are in the interests of the company and shareholders and should facilitate effective monitoring, thereby encouraging firms to use resources more efficiently.*[1]

By 'stakeholders' is meant those people who are affected in some way by the activities of the company; this includes employees, customers, lenders and members of the local community.

Two further definitions are: 'If management is about running a company then governance is about running it properly' or 'The exercise of power over the *direction of the enterprise . . .* concerns the supervision of executive actions, the duty to be accountable'.[2] This second definition points out that the internal procedures within a company, the internal systems of checks and balances, are an important element to ensure that the directors are held accountable for their actions. Perhaps the underlying reason why corporate governance is becoming important is summed up by Maw:

> *What we are afraid of is this powerful machine, which grinds out so successfully the goods we want, seems to be running without any discernible controls. A young lad learning to ride his bike may shout 'look ma no hands' but is this the way we want to see corporations run?*[3]

To sum up: corporate governance is about controlling the direction of the activities of businesses; making them more accountable to a broader constituency than shareholders. This is where the notion of stakeholders has emerged, to ensure that no one person has too much power within a company and to ensure that the directors are rewarding themselves fairly and not at the expense of the shareholders who are the real owners of the business.

The development of UK corporate governance

Why has corporate governance become a subject of growing interest in the last few years? The very first report looking into corporate governance practice was produced in the UK in 1992 under the chairmanship of Sir Adrian Cadbury[4]. The terms of reference for his committee were:

- defining the responsibility of **executives** and **non-executive directors** for reviewing and reporting on performance to shareholders

1. http://www.oecd.org/dateoecd/19/29/23888981.pdf, accessed 21/04/2004.
2. Trickier, R. L. (2000) (ed.) *Corporate Governance*. Aldershot: Ashgate.
3. Maw, G.L., Lord Lane of Horsell and Craig-Cooper, M. (1994) *Maw on Corporate Governance*. Edited by A. Alsbury. Aldershot: Dartmouth.
4. The Cadbury Report (1992) http://www.ecgi.org/codes/country_documents/uk/cadbury.pdf

- making the case for audit committees
- defining the principal responsibility of auditors
- forming links between shareholders, boards and auditors.

The Cadbury Committee was created because the sponsors (the London Stock Exchange and the professional accounting bodies) were concerned at the perceived low level of confidence in financial reporting and in the ability of auditors to provide adequate safeguards which the users of company reports sought and expected. There had been a series of financial scandals prior to the formation of the committee which brought to light the variety of accounting practices that were being adopted in order to produce accounting statements which placed companies in a favourable light. The term window dressing emerged to explain these particular practices. Of more concern was the fact that the auditors did not appear able to identify when these practices were being used and so confidence in the published accounts began to fall.

The Cadbury Report

The essential features of the report were as follows; these became known as the Cadbury Code:

- There should be in place a system of checks and balances with a view to increasing openness and transparency, and this was to be achieved by adopting the rule that companies were to declare the reasons why any of the following recommendations had not been adopted.
- There should be a division of responsibility between chairperson and chief executive.
- The board should include non-executive directors (NEDs) of sufficient calibre and number to influence decisions taken.
- NEDs should be independent, selected via a formal procedure and appointed for a specified term. Reappointment should not be automatic and fees should reflect time and commitment.
- Full disclosure should be made of directors' total remuneration including stock options and performance-related elements.
- An audit committee should be established, containing at least three NEDs.
- A remuneration committee should be established, composed mainly of NEDs.
- Directors should report on the system of internal control and whether the business is a going concern.
- Companies should disclose that they have complied with the requirements of the code.

Cadbury was clearly concerned that directors should not feel constrained by the requirements of the new code as he inserted into the report the following statement: 'Boards must have the freedom to drive their companies forward – but within a framework of accountability.'

Using published accounts

Obtain the published accounts of any FTSE 100 company (or access the accounts via the company's website) and find the section headed 'corporate governance'. Check to see how many of the features identified by Cadbury have been mentioned within this section of the report. We will refer back to this section of the report in later tasks.

Note: **No answers have been provided to any of the tasks in this chapter as each set of accounts will vary.**

We will now take some of the recommendations and look at the thinking behind them.

The division of responsibility at the head of the company

Essentially, division of responsibility at the head of the company means that there should be a clear distinction between the roles of chairperson and chief executive. Too many examples have emerged of one person at the head of a company treating the company as if it were their own fiefdom. The late Robert Maxwell of Mirror Group Newspapers was probably the best example of this. He used pension fund assets to support the share price of the company MGN.

When power is concentrated in one person it causes problems. Whilst the person is still at the top they can surround themselves with directors who are 'their' people. This ensures that any decisions they want made can be forced through without full discussion and consultation. Such power and influence can extend to business strategy, levels of remuneration and the level and types of perks. The Stock Market now reacts badly by lowering the share price of a company in response to any announcement which suggests that one person will remain as both chairperson and chief executive.

The role of non-executive directors

A clear thrust throughout the development of corporate governance systems worldwide has been a recognition of the unique position occupied by the NEDs. They have access and an insight into the workings of the company at a level which is just not available to others. A NED is a person who sits on the board but does not have a full-time executive role within the company. Essentially a NED is an independent person, appointed to the board of directors, on a part-time basis, to fulfil two particular roles.

The NEDs will bring with them a level of expertise or specialism which the board thinks will enhance the workings of the board and the company. For this reason they are often directors from other companies. Their specialism will be used to guide the strategic direction of the company. It is hoped that the NEDs will ensure that the directors do not adopt strategies which are blatantly foolish and doomed to obvious failure. The NEDs are also used to monitor the activities of the executive board. This is done via their work within the remuneration and audit committees.

There has been much comment about the increased responsibility which has been placed upon the NEDs. Now, when things do go wrong within companies, the shareholders and the financial media look to the NEDs and question why they have allowed such things to happen; for example, at Marconi (when the share price collapsed following a change in strategy), at Marks and Spencer (when they were having trouble replacing Sir Richard Greenbury) and at Enron (when the financial machinations came to light). In this latter case one of the NEDs was a UK government minister, Lord Wakeham. Some are concerned that this increased spotlight will mean that worthwhile candidates may be reluctant to come forward to serve as NEDs. The Higgs Report (2003)[5] recommended that NEDs were to be appointed via a nominations committee which would measure the balance of skills the board already had with that of the new NED to ensure they would be complementary. These recommendations were designed to combat the accusation that NEDs were being drawn from too narrow a circle; in other words, the tendency for executive directors from different companies to serve as NEDs on one another's boards. This could have an impact when they are serving on each other's remuneration committees, with salary levels being ratcheted up.

TASK 11.2

Non-executive directors

In the 'corporate governance' section of the published accounts of any plc there will be a section which discloses the names, qualifications and background of the directors. Look at the background of the NEDs and try to understand why they were chosen. Is it because they have particular expertise? Are they an ex-member of the government? Do they serve on any other boards and, if so, are there any connections between the two companies? For this last element of the task you will also have to look at the accounts of the company from which the NEDs come.

The issue of director remuneration and the use of remuneration committees

The 'problem' of director remuneration is often referred to in the popular press as the 'fat cat syndrome'. What seems particularly to irk shareholders and the general public alike is the perception that directors are able to set their own levels of pay and ensure that they are well paid irrespective of the performance of the company. Sometimes directors can even be well paid when the company has spectacularly underperformed, either by still receiving their bonuses or, if they do lose their jobs, receiving golden retirement and redundancy payments. The examples of Marconi and Railtrack illustrate the point.

The directors of Marconi embarked upon a plan to turn the former defence company into a communications and internet-based company. The strategy proved disastrous and the shareholders suffered a spectacular fall in shareholder value with the shares falling from £12 a share in September 2000 to £2.50 in June 2001. The result of the fall in share price meant that the **share options**, which were priced at £16, were now worthless. The directors came up with a plan to revalue the options to a much lower price so that they would then have some

---

5. The Higgs Report (2003) http://www.dti.gov.uk/cld/non_exec_review

value. This plan was severely criticised by the shareholders as directors would be rewarded for failure at a time when the shareholders had seen the value of their investment fall.

In 2002, Railtrack senior staff were to receive a loyalty bonus costing in total £6.7 million. This included a Mr Middleton, engineering director, who was expected to receive a £100 000 bonus. This was happening around the same time that senior managers were being charged with gross negligence, manslaughter and an offence under the Health and Safety at Work Act! If found guilty, the individuals were faced with life imprisonment and two other firms also charged could receive an unlimited fine.

A number of solutions have been put forward to combat the problems illuminated by the Marconi and Railtrack cases:

- The length of time of service contracts has been reduced. At the time of the Cadbury Report five years was the normal length of time of a director's contract. This had the effect that if a director was sacked then s/he would receive the equivalent of five years' salary as compensation. Most contracts are now two years and some even just one year.

- Directors' salaries should be set by an independent remuneration committee.

- Executive directors should play no part in decisions on their own remuneration. Boards should appoint remuneration committees consisting wholly or mainly of independent NEDs. The remuneration committee will determine the company's policy on executive remuneration and specific remuneration packages for each of the executive directors, including pension rights and any compensation payments. The members of the committee should be listed each year in the committee's report to shareholders. The remuneration chairperson should attend the company's annual general meeting to answer shareholders' questions about directors' remuneration. A **resolution** is now voted on at the shareholders' annual general meeting to approve the remuneration package being proposed for the directors. Shareholders now have the opportunity to quiz the board about their remuneration schemes and they can vote against its adoption. This happened for the first time in 2003, with Jean Paul Garnier of GSK. The shareholders were so unhappy with a proposal that Mr Garnier should receive a payout of £22 million in the event of him losing his job that they took the unprecedented step of voting against the motion. This was the very first time in UK corporate history that such a thing had happened. In the event the vote turned out to be advisory only and at the time of writing the board of directors were going to review the financial package. In the event of Mr Garnier retiring he would receive the highest annual pension of any UK director of £929 000 per annum.

Some further remuneration examples from 2002

In 2002 the average pay for a FTSE 100 chief executive was £1.6 million (up by 23 per cent), with the highest paid chief executive, that of BHP Billiton, receiving £9.1 million. The 2002 rise of 23 per cent followed increases of 17 per cent in 2001 and 28 per cent in 2000, and this occurred against a backdrop of share prices collapsing by 50 per cent over the same period. In 2003 all eight directors of Tesco earned more than £1 million; but this is not to say that these directors did not earn their salaries, as Tesco is clearly an efficient company. However, if directors' remuneration is supposedly largely based upon incentives related to maximising shareholder wealth, how did remuneration rise at a time when share prices were collapsing? It seems that the levels of reward that directors are capable of generating are far in excess of what many people believe they may be worth.

TASK 11.3

Director remuneration

Look at the section from the published accounts you have obtained for these tasks covering director remuneration. What is the balance between basic salary, bonus and share options? Why do you think it is that so much of their income is performance related?

The way in which rewards are linked to performance

Performance-related elements of remuneration should be designed to align the interests of directors and shareholders and to give directors keen incentives to perform at the highest levels. The Hampel Report[6] agreed with the view that a significant part of executive directors' remuneration should be linked to a company's performance, whether by annual bonuses, share option schemes, or **long-term incentive plans**. The real problem is in aligning the short-term interests of the directors (remember how short their contracts are) with the long-term interests of the shareholders. Shareholders will prefer directors to have lower base salaries and a higher component of performance-related pay to ensure that the directors are 'incentivised' to perform for the shareholders' benefit. Remember the quote above by Adam Smith about the problems of managers not acting quite like owners? The problem seems to be that the elements of 'incentivised' pay are out of control with no one able to moderate the inexorable rise of director remuneration.

Disclosure of director's remuneration

Stock Exchange listing rules implement most of the disclosure provisions in the Greenbury Code[7]. They require companies to include in their annual report:

- a report by the remuneration committee detailing the remuneration policy for executive directors
- details of the remuneration packages of each director by name, such as basic salary, annual bonuses and long-term incentive schemes, including share options
- information on share options, which should be given for each director in accordance with the Accounting Standards Board's Urgent Issues Task Force Abstract 10.

As an example of the way in which directors' remuneration should be reported, Exhibit 11.1 is taken from the accounts of Pearson Publications.

[6.] The Hampel Report (1998) http://www.ecgi.org/codes/country_documents/uk/hampel_index.htm

[7.] The Greenbury Report (1995) http://www.ecgi.org/codes/country_documents/uk/greenbury.pdf

The information in the following exhibit is from Pearson directors' report from the 2002 annual report. The information presented is intended merely as an example of a standard report and any names or figures have no significance.

Exhibit 11.1

Pearson – directors' report, 2002

All figures in £000s	Salaries/ fees	Bonus	Other	2002 Total	2001 Total
Chairman					
Dennis Stevenson	275	—	—	275	275
Executive directors					
Marjorie Scardino	525	273	54	852	583
David Bell	310	161	16	487	325
Rona Fairhead (appointed 1 June 2002)	193	100	8	301	—
Peter Jovanovich (appointed 1 June 2002)	325	240	5	570	—
John Makinson	419	279	157	855	396
Non-executive directors					
Terry Burns	35	—	—	35	35
Patrick Cescau (appointed 1 April 2002)	26	—	—	26	—
Reuben Mark	47	—	—	47	45
Vernon Sankey	40	—	—	40	40
Rana Talwar	35	—	—	35	35
Total	2 230	1 053	240	3 523	1 734
Total 2001†	1 653	—	94	—	1 747

† Includes amounts to former directors.

Note 1: John Makinson was the highest paid director in 2002. His total remuneration, including pension contributions, amounted to £859 607.

Note 2: For the full-year, Rona Fairhead's and Peter Jovanovich's remuneration was as follows:

All figures in £000s	Salaries/ fees	Bonus	Other	Total
Rona Fairhead	318	165	13	496
Peter Jovanovich	557	412	9	978

Note 3: Although the salaries of the executive directors were in certain cases below those of their competitors, the executive directors (along with their fellow senior managers) elected not to receive an increase in their base salaries with effect from 1 January 2002. Rona Fairhead and John Makinson received increases in their base salaries on taking up their appointments as chief financial officer and chairman and chief executive of the Penguin Group respectively with effect from 1 June 2002.

Note 4: For Pearson plc, the 2002 performance measures in the annual bonus were growth in underlying sales, growth in adjusted earnings per share, trading cash conversion and average working capital as a ratio to sales.

In the case of Peter Jovanovich and, for part of the year, John Makinson, part of their bonuses also related to the performance of Pearson Education and Penguin Group respectively. For both businesses, the performance measures were growth in underlying sales, trading margin, trading cash conversion and average working capital as a ratio to sales.

No discretionary bonuses were awarded for 2002.

Note 5: Other emoluments include company care and healthcare benefits and, in the case of Marjorie Scardino, include £36 090 in respect of housing costs.

On taking up his appontment as chairman and chief executive of the Penguin Group with effect from 1 June 2002, John Makinson also became entitled to a location and market premium in relation to the management of the business of the Penguin Group in the US. He received £130 640 for 2002.

Marjorie Scardino, Rona Fairhead, David Bell and John Makinson have the use of a chauffeur.

Note 6: No amounts in compensation for loss of office and no expense allowances chargeable to UK income tax were paid during the year.

The introduction and operation of audit committees

Audit committees are not a new phenomenon, and have been in existence in the USA since 1978. A common feature of both those in the USA and those in the UK is that they are composed solely of NEDs. The consensus of opinion has been that audit committees have proved their worth. So how does an audit committee help within the general framework of governance?

A peculiar feature of the relationship between shareholders, directors and the business is that the auditors are appointed by the directors on behalf of the shareholders, and as such the auditors then report officially to the shareholders. When we have cases of businesses suddenly being declared bankrupt or in serious financial difficulties, or if a major fraud has been uncovered (e.g. Barings Bank), the shareholders expect that the auditors should have been aware of what was going on and in some way see them as having been negligent. Firms of auditors can find themselves being sued for very large amounts of money as shareholders try to recover lost investments. In December 1995 the electronic security group ADT were awarded damages of £65 million plus costs of £40 million against BDO Binder Hamlyn. BDO had audited Britannia Security Group which ADT bought for £105m, but which was later to be found to be worth only £40m.

A further factor is that the fees firms of accountants receive for doing an audit have been falling under competitive pressure. For example, the audit fee for Cadbury-Schweppes (a typical large FTSE plc) for year ending 2002 was £3m, on a net profit of £830m. Interestingly, the fee paid to the auditors for non-audit work (consultancy and so on) was £3.1m. Six years previously, in 1996, the comparable figures were net profit £340m – audit fee £2m – non-audit fee £1m.

A number of issues are at stake here. First, there is a suspicion that firms of auditors are more keen on accessing the fee for non-audit work and are paying insufficient attention to the basic audit and this is why the job is not being done to the degree of rigour that shareholders might expect. Also that the auditors may be too closely involved with the directors, in that the audit contract is at the discretion of the directors and the auditors do not want to lose the work.

With these issues in mind, the Smith Review[8] identified the following as being the role and responsibility of the audit committee:

- monitoring the integrity of the financial statements
- reviewing the company's internal control and risk management systems
- monitoring and reviewing the internal audit function
- approving the terms of engagement of the external auditors
- monitoring and reviewing the external auditors' objectivity, independence and effectiveness
- developing and implementing policy on the engagement of the external auditor to supply non-audit services.

Any concerns that the committee may have on any of the above are to be reported to the board.

The audit committee should comprise at least three NEDs and the chairperson of the company should not be a member. No one other than members can attend meetings of the committee. They will be expected to meet with the external auditors at least once a year and to have access to funds in order to carry out their tasks. Members of the audit committee can expect additional remuneration in compensation for the extra time and responsibility that will be required. At least one member of the committee must be a qualified accountant or have considerable financial and management experience.

TASK 11.4

The audit committee

In the published accounts you have obtained, look through the governance report and see who was on the audit committee. Do their background and experience appear to comply with the requirements of the code?

Have the governance reports and codes made a difference?

Since the Cadbury Report there have been a number of other similar reports which have examined particular governance issues[9]. A key question would be: Have they made any difference to the way in which business is conducted within the UK? Surveys have been conducted to discover to what extent companies are complying with the requirements of the governance codes. The findings are in general agreement that virtually all companies, and particularly Footsie 100 companies, are in compliance. For example, in 2002, only five FTSE 100 and 11 per cent of companies outside the FTSE 350 had a joint chairperson/chief executive, and they all had audit and remuneration committees. However, such surveys miss the point. Companies may have established structures and

---

8. The Smith Review (2003) http://www.frc.org.uk/publications/content/ACReport.pdf
9. In addition to those previously mentioned in this chapter are the Turnbull Report (1999) http://www.icaew.co.uk/viewer/index.cfm?AUB=TB2I_6342, the Combined Code (2000) http://www.ecgi.org/codes/country_documents/uk/combined_code.pdf and the Myners Report (2001) http://www.hon-treasury.gov.uk/Documents/Financial_Services/Securities_and_Invest ments/ fin_sec_mynfinal.cfm

procedures merely to create the appearance of compliance. What really matters is the underlying culture within the organisation. Is governance being taken seriously?

If we return to the example of Greg Hutchings, we find that a general view emerged at the time that actions such as these had been acceptable during the 1980s but were not now acceptable during the 1990s. We may conclude that the difference between the two decades was the existence of governance as a real issue and that directors in particular and society in general were recognising that there needed to be a change and an improvement in the way in which business was conducted. Further tentative evidence might be that the financial scandals in the USA have not been repeated here in the UK. Although the main features of the governance systems in the two countries are broadly similar the UK culture is a little more open, with more voluntary compliance, and based upon self-regulation with more explanation about non-compliance. In short the UK approach to governance may be seen as more principle-based than rule-based (the US approach), and as a result creating a more positive environment in which businesses are run and managed.

FINAL COMMENTS

A major negative in this rosy scene in the UK is the issue of director pay and how to reconcile the interests of directors and shareholders. The government, via the DTI, believes that the answer lies in shareholders making full use of their votes at annual general meetings. This misses the point – what really counts is: 'Do shareholders act as if they are owners?' If they have only bought a few shares, or are making a short-term speculative punt, then they are not going to assume the role of responsible owners. This strikes at the heart of the way in which we have created large modern corporations with the privilege of limited liability. The corporations are so large that no one person or group of persons is going to own a sufficiently large stake to overrule a decision by the directors. All we can hope for is to create a climate in which the directors appreciate that if they go beyond the bounds of reasonableness in any area then they will breach the governance framework and the media will then bring this to everyone's attention. At the moment this is perhaps all we can hope for – yet it is far more than existed previously.

SUMMARY

In this chapter we have tried to show that accounting does not operate in a vacuum and that the published accounts have a real impact upon the lives of all the stakeholders who are bound in various relationships to an enterprise. The following concepts and techniques have been covered:

- The role of governance codes in creating the governance framework within the UK.
- The issue of director remuneration in terms of how difficult it is to reconcile the short-term ambitions of the directors with the long-term investment strategy of investors.
- The role of the audit committee in meeting the expectations of the owner shareholders.

- There are a number of websites you can visit to find useful reading on corporate governance. We have compiled a list of key sites for you on the companion website for this book. There are also hyperlinks to take you directly to any web pages mentioned in this chapter. Please visit the website below and click on the links section: www.thomsonlearning.co.uk/accounting andfinance/hand

Please turn to the back of the book for detailed answers to questions marked with a ❓ . Answers to the other questions can be found on the companion website at www.thomsonlearning.co.uk/accountingandfinance/hand

REVIEW QUESTIONS

❓ **RQ 11.1** Adam Smith was the first to observe that directors of companies are in a very special situation. How does this come about and what can be done to remedy the situation?

❓ **RQ 11.2** What role does a NED perform and why are they seen to be central to good governance systems?

❓ **RQ 11.3** To whom are the external auditors responsible, and how is their work assisted by the existence of an audit committee?

WEB RESOURCES   wwww

www.thomsonlearning.co.uk/accountingandfinance/hand

The companion website has free additional resources for you to use alongside this book. If you are a student you can access material to help with revision, including practice questions with answers to test how much of the material you have understood. There are also useful hyperlinks to companies and information sources mentioned in the book as well as interactive quizzes. There are additional resources for lecturers using this book on their courses; the details can be found in the preface at the front of this book.

Answer notes

Answer notes to numerical problems

NP 1.1 Shepherds – an argument about value

This warm-up exercise as to whose wealth is greater is open-ended and designed to raise some basic issues that the accountant must take into consideration in their daily job. For example, the necessity of a common unit of value (the impossibility of adding apples and pears), and how to account for promises of future value and debts that have not yet been paid but must be taken into account at some point in the future. It shows that because accounting is based on assumptions about value, it is not a precise science and different 'solutions' are possible with different assumptions.

The shepherds – notes on possible solution

Deyonne

400 sheep	400
20 acres	80
1 cabin	12
1 plough (= 2 goats, assume 3 goats = 1 sheep)	$\frac{2}{3}$
2 carts (1 poor acre, say)	3
1 ox	5
	$500\frac{2}{3}$
Less: sheep owned by another	(35)
sheep owed for services	(3)
	$462\frac{2}{3}$

Batonne

360 sheep	360
30 acres	120
10 goats	$3\frac{1}{3}$
1 ox	3
1 cart	2
1 cabin	8
	$496\frac{1}{3}$

Note: different figures may be possible with different assumptions – the solution has been produced using sheep as a unit of currency. It could be possible to create a different answer using goats. One might think that sheep are not a sensible unit of economic exchange. However, in some societies animals are used as a store of wealth and cash is not exactly a stable valuation base. Particular points to bear in mind are:

1. Do we value assets at their historic cost (the value at the time they were purchased) or do we value at current value (the value they are worth in today's prices)?

2. We do not have a rate for a poor acre of land so we have to make a guess as to its value.

3. We do not include the value of the order for the coats. Accountants take a conservative view and will only account for this transaction when the coats have been delivered to the customer.

ANSWER NOTES TO CHAPTER 2

Answer notes to tasks

Task **2.1** A retailer's costs

Fixed costs may include: energy; staff wages; rents; insurances; shop fittings and display racks; managers' wages; rates; telephone and IT costs.
Variable costs would mainly be the cost of the products bought from suppliers (e.g. for a clothing shop, the costs of shirts, tops, trousers taken from suppliers).

Task **2.2** Plate-making costs

1. Daily fixed costs = (£500 + £300 + £200) = £1000.

2. Variable cost of one plate = $\frac{(£250)}{1000}$ = £0.25 (material) + £0.10 (other) = £0.35 per plate.

3. Total cost of a plate at normal output levels = variable cost of £0.35 + fixed cost of $\frac{(£1000)}{1000}$ = £1.35.

4. Total cost of a plate at minimum level = 0.35 + $\frac{(£1000)}{800}$ = £1.60, while at maximum level the cost becomes = 0.35 + $\frac{(£1000)}{1200}$ = £1.183.

This shows how critical is the level of output for calculating the full cost of a product as fixed costs have to be 'spread over' all units produced.

Task **2.3** Margins and mark-ups

1. For the newsagent – cost £1 + mark-up 100 per cent (i.e. £1) gives selling price of £2. Gross margin would therefore be £1 on a selling price of £2 or 50 per cent.

2. Say, for example, that an item of furniture was sold for £100. Then the margin would be 20 per cent of £100 (= £20) which means that the original cost was (100 – 20) £80. The mark-up was therefore £20 on £80 or $(\frac{20}{80} \times 100)\% = 25\%$.

Task 2.4 Pottery break-even

1. Contribution = (£2.50 – £0.35) = £2.15, therefore break-even at $\frac{(£1000)}{£2.15} = 465$ plates.

2. If variable costs rise by 10p, i.e. to 45p, then contribution becomes (£2.50 – £0.45) = £2.05, and break-even = $\frac{£1000}{£2.05} = 488$ plates.

   If fixed costs rise to £1100, break-even = $\frac{(£1100)}{£2.15} = 512$ plates.

   If the selling price falls to £2.20, contribution becomes (£2.20 – £0.35) = £1.85 per plate, and break-even becomes $\frac{(£1000)}{£1.85} = 541$ plates.

3. If all three circumstances in 2. occur together, then selling price = £2.20, variable costs = £0.45, and contribution = £1.75. Fixed costs = £1100, and break-even = $\frac{(£1100)}{£1.75} = 629$ plates.

Task 2.5 Costs of running a car

Fixed costs estimates	£
Road tax	150
Insurance	450
	600

Variable costs estimates:
Petrol (say) £0.10 per mile, therefore at 12 000 miles = £1200
Maintenance (say) £0.05 per mile, therefore at 12 000 miles = £600
Thus variable cost per mile is £0.15, or £1800 per year.

Note: we have ignored the drop in value of the car, which may be called 'depreciation' as we have not yet introduced this idea within the text. This drop in value, while not a cash outlay, could be an important extra cost of running the car.

Using a graph (not to scale) the picture in the diagram below would emerge: The graph shows that the £600 of fixed costs are incurred whatever the mileage, but that the sloped line (representing variable costs of £0.15 per mile) rises as mileage increases, reaching £1800 at 12 000 miles. The total cost at that level of mileage is therefore £600 + £1800 = £2400.

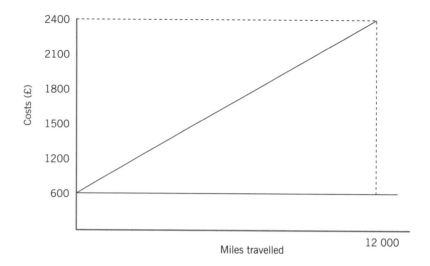

Task 2.6 Margin of safety and relevant range

Margin of safety

If 1000 plates per day are being produced and sold, and (as in Task 2.4 (1.))
break-even is at 465 plates, then the margin of safety is (1000 − 465) = 535.
Expressed as a percentage of actual output this would be

$$\frac{535}{1000} \times 100\% = 53.5\%.$$

At this level of output the pottery is well above break-even and appears to have
a low risk profile.

However, should contribution fall (as it does in task 2.4 (3.)) and break-even
becomes 629 plates, then the pottery has a smaller margin of safety (1000 −
629 = 371, or 37.1%.

Relevant range

The relevant range for the pottery is 800 to 1200 plates per day. This is the
'normally' expected level of daily output. This is quite a wide range and indicates some riskiness. Should sales drop to 800 plates for some period of time
then the firm would become higher risk, particularly if costs were rising at the
same time.

Task 2.7 Pottery selling prices, profits and costs

1. Profit for 10 days if output were 800 plates:
    Contribution = (1.75 − 0.35) = 1.40 × 800 × 10 days   11 200
    Fixed costs   10 000
    Profit   1 200

2. 10-day profit at 1000 plates per day:
    Contribution = (1.75 − 0.35) = 1.40 × 1000 × 10 days   14 000
    Fixed costs   10 000
    Profit   4 000

3. The extra £2800 (4000 − 1200) profit is simply the extra 200 plates per day × 10 days × £1.40 contribution. This demonstrates that, as the firm's output rises above break-even, all extra contribution becomes extra profit because all fixed costs have already been covered.

Answer notes to review questions

RQ 2.2

The correctness of the statement probably depends on the levels of competitiveness in the industry. Taking a sector-wide view the argument is circular: what the customer will pay is determined by general market prices which often reflect typical industry-wide cost levels. Thus there is most definitely a clear relationship (at least across the sector) between cost levels and prices. At the level of an individual company, however, the relationship may break down for a number of reasons. Examples are:

- the need to break into a new market may mean selling close to or below cost
- power in the market may lead to higher pricing by some suppliers
- brand image may allow higher prices
- competitive bidding in the public sector may force prices down to uneconomic levels.

Certainly it is true that an understanding of cost levels can assist managers to make better informed pricing decisions.

RQ 2.3

The strengths of break-even analysis include:

- causing managers to think about the relationships between activity levels and profits
- creating the need to analyse costs in more detail in order to understand how they behave (e.g. is the cost fixed, variable, or some combination?).

The limitations of break-even analysis largely relate to the assumptions within the model, which include:

- that the lines are assumed to be straight – sometimes called the 'linearity assumption'
- that the analysis copes easily with single products, while most firms are dealing with multiple products or services
- that there is only one independent variable (output).

Answer notes to numerical problems

NP 2.1 – Restaurant costs and break-even

Part 1

Basic information needed for this analysis:

Fixed costs per week	£5000
Variable costs per meal	£6
Selling price (average)	£16
Contribution (£16 − £6)	£10 per meal
Normal number of meals per week	600
Highest and lowest numbers	700 – 300
Break-even point	

$$\frac{£5000}{10}$$

500 meals

Relevant range	between 700 to 300 meals
Contribution per meal	£10 per meal

Total contribution and profit at various levels of activity:

Meals per day	300	400	600	700
Contribution	£3000	£4000	£6000	£7000
Profit or (loss) = contribution minus fixed costs	(£2000)	(£1000)	£1000	£2000

Margin of safety

$$600 - 500 = 100 \text{ meals or } \frac{100}{600} \times 100\% = 16.7\%$$

Part 2

Revised basic information for the analysis:

Fixed costs per week	£5400 (increase of £400)
Variable costs per meal	£6 (unchanged)
Selling price (average)	£18 (increase of £2)
Contribution (£18 − £6)	£12 per meal
Normal number of meals per week	550 (a reduction of 50)
Highest and lowest numbers	700 – 300 (unchanged)

Break-even point

$$\frac{£5400}{12}$$

450 meals

Although fixed costs have risen, price rises more than compensate, and the restaurant can break even at a lower level of activity.

Relevant range   between 700 to 300 meals
No change

Contribution per meal   £12 per meal
Increases in line with price rise

Total contribution and profit at various levels of activity:

Meals per day	300	400	600	700
contribution	£3600	£4800	£7200	£8400
Profit or (loss) = contribution minus fixed costs	(£1800)	(£600)	£1800	£3000

Profit levels are better at all levels of output.

Margin of safety

$$600 - 450 = 150 \text{ meals or } \frac{150}{600} \times 100\% = 25\%$$

A significant improvement. The restaurant now operates at a lower break-even point and is less vulnerable to a drop in demand, provided that the new prices do not deter too may customers.

NP 2.3 Kaplan – CVP analysis

	Machine A	Machine B
1. Contribution per unit		
	(10 − 7) = £3	(10 − 4) = £6
Maximum contribution (10000 units)	30 000	60 000
less fixed costs	20 000	50 000
Maximum profit	10 000	10 000
Minimum contribution (7000 units)	21 000	42 000
less fixed costs	20 000	50 000
Minimum profit/(loss)	1 000	(8 000)
2. Break-even points		
(i) Fixed costs for each machine	20 000	50 000
(ii) Contribution per unit	3	6
Dividing (i) by (ii) gives (units)	6 667	8 333

At these levels there will be no loss and no profit as the fixed costs are just covered by all contributions.

3. Break-even charts

Machine A

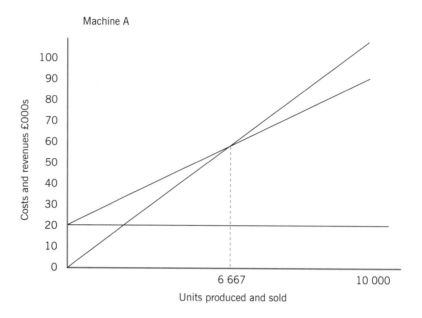

Machine B

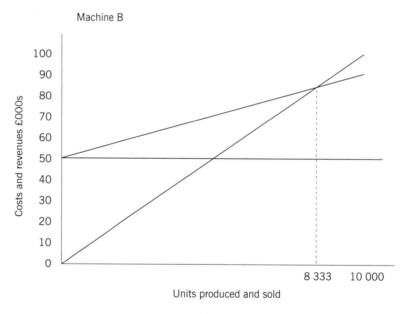

4. Discussion

The question is to some extent about risk. B is more risky in that it requires higher levels of fixed costs and therefore output has to be guaranteed to cover these costs. B breaks even at a higher point than A. However, there may be some hidden advantages in B, such as better quality, or lower rejection rates. We may also consider the longer-term questions about whether we can expect demand to hold up in the long term, and whether it is the fixed costs or the variable costs that are likely to increase beyond current levels.

In general this type of break-even analysis can help in our understanding of cost behaviour, and provides a starting point for the decision. It may help managers to ask questions about cost control, prices, demand levels and so on. However, there are a lot of assumptions in the analysis, for example:

- that costs can be predicted accurately
- that the lines on the graph will be straight (i.e. they are linear and not subject to economies of scale).

It may be, for example, that if production levels were high, then the variable cost may drop as we gain advantage of buying discounts. Also, a constant selling price is assumed.

If used with care, and seen as a good starting point but not as yielding all of the answers, such analysis can help managers to better understand their decisions.

ANSWER NOTES TO CHAPTER 3

Answer notes to tasks

Task 3.1 Personal relevant cash flows

This task, clearly, has no 'model' answer and will be specific to your own circumstances. The task encourages you to consider all relevant costs including any income foregone, which may be a very significant cost in some cases. The arguments about the funding of undergraduate education to some extent rests on the idea that students should contribute towards their education now in the expectation that their relevant cash inflows are likely to be higher in later life because of the cost sacrifices that are made during their time at university.

Task 3.2 Input constraints for Matheson

The full financial picture for Matheson, substituting numbers for ?, is as follows:

	Zaps	Gigs	Pronks
The contribution for each toy is selling price less variable costs	£3.00	£3.50	£4.00
The import cost of each toy is	£7.00	£7.50	£10.00
Thus, contribution per £ of import cost =	£0.429	£0.467	£0.400
and the ranking becomes	2nd	1st	3rd
What would be the preferred sales programme for each product?	4 000	4 000	2 200

Gigs and Zaps can be sold up to maximum demand, which only takes up import costs of £58 000 (4000 × £7 = £28 000) + (4000 × £7.50 = £30 000).

This would leave £80 000 – £58 000 = £22 000 for Pronks.

▶

The number of Pronks which could therefore be imported and sold is
$\dfrac{(£22\ 000}{£10)} = 2\ 200.$

Total contribution is	£34 800	£12 000	£14 000	£8 800
less fixed costs	£20 000			
Profit	£14 800			

The input constraint can be seen to be costing Matheson (£22 000 − £14 800) = £7200. This can be proved by seeing that 1800 fewer Pronks are to be sold at a contribution of £4, i.e. £7200. This is a significant loss of profit and could lead the managers of Matheson to consider ways of shifting the resource constraint (e.g. by extra borrowing if it is cash shortage that is restricting the supply).

Task 3.3 Allocating overheads to products

1. Perhaps by looking more closely at the *activities* which go towards making and selling the products we could gain greater insights into a 'fair' allocation. For instance, if we discovered that £30 000 of the total fixed costs related to direct selling (largely visits to customers), and that product X caused roughly 100 customer visits while Y only caused 20, then that particular cost (£30 000) could be 'fairly' spread:

   $\dfrac{£30\ 000}{120} = £250$ per visit

   thus X picks up 250 × 100 = £25 000, while Y carries only £250 × 20 = £5000.

2. It can be argued that while, in the long run, the firm needs to cover all costs including fixed costs, in the short run only marginal cost matters. The key question is: How will this information be used? For instance, for a very short-term decision about selling a special one-off order; maybe only variable costs count, but if the concern is for long-run viability of the product then all costs should be considered.

3. Maybe not at all if the price is market driven. But cost will probably impact on price to some extent (even if only at the margin). If the firm has a monopoly then cost could be a major factor in price determination. And this also poses the question: what profit might be considered 'reasonable' (i.e. difference between total cost and selling price) for this particular firm/industry?

Answer notes to review questions

RQ 3.2

If, for example, you recently spent £300 on having your car repaired, and it let you down again immediately afterwards – would the £300 weigh in your decision whether to change or hold on to the car?

Again, if a manager buys a computer for £10 000 and two months later a vastly more efficient machine becomes available, does the £10 000 influence his/her decision whether to opt for a replacement?

The relevant cash flow argument suggests that both costs are *sunk* and should be disregarded (from an economic point of view). However, there is a deeper behavioural point that decisions are taken by people who may feel 'attached' to prior decisions (e.g. they don't wish to admit previous errors).

RQ 3.3

The question takes us into the 'externalities' debate. It is taken for granted (in accounting practice at least) that business reports only account for transactions from the business viewpoint. Many people have questioned whether this is good enough from a wider social viewpoint. The classic case is of the chemical firm tipping poisons into local water supplies. The clean-up costs may be borne, at least in part, by the local or central government, and non-financial costs of poor health may fall on the members of the local community.

Answer notes to numerical problems

NP 3.1 School catering

Financial analysis to show whether or not it makes sense to bring the meals service within the school

Expected number of meals = 500 pupils × 200 days		100 000 meals
	£	
Revenue at £1.50 per meal		150 000
Variable costs at £0.80 per meal		80 000
Contribution (£0.70 per meal)		70 000
Relevant fixed costs		
staff	30 000	
other relevant	10 000	
And school general costs that would be only incurred if the plan goes ahead (20 000 − 15 000)	5 000	45 000
Overall increase in school profits		25 000

Advice for head teacher and governors

The plan appears to be sound according to these figures, showing a healthy profit of £25 000, in addition to the non-financial benefits outlined in the problem. Some of the costs that are being allocated to the plan are ignored (£15 000) as they will be incurred whether or not the plan goes ahead and are not relevant to the decision.

Questions and other factors for the governors to attend to before proceeding would include:

- How sure can they be about the forecasts?
- Have they included all costs (e.g. health and safety)?
- Do they have the managerial resources to make it work?

NP 3.2 GH Ltd – making or buying?

1. Change in profits

Assuming that there is no other use for the facilities

Bought cost = 3.5 × 20 000		£70 000
Saving variable costs (2.90 × 20 000)	58 000	
fixed costs	8 000	66 000
Therefore profit decreases by		(4 000)

Assuming that resources released can be used for another product (10 000 units at £2 contribution)

Bought-in cost = £3.5 × 20 000 =		£70 000
Saving variable costs (£2.90 × 20 000)	58 000	
new contribution (10 000 × £2)	20 000	
		78 000
Therefore profit improves by		8 000

2. Other factors that should be considered include:

- What is the potential for future cost increases.?
- How certain is GH about demand for products?
- How important is the component to the total production run (in that, by subcontracting, GH loses some control over the process)?
- Are there any stockholding costs that should be factored into the analysis?

ANSWER NOTES TO CHAPTER 4

Answer notes to tasks

Task 4.1 Pictures of an organisation

People are not shown in the accounts, although their costs are reflected as an expense of the business. The intangible values of product brand names or the premium a buyer may be prepared to pay to acquire an established business are not shown either. This value is often referred to as the figure for goodwill. This task aims to show you that the accounting 'picture', like any other, is only partial.

Task 4.2 Reviewing the quadrants

Each transaction affected two items in the quadrant and always by the same amount. Accountants call this the 'rule of duality'. This is the 'power' of the basic accounting system: after each and every transaction all the numbers should total and be equal to one another, that is they should balance. When items balance we then know that they have been entered correctly.

Task 4.3 What if?

1. In this case we have entered into a trading relationship with a customer whom we call a debtor. (They are in our debt to the value of the goods we have sold them.) Effect upon the quadrant: cash would not change but an item, 'Debtors £1400', would now appear as part of the assets of the business – money that will be received in the future.

2. Effect upon the quadrant: cash would increase by £500 and loans (liability) would increase by £500.

3. Effect upon the quadrant: cash would be reduced by £250 and the liability to the creditor would be reduced by £250.

Task 4.4 Footballers – expense or asset?

In the accounts of some Premier League clubs the players are written off as an expense. This is taking a very prudent view of the playing life of the player. They are assuming that the player may not play for more than one year, potentially even less than one year. Other clubs treat the player as an asset and write him off to the profit and loss account over the life of the player's contract. They are taking a less pessimistic view of the playing life of the player.

A suspicion has been voiced that it is those clubs who are highly profitable and can afford to take the full cost of the player in Year 1 who are adopting the former policy.

Task 4.5 A second quadrant example

ASSETS				LIABILITIES
Cash + 1000 (1) − 500 (2) − 350 (4) + 500 (6)	650		Shareholders 1000	(1)
Equipment	500	(2)		
Stock 400 (3) − 400 (5)	0		Creditors 400 (3) − 350 (4) 50	
Debtors 700 (5) − 500 (6)	200			
EXPENSES				**REVENUES**
Cost of sales	400	(5)	Sales	700 (5)
Totals	1750			1750

Task 4.6 County Brewery

Updated quadrant with additional information (questions 1 and 2):

ASSETS		LIABILITIES	
Property	100	Shareholders' funds	110
Machines and vehicles 50 + 32 − 6	76	Long-term loans	23
Stocks 8 + 30 − 25	13	Creditors 40 + 30 + 55 + 20 − 96	49
Debtors 1 + 125 − 117	19	Tax	4
Cash/bank 4 − 32 + 117 − 96 + 15 − 6	2	Dividends	2
	210		210
EXPENSES		REVENUES	
Cost of sales	25	Sales	125
Production costs	55		
Marketing	20		
Interest	6		
Depreciation	6		
Tax	4		
Dividends	2		
Retained Profit	7		
	125		125

3. The company has made a profit for the year which has added to the net assets of the business. However, at present the loans and creditors outweigh the current assets (stock, debtors and cash) of the business, which is potentially a concern if those liabilities need to be paid soon.

Task 4.7 Vertical layout for County Brewery

Profit and loss account (£m)		
Sales		125
Less material cost	25	
other production costs	55	
marketing/administration	20	
depreciation	6	106
Operating profit	19	
Interest cost	6	
Profit before tax		13
Tax		4
Profit after tax	9	
Dividends		2
Profit left after charging all costs and claims	7	

Balance sheet

Fixed assets	property			100
	machines and vehicles			76
				176
Stocks		13		
Debtors		19		
Cash		2	34	
Loans			38	
Creditors			55	
			93	
				(59)
				117
Shareholders' capital (110 + 7 profit)				117

Answer notes to review questions

RQ 4.2

A balance sheet is a picture of a business at a single point in time. Within the statement one can make some assessment in terms of the values of assets and liabilities; also, how the business has been funded in terms of the balance between owner equity and debt.

RQ 4.3

All transactions have a double or dual aspect with both 'sides' of the transaction being recorded. This 'double-entry' simply reflects the natural exchange nature of transactions and as a result both sides will always be in balance (assuming the recording was done correctly).

RQ 4.4

Profit is the difference between the total of expenses and the total of revenues within a particular time period. Cash is the net balance of cash inflows and outflows over the same period. It is not unusual for a company to be highly profitable but not to have any cash, and in some rare and unusual cases *vice versa*.

Balance sheet

Fixed assets	property		100
	machines and vehicles		76
			176
Stocks		13	
Debtors		19	
Cash		2	
		34	
Creditors		(55)	
			(21)
			155
Shareholders capital (110 + 7 profit)			117
Loans			38
			155

Answer notes to numerical problems

NP 4.1 Albert Adey – a quadrant problem

1. An Accounting Quadrant

ASSETS				LIABILITIES
Cash				
1 000 − 2 000 − 400 + 1 000		Capital		1 000
(becomes overdraft)				
Equipment	400	Creditor		10 000
Stock 10 000 − 5 000	5000	Overdraft		400
Debtors 5 500 − 1 000	4 500			
Prepaid	1 817			
EXPENSES				**REVENUES**
Cost of sales	5 000			
Rent 2 000 − 1 817	183	Sales		5 500
	16 900			16 900

Note the calculation of the rent. Although we have paid for the rent upfront we only charge as an expense that amount of the rent we have used. We have used 11 days so this is the amount that is charged with the balance being carried forward as an asset. This future rent already paid will then be charged as an expense to the relevant period as this occurs.

Rent $\frac{(2000}{120)} \times 11 = 183$

Rent 2000 − 183 = 1817 prepaid

2. Albert Adey profit and loss account for 11 days of January

	£
Sales	5 500
Cost of sales	5 000
Gross profit	500
Rent	183
Profit	317

Albert Adey balance sheet at 11 January

	£	£
Equipment		400
Stock	5 000	
Debtors	4 500	
Prepaid rent	1 817	
Cash	—	
	11 317	
Creditors	10 000	
Overdraft	400	
	10 400	917
		1 317
Capital		1 000
Profit		317
		1 317

NP 4.2 Adam Astaron – opening and closing financial positions

1. Adam Asteron opening equity

Equity is another term for 'investments in the business' or 'net assets'; in other words, add the assets and take away the liabilities:

$$975 + 4274 + 328 - 953 = 4624$$

Opening quadrant			
ASSETS			LIABILITIES
Stock	4 274	Capital	4 624
Debtors	328	Creditors	953
Bank	975		
	5 577		5 577
EXPENSES	Nil	REVENUES	Nil

Closing quadrant			
ASSETS			LIABILITIES
Bank 975 – 246 – 352 – 256 – 165 + 525 – 250	231	Capital	4 624
Stock 4 247 + 256 + 1153 – 423 – 890	4 370	Creditors 953 – 352	1 754
Debtors 328 + 1 135	1 463		
EXPENSES		REVENUES	
Telephone	246	Sales 525 + 1 135	1 660
Rent	165		
Salaries	250		
Cost of sales 423 + 890	1 313		
	8 038		8 038

ANSWER NOTES TO CHAPTER 5

Answer notes to tasks

Task 5.1 Hicks and Fisher

Although their work was about individuals rather than the artificial persons that are companies, Fisher was talking about proprietary capital maintenance – what you can buy even if there has been price inflation – whereas Hicks was talking about operating capital maintenance – what you can do with your capital.

Task 5.2 Capital maintenance

In cash terms you made a profit of $2000 - 1900 = 100$ for this year.
Since you had £500 to start with, you now have £600.

But it would be a mistake to take either £100 or more out of the business if you hope to continue on the same scale as you did this year. The initial capital of £500 enabled you to generate the earnings of £2000 this year. Even if all other conditions were the same you therefore should need £500 again to generate similar-sized earnings and profits next year and so might be thinking of taking out 600 − 500 = 100.

But we have been told that there has been inflation during the year and so now expect that you would need 5 per cent more in starting capital:

$$500 \times 1.05 = 525$$

Therefore you could take 600 − 525 = 75 out of the business and still be able to operate on the same scale next year.

Task 5.3 Stocks and depreciation effect on the balance sheet

Looking at the balance sheet you should have noticed that a change in the stock value would have a significant impact on the net current assets position and therefore on the total assets in the top part of the balance sheet.

The depreciation figure affects the fixed asset figure (the non-current assets section), and so also the total assets in the top of the balance sheet.

Changes in either stock or depreciation would affect the profit figure, seen by looking at the profit and loss account; and the profit for the year is incorporated into the accumulated profit and loss figure which appears in the bottom of the balance sheet.

Task 5.4 The effect of different closing stock values

Opening stock	8 000
Purchases	200 000
	208 000
Closing stock	25 000
Cost of sales	183 000

Cost of sales has fallen by £5000 – therefore the gross profit and net profit will rise by £5000. A higher tax bill will result but higher profits will be available for distribution to the shareholders.

Task 5.5 Quadrant entries reflecting accruals and prepayments

ASSETS				LIABILITIES
Cash	− 360	Accrual − rates		+100
prepaid rent	+180	Accrual − wages		+500
EXPENSES				REVENUE
Business rates	+100			
Rent	+360 − 180			
Wages	+500			

Task 5.6 Straight line depreciation calculation

The annual depreciation charge would be:

$$\frac{10\ 000 - 1\ 000}{5} = 1\ 800 \text{ per year}$$

Task 5.7 Effect of alternative assumptions

1. This will depend upon the time we became certain that the asset would last for a further five years. Over the life of the asset the current annual depreciation charge will be halved and therefore the figure for net profit will need to be amended for each of the relevant years.

2. If we do not discover this until we try to sell the asset and receive zero scrap value, we will incur a loss on disposal which will affect the reported figure in the final year. In theory at least this means that the amounts charged for depreciation have been incorrect over the current life of the asset. Alternatively, we might discover that we will receive zero scrap value before the end of the useful life; in which case, as in 1., we will change the rate of depreciation. In this case we will increase depreciation so that the full cost of the asset is charged to expenses in the profit and loss account during its life.

3. This will depend upon when we discover that the furniture is of inferior quality. If we do not know this before it disintegrates in the third year then we will have a situation similar to the previous example but with a huge loss on disposal. If it were decided that the asset were to have a reduced life early in its life then the depreciation charge would be amended accordingly depending upon the point in time the adjustment were to be made. Assuming we were to adjust after two years from a previously assumed life of ten years and residual value of £1000 to a revised life of three years:

Year 1 $900\ (10\ 000 - \frac{1\ 000}{10}) =$ 900 per annum, so written down value is £9 100

Year 2 $4\ 050\ (9\ 100 - \frac{1\ 000}{2}) =$ 4 050 per annum, so written down value is £5 050

Therefore, in Year 3, the expected amount of depreciation is also £4050 which will leave a final written down value of £1000 which should be covered by the £1000 expected scrap value.

If it were decided that this would be such a relatively huge change in depreciation charge between Year 1 and Year 2 in the context of this company that the accounts would otherwise look rather odd, a prior year adjustment might be made so that when a person read the accounts at the end of Year 2 they would look as if the company had always expected the life to be only three years. In other words, the Year 1 accounts, shown as comparative in the Year 2 report, would be retrospectively amended. This would not normally happen in the case of a change in depreciation *estimate* as prior-year adjustments are intended to be used only to correct fundamental errors or changes in policy in the accounts. A note to the accounts has to explain what has happened and thus draw the user's attention to it. This demonstrates again that accounting profit is far from an absolute number!

Answer notes to review questions

RQ 5.2

Note: There is often scope for debate and judgement in these matters:

- sales representative's car – probably reducing balance: loses most value early on
- microcomputer – probably reducing balance: volatile market means early obsolescence likely, so short life appropriate
- printer – probably straight line: consider length of useful life – when do you intend to replace with laser printer?
- packing machine – consider depreciating over hours used? or parcels packed? Probably straight line
- photocopier – relate depreciation rate to copies made? Upgrades are constantly available – same comments as microcomputer
- lease on land and buildings – over life of lease, but speed up if near end of life.

RQ 5.3

1. Choice of depreciation method/life/residual value.
2. Valuation of stocks, depends on identification of cost and NRV in each set of circumstances.
3. Accounts usually only include things measured historically in money terms – they rarely reflect inflation and non-money value events, e.g. recruitment of wonderful new staff.

Does this matter?
It is essential – the accounts aim to give a true and fair view so appropriate decisions need to be made for each business, although we expect consistency from period to period. However, beware when comparing businesses because you may find, on closer inspection, that they have made very different subjective choices and thus present widely varying results.

NP 5.1 Gross profit and cost of sales

Gross profit and cost of sales worksheet

	Year 1 (£)	Year 2 (£)	Year 3 (£)
Sales	1 000	1 200	2 000
Opening stock	100	200	300
Purchases	600	800	1 600
Closing stock	(200)	(100)	(400)
Cost of sales	500	900	1 500
Gross profit	500	300	500
Gross profit as % of sales	50%	25%	25%

It might seem that the higher the gross profit percentage the better – therefore 50 per cent in Year 1 might sound better than 25 per cent in Years 2 and 3 – but you need to ask, 50 per cent of what? In fact, 50 per cent of 1000 in Year 1 is the same as 25 per cent of 2000 in Year 3. If the same profit percentage had been maintained as in Year 1, 50 per cent of 2000 in Year 3 would have been even better!

NP 5.2 Straight line depreciation

Straight line depreciation

Fixed asset (£)	Year 1 (£)	Year 2 (£)	Year 3
Original cost	500	000	3 300
Expected salvage value	100	100	300
Cost less salvage value	400	900	3 000
Expected life	4	3	5
Years used so far	1	2	3
Annual depreciation	100	300	600
Depreciation to date	100	600	1 800
Cost less depn to date	400	400	1 500

The cost less depreciation to date is the figure that appears in the balance sheet.

NP 5.3 Hire and buy

ASSETS			LIABILITIES
Machine		100 000	
less depreciation		20 000	
NBV		80 000	
Cash	100 000 −	30 000	
EXPENSES			REVENUES
Depreciation		20 000	
Hire		30 000	

When a company owns an asset this is reflected by showing a fixed asset in the balance sheet and an item of expense appears in the profit and loss account – depreciation. If the company hires the asset the company has an expense in the profit and loss account – the rental charge – but no fixed asset is owned, although the company may acknowledge the position in the notes to the accounts.

NP 5.5 John Franks – depreciation and profit calculation

John Franks trading and profit and loss account for year end

Sales			120 000
O/stock		0	
Purchases		45 000	
		45 000	
C/stock		5 000	
			40 000
Gross profit			80 000
Less:			
Rent		12 000	
Other expenses		30 000	
Less: depreciation			
Machinery – straight line method			

$$\frac{28000 - 3000}{5}$$

		5000	
(or 20% on cost??	5600)		
* Vehicle	£20 000 × 0.3 =	6000	
			53 000
	Net Profit		27 000

*These are assumed rates. You need to justify the choice.

John Franks balance sheet

Fixed assets
Machinery	28 000 – 5 000 =	23 000
Vehicle	20 000 – 6 000 =	14 000
		37 000

Current assets
Stocks	5 000	
Bank	4 800	9 800
		46 800

Capital		
	25 000	
Net profit	27 000	
	52 000	
Drawings	5 200	46 800

ANSWER NOTES TO CHAPTER 6

Answer notes to tasks

Task 6.1 The users of financial statements

- Managers/directors – should have unfettered access to information appropriate to their status within the business, usually much more than an outsider can access. Therefore, managers are not main recipients of the published annual reports – they tend to rely upon the management accounts; but the directors are legally responsible for producing the published information.

- Investors (shareholders in the case of companies) and potential shareholders including financial analysts and advisers – this group is seen as a major recipient of published financial information by all regulators. As they provide a large part of the finance in many companies they are also seen as important users by the management of the company. Their main aim is to work out whether making an investment in a company, or continuing to hold an investment in a company, is a good idea for them (whether it is financially profitable, in terms of dividends they will receive or increases in the value of their shareholding). So they are using the accounts to make decisions about being an investor. Large investors and analysts and advisers are often seen as so important to the company that they are courted and kept informed through meetings and other media in addition to the annual financial reports.

- Lenders and banks – these are a group that has loaned money to the business and so they need to be reassured as to the business's ability to pay interest and repay capital.

- Suppliers and trade creditors – this group is similar to the lenders group above. They need information to decide how good a customer the company is likely to be in future and whether it is able to repay any outstanding amounts from past dealings.

- Government, Inland Revenue and other agencies – the financial reports are used to check taxation computations and gather statistics which form part of government forecasts and reports.

- Employees and trade unions – although not financial investors this group has a great interest in the progress of the business, its stability as an employer and the size of the profits for paying future wage claims etc. Not all of this information will necessarily be financially based.

- Customers – if a large customer is buying from a small supplier they will want reassurance that the supplier is going to be able to deliver. Information will reassure them that any deposit they pay is safe and that the goods or services will arrive in time for their own business to continue functioning smoothly.

- The general public, including environmental pressure groups – a company may be seen as part of the wider community. A large business can have a big impact on a town or city's prosperity and physical environment and that wider community will also expect to be consulted and involved when the business has plans to change size or activity level. Again, not all the information they want will be financial but may be more fact based.

Task 6.2 The skills of users of accounts

Some writers argue that business is complex and so cannot always be reported in very simple terms. It is more important to report a true picture of what has happened than to cater to the lowest common denominator. It should be possible for a non-expert to pay a financial adviser to interpret information for them and so gain the benefit of the information contained in the annual report, rather than investing their own time and money in becoming expert themselves.

Task 6.3 Look at a set of published accounts

In simple terms the report can be broken down into the following:

- Public relations material – this is often in the form of colourful pictures and explanations of what the business does. It is not part of the accounts.
- The accounts – the numerical reports including balance sheet and profit and loss account and explanatory notes.
- Various reviews of the year by the chairman and chief executive.
- Information required by the Stock Exchange, including summarised financial information from the last five years, corporate information about the financial calendar and company financial advisers.

Answer notes to review questions

RQ 6.1

The stock market obtains information from a variety of sources. Because of the time delay involved, the annual report is more of a confirmation or check on earlier estimates by analysts. During the accounting year information is also obtained through press reports of any activities a company is undertaking which may affect their future results, special analyst briefings made by the company concerned, the release of interim accounts, and rumour and gossip!

The share price is simply the view of the market at a point in time of how much a share may be worth; that price will rise or fall dependent on demand for the shares in the market.

RQ 6.2

The question aims to provoke thought about the nature of 'accounting rules'. Physical laws (e.g. the law of gravity) are unchanging, but accounting is a social science subject to the changing nature of social demands on, economic and business conditions, etc. So profit is redefined in different periods of history, for example:

1. the matching concept overtook cash-based accounting when businesses moved from a single-venture base towards long-term organisations

2. attempts (not always successful) to redefine profit have been made to cope with inflationary trends.

ANSWER NOTES TO CHAPTER 7

Answer notes to tasks

Task 7.1 Profits are not the same as cash

The accruals or matching concept (accruals, prepayments, stocks, deprecia-tion, use of provisions) and the use of credit (purchases and sales) means that profit is not the same as the cash balance of the business at any particular point in time.

Task 7.2 Builder Group cash-flow statement – Year 3

Profit before tax	52
Add depreciation	3
	55
Changes in working capital:	
Stocks increase	(41)
Debtors increase	(12)
Creditors increase	21
Net inflow from operating activities	23
Returns on investment and servicing of finance	
Dividends paid	9
Taxation paid	8
Capital expenditure Fixed assets bought	17
Net cash flow before finance	(11)
Financing activities	
Shares issued	46
Loans increased	12
Net increase in cash and cash equivalents	47

Note the fact that the 'net inflow from operating activities' is the profit before tax figure adjusted for the things listed in Task 7.1 above (the things that make profits not equal to cash); all the other things in the statement then list the amount of cash actually paid and received to come down to the total movement of cash in the year; note that the fixed assets bought figure has to be derived in this example (Year 1 property = 54; Year 2 property = 80; but also in Year 2 there was a £2m depreciation charge).

Note that the emboldened headings are prescribed format required by FRS1 CFSs.

Task 7.3 Use of the cash-flow statement

The CFS focuses on *cash* changes in the period, which is a useful addition when you consider that profit does not equal cash. It allows the user to think of the solvency of the business and assess its likely ability to pay bills. It is another way of looking at the changes in assets held by the business from last year to this (between the balance sheets).

Answer notes to review questions

RQ7.3

The CFS is historical – it is quite technical in construction so the uninitiated may see an increase in cash and cash equivalent as a good thing even though that could have been achieved simply by taking on a new loan (which may not be 'a good thing').

Answer notes to numerical problems

NP 7.1 County Brewery revisited

Profit from operations	19
Add depreciation	6
	25
Increase in stock	(5)
Increase in debtors	(8)
Increase in creditors	9
Net inflow from operating activities	21
Returns on investment and servicing of finance	
Interest	(6)
Dividend paid (unknown – assume nil)	
Taxation paid ditto	
Investing activities	
Purchase of new machines	(32)
Net cash outflow before financing	(17)

▶

Financing activities	
Increase in loans	15
(Owners did not pay in any more cash)	
Decrease in cash and cash equivalents	(2)

NP 7.2 Health and pharmaceutical retailer – cash-flow statements

Note: figures are in £m.

Decrease in cash position in Year 1 is recovered by Year 2 performance (ignoring inflation, the cash has been replaced).

The net cash inflow from operating activities of 179 is a 74 per cent improvement on Year 1, apparently largely achieved through de-stocking and increasing the amount owed to creditors. Check this is a sensible thing for this company to do and does not endanger future trading.

A higher dividend was paid in Year 2 – passing on some of the improved profit to shareholders.

There is lower investment in new fixed assets in Year 2. Is this wise/according to plan?

Some new subsidiaries; some loans repaid in Year 2.

NP 7.4 Colours

Red

- High proportion of assets in cash investments and debtors.
- High proportion of liabilities are trade creditors.
- No stock, overdraft or intangible assets.
- Land and buildings make up majority of fixed assets.
- But all fixed assets are small in relation to trade debtors and creditors.

Red is likely to be the high street banker:

- lots of money owed to/from customers
- substantial investment in property (the branches and head office)
- unlikely to have lots of stocks (except stationery) or anything else associated with production, like machinery or patents, etc.

Orange

- Very large proportion of total assets are current assets.
- Suggest this is a service industry company, which would need good staff rather than fixed assets.

Therefore Orange is probably a PR and advertising company:

- main fixed assets likely to be nice office furnishings and computers
- may not own its own buildings

- likely to have much work in progress (jobs under way) and goodwill could arise from having taken over other similar businesses and paid more than the cost of the assets acquired to do so
- main expenses likely to be payroll which it could finance by the overdraft until it gets paid by customers.

Yellow

- More cash and investments than debtors
- but trade and other creditors are high
- suggests the company can sell mainly for cash but is able to get supplies on credit.

Probably Yellow is a retailer, who would therefore have stock and fixed assets (shops?). The other creditors might represent the wages due to staff and National Insurance and tax due to the Inland Revenue.

ANSWER NOTES TO CHAPTER 8

Answer notes to tasks

Task 8.1 Customer debts

1. They may consider only granting credit to those customers who have a good credit record, e.g. those who currently pay within the prescribed time period.
2. They may wish to consider offering incentives and inducements in order to encourage their debtors to pay more promptly: a cash discount perhaps.
3. They should be more efficient at sending invoices out on time.
4. They might use the accounting system to produce a schedule list of debtors by date so that management attention can be focused on outstanding debtors.
5. They may consider factoring in those debtors from whom it is proving difficult to obtain funds.

Task 8.2 Debtor investment

One day's sales $= \frac{£5m}{365} = £13\ 699$.

Thus, if debts are 80 days then debtor total $= £13\ 699 \times 80 = 1\ 095\ 920$, an increase of £95 920 and an extra cost (at 20 per cent) of just over £19 000 annually.

Task 8.3 Cash conversion

1. $60 + 50 - 40 = 70$

2. Stocks £1m $\times$ 0.75 $\times \dfrac{50}{365}$ 102 740

     Debtors £1m $\times \dfrac{60}{365}$ 164 384

     Less creditors £700 000 $\times \dfrac{40}{365}$ $\underline{76\ 712}$

                                            $\underline{190\ 412}$

Answer notes to review questions

RQ 8.1

The accounting numbers are based upon historic cost and so do not represent the current value of the assets to the business.

The analysis is based upon only two years' figures so it is difficult to identify any long-term trends. Also we do not have access to any competitors figures against which we could benchmark the performance of Jondoe, nor do we have any industry averages so that we could judge the performance of the sector.

RQ 8.2

You would probably be concerned with ratios which focused upon liquidity, as your concern would be the ability of the customer to make the repayments as and when they were due. So, you would focus upon the current and liquidity ratios. You would also look at the amount of borrowing they already had to see if they were not financially overstretched. So, you would also be looking at balance sheet gearing and interest cover.

RQ 8.3

What does Aunt Agatha wants from the investment: short-term cash returns or long-term growth? This will determine the ratios which matter. For the short term, the levels of profitability allied to P/E ratio and EPS, dividend yield and dividend cover are the important ones. For the long term, in addition to the trends of the ratios already mentioned, you would be interested in those ratios which focused upon the use of assets, e.g. sales, fixed assets, liquidity ratios, ROCE and returns on shareholders' funds.

RQ 8.4

Ratios offer a partial picture of past performance and can suggest areas for improvement. They also allow comparisons to be made between different investments and, if used sensibly (and supplemented with other non-financial information), ratios can offer insights; but clearly the historic nature/absence of predicted figures is a drawback.

Answer notes to numerical problems

NP 8.1 Trenton plc – missing numbers and ratios

Balance sheets at the end of	2001		2002	
		(£m)		
Fixed assets				
Factories	50		20	
Less depreciation	10	40	5	15
Retail outlets	70		130	
Less depreciation	10	60	20	110
		100		125
Current assets				
Stocks		50		35
Debtors		40		25
Cash		=		2
		90		62
Current liabilities				
Trade creditors		20		35
Taxation		1		9
Dividends		1		4
Bank overdrafts		30		0
		52		48
Working capital		38		14
Loans		10		5
Net assets		128		134
Share capital (£1 shares)		40		40
Reserves		88		94
Equity		128		134
Market value of one £1 share		£1.00		£4.00

Income statements	2001	2002
	(£m)	
Sales	200	250
Cost of sales	150	175
Gross profit	50	75
Depreciation	4	10
Cash-based expenses	40	45
Profit before interest	6	20
Interest	3	1
Profit before tax	3	19
Taxation	1	9
Profit after tax	2	10
Dividends	1	4
Profit retained	1	6

Cash-flow statement		2002
Profit before tax		19
Depreciation (all on retail outlets)		10
		29
Reduction in stocks		15
Reduction in debtors		15
Increase in creditors		15
Operating funds		74
Dividends paid		(1)
Taxation paid		(1)
Factories sold		25
Purchase of retail outlets		(60)
Loans repaid		(5)
Increase in cash	(30 + 2)	32

Profitability

Return on shareholders' funds	14.18%
Gross margin	30.00%
Net profit to sales	7.60%
Asset turnover	1.865

Liquidity

Current ratio	1.29
Quick ratio	0.56
Stock turnover	5.00
Debtor turnover	10.00
Creditor turnover	5.00

Gearing

Interest cover	20.00
Balance sheet gearing	3.60%

Investment

EPS	25p
Dividend per share	10p
Dividend yield	2.50%
P/E	16.00

NP 8.3 Little and Large

1. The gearing of Large is much greater than Little: 76% compared to 28%. Therefore, Large will have a much greater interest charge to meet.
2. Large has a profit margin of 25 per cent as opposed to 20 per cent in spite of higher debt/interest.
3. The ROCE is lower for Large, but a higher gearing has had the effect of increasing return on equity above Little.
4. The EPS is greater for Large, but Large has a much lower P/E ratio. The market price of Large's share must therefore be correspondingly lower: Large's share is 184p compared to Little's of 238p. The market therefore rates Little as a 'better' investment than 'Large'.
5. Little, with the higher dividend cover, is retaining more profit than Large.

Conclusion

Little offers a less risky investment with much lower levels of gearing yet offering similar returns in terms of ROCE and return on equity. However, should the economy move out of recession then the shareholders of Large will begin to experience the gearing effects upon their returns.

NP 8.4 Hayfor and Caxton

Various answers are possible of course – but they should focus on the scenario in the question, i.e. a supplier worried about a major customer, not just calculate all the possible ratios.

What do suppliers worry about? Liquidity, links to gearing and profitability, while EPS and other investment ratios are less important.

Calculations	20−4	20−5
Current ratio	1.25	$\dfrac{9\ 173}{11\ 068} = 0.83$
Acid test	0.94	$\dfrac{9\ 173 - 2\ 003}{11\ 068} = 0.65$
Stock days		Not possible
Debtor days	105.00	$\dfrac{70\ 980 \times 36.5}{27\ 663} = 94$
Creditor days		Not possible
Net profit to sales	2.5%	$\dfrac{(2\ 311)}{27\ 663} = (8.3\%)$
Gearing $= \dfrac{\text{Debt}}{\text{Debt + equity}}$	$\dfrac{420 + 2931}{10\ 426} = 32\%$	$\dfrac{4\ 608}{8\ 624} = 53\%$
Interest cover $= \dfrac{\text{PBIT}}{\text{Interest}}$	1.94	$\dfrac{(2\ 311)}{712} = (3.24\%)$

Commentary

The report should refer to the fact that historical data is no guarantee of future performance.

Falling liquidity could be dangerous, especially as it appears to be quite a bit worse than the industry average.

The collection period is also significantly slower than average, suggesting that problems with credit control and an inability to collect the debts may be causing the problem. This is supported by the fact that creditors and stocks are not wildly different from $20-4$ to $20-5$.

Hayfor's managers should be worried by the fact that not only have profits turned to losses between the years, leading to the inability to pay interest (long-term lenders tend to give secured loans, making it dangerous for suppliers who are normally unsecured – may need to discuss this a bit further) but the company appears to have taken on more debt to try to combat the liquidity problem – hence the increase in balance sheet gearing.

Caxton appears a bad risk for Hayfor – but perhaps they can work together to get the debt collection problems sorted out; maybe even a merger/takeover in the longer term.

ANSWER NOTES TO CHAPTER 9

Answer notes to tasks

Task 9.1 A personal financial prediction

A very personal task to which, clearly, we can offer no 'model' answer!

Task 9.2 A balance sheet budget

1. Budgeted balance s heet at the end of the first year

Balance sheet			(£)
Fixed assets (9 000 + 6 000 − 2 000)			13 000
Current assets			
Stocks (8 000 + 2 000)		10 000	
Debtors (20% of 150 000)		30 000	
		40 000	
Less current liabilities			
Creditors (0.5 × (10 000 + 30 000)) =	20 000		
Overdraft (the missing figure − see below for explanation)	11 000	31 000	
Net current assets (or working capital)			9 000
Net assets			22 000
Financed by			
Loans			6 000
Owners' capital			
At start of year		10 000	
Retained this year (4% of £150k)		6 000	16 000
			22 000

2. A discussion would cover the short- and long-term prospects as revealed by the numbers above. Profitability looks modest (but there may be 'start-up' factors, and prospects may be better for the second year). The cash flow is pretty dire (moving from £2000 positive to £11 000 overdraft), although the extra investment in fixed assets accounts for £6000 of this. There is a possible need to consider control of stock and debtor levels.

We did not ask for this, but a useful way of seeing the cash movements in this first year would be a cash-flow budget statement that highlights the main factors affecting the liquidity of the business:

Sources of cash are expected to be:

	(£)
Profits	6 000
+ depreciation (a non-cash expense, and therefore added back)	2 000
	8 000

However, working capital changes will be negative on cash flow:

Stock increase	(2 000)	
Debtor increase	(30 000)	
Less creditor increase	17 000	(15 000)

And extra fixed assets also reduce liquidity by	(6 000)

Which would suggest an overall worsening of the bank position by	(13 000)

If the opening bank position is	2 000
Then the closing overdraft will become	(11 000)
A negative swing of	(13 000)

Task 9.3 The printer's costs

The basic cost analysis for this task is:

Fixed and variable elements of costs	Variable cost per book (£)	Fixed cost per week (£)
Paper	5	
Royalty	3	
Semi-variable costs		
Agent's costs	2	100
Total variable cost elements	10	
Fixed costs		50 000
Stepped fixed costs (labour) (rising by £400 for each 1 000 books above 5 000)		4 000
Selling price is £40 per book		

From this basic data we can construct an answer to the task:

Books published and sold	1 000	3 000	7 000
Variable costs (£10 per book)	10 000	30 000	70 000
Revenues (£40 per book)	40 000	120 000	280 000
Contribution (£30 per book)	30 000	90 000	210 000
Fixed costs	50 000	50 000	50 000
Fixed element of semi-variable costs (£)	100	100	100
Stepped fixed costs (£)	4 000	4 000	5 200
Total fixed costs (£)	54 100	54 100	55 300
Profit (or loss) for a week (£)	(24 100)	35 900	154 700

Task 9.4 Cost budgeting

Cost headings will probably include:

- Salaries
- Travel expenses – including accommodation
- Motor car costs
- Promotional costs – e.g. customer promotion packs, free handouts, etc.
- Bad debts – i.e. the costs of customers failing to pay for sales made.

Budgeting for these costs would include some 'top-down' thinking (i.e. you, as manager, would be expected to lay down some criteria and restrictions on levels of spend) and 'bottom-up' bidding from your salespeople who would, presumably, be explaining how costs were incurred, and how different customers require different levels of service and hence costs. Past cost levels may be helpful in providing a guide for the new estimates.

Task 9.5 Your personal financial predictions: how did they turn out?

Another very personal task, and therefore impossible for us to provide an answer. However, we hope that the task will demonstrate the difficulties that you may have had in making predictions about spending even at this 'one-person' level. A complex organisation, we may expect, will have similar difficulties but over many more cost headings: hence the need for a robust system of budgetary control to allow for monitoring of cost levels.

Task 9.6 Explaining cost variances – furniture

Costs for 120 chairs should be (120 × £10) = £1200 in timber. Prices fell by 10 per cent, thus saving £120. We would therefore expect to have spent (after the price reduction) £1200 − £120, or £1080.
The actual spend on timber was £1300, and thus the inefficiency of the new employee cost = (£1300 − £1080) = £220. In summary:

	(£)	
Price variance	120	(favourable)
Efficiency variance (cost of the wastage)	220	(unfavourable)
Total material cost variance	100	(unfavourable)

The task demonstrates that we should not take variances at face value, as there may be more than one underlying cause contained within them.

Task 9.7 Jane Roser – when plans go wrong

1. Profits – budget and actual

		Budget	Actual
Sales quantity		30 shirts	20 shirts
Price		£15	£15
		(£)	
Sales revenue		450	300
Cost of shirts sold			
budget	30 × £10	300	
actual	20 × £9	180	
Contribution		150	120
Fixed costs			
Wages		20	10
Rent		30	40
Profit		100	70

2. Explaining the difference in profits

The £30 reduction in profit can be explained as follows:

Volume of sales was down Jane lost (10 shirts × £5) budgeted contribution	(£50)	(unfavourable)
But shirts cost £1 less giving an improved contribution On the shirts sold of £1 × 20	£20	(favourable)
Rent exceeded budget	(£10)	(unfavourable)
Wages saved against budget	£10	(favourable)
Giving an overall unfavourable variance of	£30	

3. Why did the cash balance reduce by £20?

	(£)
Opening cash balance	400
Less new shirts bought	(270)
Less wages and rent paid	(50)
Plus cash received from customers	300
Cash left at close of business	380

4. Why was there a profit of £70 but cash reduction of £20?

	(£)
Profit made	70
Stock bought but not sold	(90)
Overall reduction in cash	(20)

Answer notes to review questions

RQ 9.1

It's a fair point! However, planning within an uncertain environment remains a key feature of the work of many managers, and it can be argued that some plans (even though inevitably inaccurate) are better than none.

Plans can be modified as events unfold, and planning at least allows us to know how far we are away from the desired position.

At a deeper level, plans and budgets may be seen as a 'comfort blanket' which provide the illusion that we are in control, when clearly we are not!

RQ 9.4

The major aspects are likely to include higher turnover, costs, profits and working capital levels.

The major issue will almost certainly be the effect on liquidity, bank balance and loans. Building firms operate on a long lead time which requires a significant outlay on stocks/debtors before cash is returned from sales. Hence it is perfectly possible for success, in the form of increased demand and sales, to lead to problems in reduced liquidity.

Answer notes to numerical problems

NP 9.1 Magic Lantern – cash budget

	May	June	July	Aug	Sept	Oct	Nov	Dec
Sales units × £40	40 000	48 000	56 000	64 000	72 000	80 000	88 000	104 000
Production units × £26	31 200	36 400	41 600	52 000	62 400	67 600	62 400	57 200

Cash budget

Receipts		July	Aug	Sept	Oct	Nov	Dec
(£)		40 000	48 000	56 000	64 000	72 000	80 000

Payments		July	Aug	Sept	Oct	Nov	Dec
Materials		31 200	36 400	41 600	52 000	62 400	67 600
Fixed costs		6 000	6 000	6 000	6 000	6 000	6 000
Tax/vehicle			8 000		18 000		
Total payments		37 200	50 400	47 600	76 000	68 400	73 600
Surplus/(deficit)		2 800	(2 400)	8 400	(12 000)	3 600	6400
Cash/(overdraft) Beginning		(3 000)	(200)	(2 600)	5 800	(6 200)	(2 600)
Cash/(overdraft) End	(3 000)	(200)	(2 600)	5 800	(6 200)	(2 600)	3 800

NP 9.3 Gunners – an exercise in budget presentation

1. A possible revision of the information that would be more helpful for managers follows:

Income statement Year 1

	Vizi Unit	Vizi Total	Ordi Unit	Ordi Total	Funi Unit	Funi Total	All products
Sales (000 units)		250		100		150	500
Selling price (£)	100		80		120		
Sales revenue (£000)		25 000		8 000		18 000	51000

Expenses	£	£000	£	£000	£	£000	£000
Cost of imported goods sold (50%)	50	12 500	40	4 000	60	9 000	25 500
Product contribution	50	12 500	40	4 000	60	9 000	25 500
Separable fixed costs		4 500		1 000		5 000	10 500
Product profit		8 000		3 000		4 000	15 000
General fixed costs		5 000		2 000		3 000	10 000
Net profit/(loss)		3 000		1 000		1 000	5 000

Budget income statement Year 2

	Vizi		Ordi		Funi		All products
	Unit	Total	Unit	Total	Unit	Total	
Sales (000 units)		237.5		95		142.5	475
Selling Price (£)	110		88		132		
Sales Revenue (£000)		26 125		8 360		18 810	53 295
Expenses	£	£000	£	£000	£	£000	£000
Cost of imported goods sold (60%)	66	15 675	52.8	5 016	79.2	11 286	31 977
Product contribution	44	10 450	35.2	3 344	52.8	7 524	21 318
Separable fixed costs		4 950		1 100		5 500	11 550
Product profit		5 500		2 244		2 024	9 768
General fixed costs		5 500		2 200		3 300	11 000
Net profit/(loss)		—		44		(1 276)	(1 232)

2. The effect on profit budgets of various changes

	Vizi	Ordi	Funi	Total
(a) Separable fixed costs at 90%				
Original budget	4 950	1 100	5 500	11 550
90% of last year	4 050	900	4 500	9 450
Profit increase (£000)	900	200	1 000	2 100
(b) Funi product (cease to import)				
Original budget product profit			2 024	
Revised budget product profit			—	
Loss of profit (£000)				(2 024)
(c) Selling prices + 25%;				
quantity 90%	£	£	£	£
Revised selling price	125	100	150	
Revised quantities (£000)	225	90	135	
Revised revenue (£000)	28 125	9 000	20 250	
Imported cost per unit	66.0	52.8	79.2	
Imported cost total (£000)	14 850	4 752	10 692	
Revised product contribution	13 275	4 248	9 558	
Original product contribution	10 450	3 344	7 524	
Increased profit (£000)	2 825	904	2 034	5 763

3. Comments

- The company is caught in a 'squeeze': reduced demand is coupled with cost inflation leading to profit reduction.

- Elimination of the Funi product is harmful, as all products provide a contribution towards the general fixed costs.

- 2(a) would help if that level of cost reduction can be sustained without damaging quality of service and possibly demand.

■ 2(c) looks attractive – however, how certain is it that markets can sustain a 25 per cent price increase with demand reduced to only 90 per cent? If demand falls further then profits may drop below the original position.

NP 9.5 Genesis – variances from standard cost

Variance summary based on actual sales and production of 1400 units

	Standard quantity	Standard cost/ revenue (£)	Cost/ revenue per unit (£)	Flexed budget (£)	Actual costs/ revenues (£)	Total variances (£)
Material	15 sq m	3	45	63 000	88 000	(25 000)
Labour	5 hours	4	20	28 000	34 000	(6 000)
Cost of production			65	91 000	122 000	(31 000)
Sales	1	100	100	140 000	142 800	2 800
Contribution			35	49 000	20 800	(28 200)

The overall picture of Genesis' profit performance is therefore:

		£
Original budget contribution	1 000 units @ £35	35 000
Sales volume variance	400 units @ £35	14 000
Flexed budget profit	1 400 units @ £35	49 000
Other variances		(28 200)
Actual contribution		20 800

It is now possible to analyse the 'other variances' in more detail.

Variance analysis

	Material variances			Labour variances		
	sq m	£	£	hours	£	£
Actual costs	22 000	4	88 000	6 800	5	34 000
Price/rate variance	22 000	(1)	(22 000)	6 800	(1)	(6 800)
Actual inputs at standard cost	22 000	3	66 000	6 800	4	27 200
Usage/efficiency variance	(1 000)	3	(3 000)	200	4	800
Fixed budget (1 400 units)	21 000	3	63 000	7 000	4	28 000

Clearly, Genesis has suffered significant extra costs. Material and labour prices are above standard. Materials have been overused, compared to standard. There is a small saving on labour usage. It is important to remember that a variance *may* be due to improved or deteriorating levels of efficiency. Equally, it may be caused by the inaccurate setting of standards. The variance analysis only provides a series of initial questions (i.e. the variances). Further investigation and discussions will be necessary to discover answers.

Sales variances

The sales variances have already been calculated. On the variance summary we can see a sales variance of £2800. This is the price variance: 1400 units sold at a price £2 above standard. We have also seen that the sales volume variance, which explains the difference between original and flexed budget profits, is 400 units at £35 standard contribution = £14 000.

ANSWER NOTES TO CHAPTER 10

Answer notes to tasks

Task 10.1 A personal long-term decision

Clearly, this is personal to you, and we cannot offer a 'model' answer, but the kinds of costs and benefits that may appear (depending on your course of study) include:

Costs and benefits	Immediate	Next year	More than one year ahead
Course fees	££		
Textbooks and other resources	££		
Travel and accommodation	££		
Income given up through being on the course	££		
Costs of a follow-up course or later stage		££	
of the programme		££	
Improved earnings			££

Task 10.2 Predicting cash flows

Cash flows for the retailer of books and stationery could include:

Cash flows	Predictability?
Sales income	Weak predictability at first until patterns are established
Staff wages	Moderately predictable – depending on levels of sales
Rent and business rates	High level of predictability
Telephone	Fairly predictable
Energy costs	Fairly predictable
Initial promotion costs	Highly predictable
Bank interest	Low level of predictability – depends upon cash flow management, sales levels and interest rates

Task 10.3 Your own personal cost of capital?

The answer to this task will, of course, be personal to the reader! The task is set to get you thinking about how you 'fund' your major spending decisions – i.e., from what source you get the money. Following that, we invite you to think about the costs that attach to that form of funding.

Task 10.4 Retail therapy

This is a very personal question, and we cannot offer a suggested solution! The question is set to get you thinking about non-financial considerations that may play a part in decision-making. If it can apply at a personal level, then it may be equally true that some business decisions include a non-financial and non-rational element.

Task 10.5 FlyCheap

Assuming that FlyCheap sell 20 per cent of all tickets at £10, the price of other tickets could be calculated as follows:

	££
Fixed costs per day	18 000
Variable costs (720 × £5)	3 600
	21 600
Profit expected (20% on costs)	4 320
Revenues needed for each day	25 920
Revenues from very low price tickets (20% × 720 × £10)	1 440
Revenue needed from other tickets	24 480

The price for other 576 tickets (i.e. 80 per cent of 720) would therefore have to be around:

$$\frac{(£24480)}{576} = £42.50$$

Task 10.6 Strategy and profit analysis

1. The analysis suggests that the closure of in-company courses would, at best, bring marginally more profit into the faculty in the short term. However, the decision should be taken with a long-term view of the strategy in mind. If the Business School wants to be a player in all parts of the education market then it is likely to make sense to stick with the in-company market as it is expected to expand, while undergraduate funding is expected to become less profitable.

    There is clearly some competition from other universities, but this would be unlikely to deter UME from grappling with the potentially good in-company market.

2. Other information that would help to inform the decision includes:

   - more detailed financial projections for undergraduate and postgraduate courses
   - historic data covering more than one year
   - information about the competition
   - strategic plans for UME as a whole
   - political information about the future funding of HE.

3. The accounting numbers are likely to be important, but not the only basis for the decision. The key is likely to be the strategic goals for UME and where the Business School fits within that overall plan. Most university business schools would expect to be involved in the in-company market as it is seen as a way of 'freeing' the university from reliance on (reduced) public funding.

Answers to review questions

RQ 10.1

Apart from the financial implications of any decision, other factors that may have an impact on the final decision outcome include:

- *Environmental* – for example, the impact of building a new road on wildlife and the countryside.
- *Employment* – it may be politically unacceptable for a public body to make redundancies within an area of high unemployment.
- *Personal* – in a takeover 'battle' or a newspaper price 'war', the main wealthy players involved may be prepared to suffer financial losses in order to gain ownership of other treasured companies.
- *Political* – the closing of coal mines in the 1980s was, some commentators suggested, driven in part by a political agenda as much as by the economics of mining coal.

RQ 10.2

Both payback and NPV are based upon the relevant cash flows expected to arise from a decision.

Payback calculates the approximate time that it takes to recover the initial investment (e.g 3.5 years' payback period) and ignores any cash flows that occur after that point.

NPV applies a discount rate to the future cash flows, effectively allowing for the opportunity cost of money (known as the cost of capital in the case of companies). Thus cash received in the future has a lower (discounted) value as the business, in waiting for the cash, loses the earnings that could have been gained on that money had it been received earlier.

NPV is said to align with the goal of shareholder wealth maximisation; in theory, a positive NPV means that the decision will raise the value of the business.

In summary, while payback is relatively simple, it ignores the fact that cash flows occur in different time periods. NPV attempts to recognise that fact.

Answer notes to numerical problems

NP 10.1 JRC Cars

1. Financial analysis of the two projects

Robotics (relevant cash flows)

			£000
Year	Labour costs (see below)	Materials (see below)	Total relevant cash flows
1	40	10	50
2	50	10	60
3	50	10	60

Labour = £10 × 80 × 50 = £40 000 (Year 1)
= 10 × 100 × 50 = £50 000 (Years 2 and 3)

Material = 200 × 50 = £10 000

Project comparison (£000)

Year	XR9			Robotics		
	RCF	Factor (20%)	NPV	RCF	Factor (20%)	NPV
0	(200)	1	(200)	(70)	1.	(70)
1	50	0.833	41.65	50	0.833	41.65
2	90	0.694	62.46	60	0.694	41.64
3	90	0.579	52.11	60	0.579	34.74
4	60	0.482	28.92			
5	60	0.402	24.12			
		Total NPV	9.26		Total NPV	48.03

Payback periods (approximate)

2.69 years   1.33 years

2. NPV of XR9 if there are no cash flows in years 4 & 5
= 9.26 − (28.92 + 24.12) = −43.78 (i.e. a large negative NPV)

3. Comments and discussion could include:

Robotics clearly offers a better return *plus* it involves less risk; the cash flows are easier to predict than for XR9. Both projects shows positive NPVs, therefore it may be possible to do both unless cash is rationed. Alternatively, one project could be deferred until cash became available. For strategic reasons it may be that the XR9 *must* be done to stay in line with competition.

Answer to review questions

RQ 11.1

This situation arises due to the separation of ownership and control via the dispersed share ownership across a wide number of shareholders, none of whom individually has the power to impose their individual wishes upon the directors.

The way in which this problem is remedied is by trying to ensure that there are systems in place which control how the directors might try to consume the assets of the business for their own use. In addition, the directors' terms of remuneration are aligned to the longer-term growth preferences of the shareholders. This is done by having performance targets which look to long-term growth set as part of the directors long-term incentive plans.

RQ 11.2

NEDs perform two roles. One is to bring their particular expertise to the decision-making process at board level. The other is to monitor the activities of the directors and to serve on the committees which form the backbone of the company's corporate governance system, e.g. audit and remuneration committees.

RQ 11.3

The external auditors are appointed by the board of directors on behalf of the shareholders. The auditors report to the directors but in addition they issue a report to the shareholders on the validity of the accounting statements. They are assisted in their work by the existence of the internal auditors and the independent work of the audit committee who are responsible for ensuring that the company's internal control procedures are robust.

Glossary

accept or reject decision (p.31) a decision in which it is only possible to accept or reject an option.

Accounting Quadrant (p.47) a simple learning device for illustrating the basic principles upon which transactions are recorded and processed within the accounting system, and upon which the main financial statements are based.

Accounting Standards Board (ASB) (p.92) the ASB is the body that produces UK Financial Reporting Standards (FRS).

accrual (p.78) a liability, which shows that the business has already benefited from goods/services that have not yet been paid for, e.g. a telephone bill outstanding at the end of an accounting year.

allocation of fixed costs (p.36) sometimes called overhead recovery, these techniques allow allocation or 'recovery' of some amount of fixed costs within the cost of the product or service.

asset (p.48) a resource that a business owns or has a right to use.

asset turnover ratio (p.130) measures the efficiency with which assets have been used to generate sales.

audit (p.3) the statutory checking of financial records and statements by an auditor.

audit committee (p.230) oversees the relationship between the board and the internal and external auditors.

auditor's report (p.95) a formal statement in the company's annual report by its auditors on whether the accounts show a true and fair view (q.v.).

balance sheet (p.50) the financial statement that gives a snapshot of the assets and liabilities of a business at a particular point in time.

balance sheet gearing ratio (p.136) measures the proportion of debt to equity capital used by a business.

'best or worst' analysis (p.38) within decision analysis, an attempt to calculate the best and worst outcomes in order to provide the decision-maker with a sense of risk.

bookkeeping (p.68) the process of recording financial transactions in a systematic manner.

books of account (p.46) records of the financial transactions that have been undertaken by the business.

'bottom line' (p.58) the profit or loss figure displayed at the bottom of the profit and loss account (q.v.).

bottom-up budget (p.166) a budget set by involving of all levels of management.

break-even chart (p.15) a graphical representation of costs against revenues for an activity, to determine when break-even point (q.v.) is reached.

break-even point (p.12) the level of activity at which revenues exactly equal costs and neither profit nor loss is made.

budget process (p.158) a process that includes the preparation of budgets and the monitoring of actual performance against those budgets.

budgetary control (p.158) the use of budgets as a control on the activities of all areas of the business. Control is achieved through the monitoring of actual performance against agreed budgets.

budgeting (p.157) financial planning which reflects the impact of strategic and project plans over the short term (usually a period of one year). Budgets normally include financial projections for revenues, expenses, assets, liabilities and sources of finance.

budgets (p.156) organisational plans that are quantified in financial terms. Normally the budgets cover a period at least 12 months ahead.

business plan (p.156) an overall review of the strategy and plans for the business, including key targets and financial budgets.

capital expenditure (p.2) expenditure on fixed assets.

capital expenditure budget (p.163) the budgeted spend on fixed assets during the budget period.

carrying value (p.113) the amount at which an asset is shown in the accounts – this may have been subject to revaluation, devaluation and/or depreciation since the asset was first acquired.

cash budget (p.170) a detailed budget showing expected flows of cash in to and out of the bank account during the budget period.

cash-flow budget (p.170) an overall view of the business's cash flows – essentially a statement of changes between two balance sheets (q.v.). This budget indicates the total anticipated change to working capital and cash balances during the budget period.

cash-flow cycle (p.106) a representation of how cash is used in the operations of the business.

cash-flow statement (CFS) (p.50) a financial statement which gives a complementary view to the profit and loss account (q.v.) in explaining what has happened in terms of cash flows in and out of the business during the accounting period.

chairman's statement (p.116) a non-statutory address to shareholders by a company's chairman included with the annual report.

chairperson (p.230) senior director who acts as the chairperson of the board.

chief executive (p.230) senior executive director who directs the company on a day-to-day basis.

closing stock (p.73) the total stock held by the business at the end of the financial period.

comparability (p.97) the feature of accounting information which allows a user to compare between companies and between accounting periods within an organisation because the same principles and policies have been used in preparing the information.

concepts (p.96) general rules that people have agreed to abide by.

consolidated accounts (p.116) the annual report produced by a parent company giving the overview for a group of commonly owned companies.

contribution (p.11) the amount left over from revenues (after paying all variable costs) which 'contributes' towards paying for the fixed costs and giving the business a profit.

corporate (p.17) relating to a company or business activity.

corporate governance (p.229) controlling the direction of the activities of businesses to make them more accountable to a broader constituency than shareholders (q.v.) alone.

cost behaviour (p.10) the set of techniques and concepts that attempt to explain how business costs relate to levels of activity.

cost of capital (p.202) the overall opportunity cost of money for a business, weighted according to the various sources of funds used.

cost of goods sold (p.50) the input or purchase price of items sold during one accounting period.

cost-volume-profit (CVP) analysis (p.15) the graphical representation of costs, revenues, and profit levels (dependent variables) against activity or output (independent variable).

credit (p.57) in double-entry bookkeeping an entry on the right-hand side of the ledger, recording income or liabilities.

creditor turnover (p.134) measures how many days on average a business takes to receive funds from its creditors.

creditors (p.50) businesses or persons who supply the business with goods on credit terms; usually payable one month after delivery – in short, people or businesses to whom the business owes money.

current ratio (p1.31) a liquidity ratio – the ratio of current assets to current liabilities. It measures how easily a firm is able to meet its short-term financial obligations or in other words the extent of working capital held within a business.

debit (p.57) in double-entry bookkeeping an entry on the left-hand side of the ledger, assets or expenses (q.v.).

debtor turnover (p.133) measures how many days on average the business takes to collect money owing from its debtors.

debtors (p.52) persons or businesses to whom we sell goods on credit, i.e. people or businesses who owe money to the business.

decision analysis (p.28) the process of analysis that demonstrates the impact of a decision on the organisation.

decision usefulness (p.1) the extent to which a piece of financial information is used by users in making informed financial decisions.

deficit (p.50) the result when expenses are greater than revenues.

dependent variable (p.13) used within this book to describe the variable costs and revenues that will change according to changes in a measure of activity (the independent variable).

depreciation (p.57) the fall in the value of a fixed asset due to use.

directors (p.68) the senior managers involved in making policy and executive decisions about running the business. They may also be part-owners of the business or they may simply be employees who are responsible for reporting to the owners how they have managed the business.

directors' report (p.114) a part of the annual report which is a statement of various factual matters by the directors, largely in fulfilment of their obligations under the Companies Acts.

discounted cash flows (p.204) future cash flows that have been reduced (discounted) to allow for the time that will elapse before they are received.

dividend per share (p.138) the amount of earnings per share declared as a dividend to the shareholders – a ratio of total dividend divided by the number of shares issued.

dividend yield ratio (p.139) the earnings per share expressed as a ratio of the share's market value.

dividends (p.50) payments to shareholders of the business from profits made, usually yearly or twice yearly.

earnings per share (p.138) the amount of profit after tax attributable to one share.

economic decisions (p.123) decisions for shareholders which involve the investment of funds in businesses.

equity (p.65) finance provided by shareholders, sometimes known as share capital (*q.v.*).

Exchequer (p.62) the government's finance department.

executives (p.229) board members who also work full time for the company.

expenses (p.41) resources used up in running the business, which might include rents, cost of goods sold, wages, energy costs, etc.

finance (p.91) the funding of a business – this may come from shareholders (equity or share capital), from various forms of borrowing (debt finance) or from past profits retained within the business (reserves).

financial accounting (p.46) recording and reporting of financial information to meet the external information needs of shareholders and other interested parties external to the business.

financial reporting standards (FRSs) (p.95) FRSs are the current non-statutory regulations by which UK professional accounting bodies state what is best practice in financial reporting.

financial year (p.50) for many companies the financial year will end on either 31 December or 31 March – the date to which they regularly prepare their accounts.

finished goods (p.74) fully completed goods, manufactured by the organisation but not yet sold. These form part of the asset called stock.

First In First Out (FIFO) (p.75) when a business makes lots of purchases of similar stocks this is a way of valuing stocks held at the end of the period. FIFO assumes that stocks are used in rotation so that the oldest stock (first in) is used first (first out) and so that what is left is valued at the most recent purchase price(s).

fixed assets (p.53) assets held by the business for more than one accounting year – they are used

to create wealth for the business but are not for resale.

fixed costs (p.158) costs which tend to remain the same even though output may change. Fixed costs remain (generally) unchanged in total, but fixed costs per unit reduce as output rises because the same level of fixed costs are spread across more units.

flexed budget (p.176) the budgeted costs that should have been incurred based on a budget adjusted to actual output achieved.

flexing the budget (p.176) revising the budget in line with actual levels of output prior to calculating variances. Flexing allows for a comparison of like-with-like costs.

FTSE 100 index or 'footsie' (p.48) the *Financial Times* Stock Exchange 100 index is a list of the top 100 companies quoted on the Stock Exchange, by market capitalisation. It is an index (i.e. a relative measure) that rises and falls according to the average share price movements of its constituent 100 companies.

future incremental cash flows (p.28) an alternative term for relevant cash flows: 'future' because past flows cannot be changed by future decisions, 'incremental' because we are only concerned with the extra cash flows generated by the decision.

gearing (p.135) the degree by which the firm has been financed by debt relative to equity. A highly geared firm has a higher proportion of debt to equity finance. It may be in a vulnerable position if it is unable to make regular interest payments to the suppliers of the debt.

graphic analysis (p.12) graphs can often be used to illustrate the relationship between activity levels, costs, revenues and profits.

gross margin/gross profit margin (p.128) gross profit expressed as a percentage of sales revenue.

gross profit (p.63) the difference between the cost that goods are bought for, and their selling price.

historic cost (p.90) the original cost, or cost at the time that a transaction first took place – this may be quite different from what a good or service might cost at current prices.

holding company (p.116) also known as a parent company – a company which has control over subsidiary companies.

income statement (p.50) representation of a business's gain or loss over a period which makes an effort to explain the sources of earnings and the main areas of expenditure incurred. Also known as profit and loss account (*q.v.*).

independent variable (p.13) used within the text to describe measures of activity (e.g. sales, production). The dependent variables (e.g. costs and revenues) are expected to change in response to changes in the independent variable.

insolvency (p.145) when the business owns assets but does not have sufficient cash to meet immediate financial obligations.

interest (p.60) the cost to the business of using debt finance – normally calculated by taking a fixed percentage of the capital sum borrowed.

interest cover (p.136) measures how many times the business could have paid interest charges from the 'profit before interest' figure.

internal control (p.230) system of checks and balances designed to minimise fraud and sudden bankruptcy or insolvency within a business.

internal rate of return (IRR) (p.207) the cost of capital for any decision, which if applied would yield a net present value (*q.v.*) of zero.

International accounting standards (IASs) (p.95) IASs are the international pronouncements on best practice in financial reporting. Still used as a general term for international standards rather than national standards, the official name of the standards was changed in 2003 to IFRSs.

International Accounting Standards Board (IASB) (p.95) the IASB is the body that sets international accounting standards.

International financial reporting standards (IFRSs) (p.96) IFRSs is the current name for the international accounting standards produced by the IASB.

Last In First Out (LIFO) (p.76) when a business makes lots of purchases of similar stocks this is a way of valuing stocks held at the end of the period. For the purpose of valuing the stock on hand at the year end it assumes that the most recently purchased stocks (last in) are used first (first out) so that the oldest stock is what remains. In a time of inflation the effect might be to use outdated prices to value stock.

liabilities (p.50) amounts owed to others by the business – for example creditors, loans and owners' funds.

limited company (p.59) a legal entity created to run a business. Its owners' liabilities are limited to the amount they paid for their shares. See also public limited company.

limiting factor (p.31) the factor (e.g. sales, finance, scarce materials) that limits the activity of the organisation.

linearity assumption (p.175) within standard costing it is assumed that costs can be distinguished between variable and fixed elements, and hence can be drawn as a straight line on a graph.

liquidity (p.130) the amount of working capital held in resources which are cash or which are readily convertible to cash.

long-term decisions (p.37) a relative term, but generally within financial analysis regarded as decisions whose outcomes have an impact over more than one year. See also short-term decisions.

long-term incentive plans (p.234) a particular mix of remuneration designed to make directors perform over a longer time scale.

long-term loan (p.65) borrowing by the firm not due to be repaid for at least one year.

management accounting (p.4) the use of accounting information to meet the business's internal management needs.

margin of safety (p.15) the difference between the activity level at which break-even is achieved and the expected level of activity. Often expressed as a percentage of the expected level of activity.

marginal cost (p.16) the cost at the margin, or the cost of making and selling one extra unit. Will often (although not always) equate to the variable cost per unit.

mark up (p.11) the amount (or percentage) added by a retailer to the cost of goods in arriving at the selling price.

market capitalisation (p.48) market capitalisation or value is the economic value of monetary and other assets owned by the business.

master budgets (p.163) the 'top' layer of budget statements, including profit and loss budget, balance sheet budget, cash budget and cash-flow budget.

materiality (p.97) the threshold criteria set by the ASB (*q.v.*) for deciding if information is useful. Materiality means information must be of enough significance to affect the user's decision.

multinational conglomerates (p.97) a group of companies which are based in different countries and trade across national boundaries.

net assets (p.65) the net (total assets less total liabilities) assets represent the book value of the business.

net present value (NPV) (p.200) the equivalent present value of future cash flows taking into account the time value of money (*q.v.*) – i.e. future cash flows are less valuable than those received immediately.

net profit (p.58) the net excess of revenues over expenditure.

net profit to sales ratio (p.129) the ratio of net profit earned to the level of sales.

net realisable value (p.77) the net amount the business would receive if they were to sell the stock at its current market value excluding any costs of selling and distributing.

non-executive director (p.229) a part-time board member who is independent and does not work full time for the company.

opening stock (p.73) the total stock held by the organisation at the start of the financial period.

operating activities (p.110) the normal business transactions, as opposed to those which occur very rarely and not in the normal course of business.

operating budgets (p.164) a general term covering all cost budgets for departments, functions and sections of the business. Operating budgets are used to monitor managers' expenditure.

opportunity cost of money (p.202) money received in the future is less valuable than money received immediately, as the investor has been unable to invest that money in the intervening period.

opportunity costs (p.28) benefits sacrificed by choosing one alternative over another.

organisational goals (p.214) the strategic aims of the business, e.g. to maximise profit or to be the biggest in terms of sales or employees.

overhead recovery (p.36) the accounting technique that allocates (or recovers) fixed costs to products or services. Also known as allocation of fixed costs (q.v.).

paralysis-by-analysis (p.212) term used by some business commentators to describe an over-obsession with financial number-crunching at the expense of more qualitative analysis.

parent company (p.116) owner of one or more subsidiary companies, obliged to prepare consolidated accounts. Also known as a holding company (q.v.).

payback (p.200) technique that calculates how long it takes for an investment outlay to be recovered.

postulate (p.96) a truth which is not readily verifiable but is generally agreed.

prepayment (p.78) an asset which shows that expenditure that has already taken place was actually payment in advance for goods or services that will not be benefited from until a future accounting period. For example, where an insurance premium has been paid for a period that straddles one accounting period and the next, the prepayment is the part that relates to next year.

present value (p.203) a shortened form of the term net present value (q.v.).

price/earnings ratio (P/E ratio) (p.140) an investment ratio which relates market value of a share to earnings per share.

pricing theories (p.17) theories attempting to explain how organisations arrive at selling prices for products and services, including accounting, economic and behavioural theories.

principal budget factor (p.165) another term for 'limiting factor' or the main constraining factor on the budget during the budget period. Examples include demand for goods or services, finance, scarce labour or materials.

principle (p.96) a rule that has been empirically proven over time.

products and services (p.8) all firms provide a service or a tangible product to customers. Examples include food and drink, computers, entertainment, newspapers, educational courses, books, travel, clothes and cars.

profit and loss account (p.50) the financial statement that gives a view of the accumulated revenues earned less expenses incurred by a business over a period of time, usually one year.

profitability (p.125) the measure of financial success when revenues exceed expenses.

public limited company (plc) (p.58) a company permitted to issue shares to the general public and also to have its shares quoted on a stock exchange. An advantage of this is the extra finance made available for investment by the company.

published accounts (p.69) the package of publicly available information about a business, including the financial statements.

purchases (p.75) term that specifically identifies the total amount of goods/services bought for resale by the business during the accounting period (an element of cost of sales).

quick ratio (p.131) the ratio of current assets (minus stock) to current liabilities. Measures the extent of working capital available to meet short-term debts. Also known as the acid-test ratio.

ranking decision (p.31) decision that involves ranking of alternatives from best to worst.

raw materials (p.74) basic ingredients which the organisation incorporates into its finished product.

realised profits and losses (p.113) profits and losses from completed transactions which are gathered in the profit and loss account.

relevance (p.97) to be useful, information must be relevant to the decision-making needs of a particular user.

relevant cash flows (p.28) the cash flows that will be changed because of a particular course of action or decision.

relevant range (p.15) the levels of activity between which the firm would normally expect to operate.

reliablity (p.97) to be useful, information must be reliable. The user must have confidence in how it has been produced.

remuneration committee (p.230) committee that oversees the terms and conditions of remuneration offered to directors.

resolution (p.233) an item on the agenda of the annual meeting of shareholders.

retail business (p.53) business which does not manufacture but buys and sells goods on at a higher price than purchased.

retained profits (p.61) profits left over after paying out dividends and tax. Retained profits enable the company to expand.

return on capital employed (ROCE) (p.127) a profitability ratio – the ratio of profit earned before interest and tax to long-term capital, i.e. funds provided by shareholders and debt providers.

return on equity (p.125) a profitability ratio – the ratio of profit earned before tax to shareholders' funds.

revaluation (p.84) a voluntary adjustment to the value of an asset or liability in the accounts to show the item at a value that more accurately reflects current worth.

revenue (p.11) the value of sales of goods and services.

revenue recognition (p.68) 'recognition' in this context means putting something in the accounts for the first time, so 'recognising revenue' means deciding when to include revenue earned in the profit and loss account.

semi-variable costs (p.20) costs that have both a variable element and a fixed element.

services and products (p.9) all firms provide a service or a tangible product to customers. Examples include food and drink, computers, entertainment, newspapers, educational courses, books, travel, clothes, cars.

share capital (p.65) funds provided by the owners of the business.

share option (p.232) a contract which allows a person to buy shares at some time in the future at a particular price.

shareholder (p.46) person who has made a financial investment in a business – a part owner.

shareholders' funds (p.59) the total investment made by the owners directly via shares and indirectly by retained profits.

short-term decisions (p.37) a relative term but generally within financial analysis regarded as those decisions whose outcomes can be measured within one year. See also long-term decisions.

social role of accounting information (p.2) is when accounting information is used as the basis for the allocation of scarce resources throughout society.

standard cost (p.175) the budgeted cost of one unit of product or service.

standard costing (p.175) traditional name for the approach to record keeping that uses standard costs as a way of setting budgets.

statement of historical cost profits and losses (p.113) a secondary financial statement which highlights what the results would have been if there had been no revaluation of assets by the business.

statement of total recognised gains and losses (p.113) a financial statement which gives a wider view than the profit and loss account, in that it also includes unrealised gains and losses for the same period.

statements of standard accounting practice (SSAPs) (p.95) SSAPs were the original voluntary regulation documents by which UK professional accounting bodies strove to impose consistency on elements of financial reporting. Some SSAPs still exist but they are gradually being replaced by financial reporting standards (q.v.).

statutory (p.91) legal, or required by law.

stepped fixed costs (p.20) costs that are fixed within a range of activity, but which rise by some additional amount when a new level of activity is reached.

stewardship (p.46) the managers of the business are stewards who look after the owners' investment in the business.

Stock Market (p.69) the physical or virtual space where trading in new or second-hand company shares takes place. Also known as Stock Exchange.

stock turnover (p.132) measures how many times in one year stock has been replenished.

stock (p.52) current asset – either raw materials or finished goods held for resale to the business's customers.

subsidiary (p.116) a company that is controlled by another company. Usually this is established by the number of shares that are owned, but it may be determined by rights to sit on the board, etc.

sunk costs (p.30) costs that have already been incurred and therefore will not be changed whatever business decision is taken in the future.

suppliers (p.50) people who provide a business with stock, often on credit.

surplus (p.63) what is left after deducting both cash and non-cash expenses from the gross profit to give the level of profits.

tax (p.50) charge made by governments on businesses (usually related to profit) and individuals (often related to income).

time value of money (TVoM) (p.201) describes the opportunity cost of money, based on the idea that money received in the future is less valuable than money received immediately.

top-down budgets (p.166) budgets that are, primarily, set by the higher levels of management. Implies little involvement of lower levels of management in the budget-setting process.

transaction (p.46) financial economic exchange between firms and/or individuals.

true and fair view (p.50) term used by auditors to designate that accounts have been prepared following relevant regulations and making reasonable assumptions and judgements.

understandability (p.97) to be useful, information must be understandable to the reasonably well-informed user. A subjective statement but it affects the complexity of what can/should be provided.

unrealised profits and losses (p.113) profits and losses from transactions which are not necessarily complete and therefore cannot be included in the profit and loss account, such as revaluation of assets still owned by the business, but which will be included in the statement of total recognised gains and losses.

user view (p.1) people external to the business who will 'use' accounting information reported externally by the business.

value-free (p.2) means that the information process is completely free from bias and can present information on a 'clean' basis.

variable costs (p.158) costs which rise or fall in line with activity. Examples could be bought-in components, raw materials, power, and some forms of direct labour where labour is paid according to items produced.

variance analysis (p.173) technique in standard costing to calculate differences between expected and actual costs or revenues.

variances (p.173) used in accounting to refer to differences between budgets and actual performance levels.

wealth maximisation (p.213) it is sometimes assumed that companies are acting to maximise the wealth of the shareholder group. Although problematic, this assumption underpins much financial analysis.

weighted average cost (WAC) (p.77) when a business makes lots of purchases of similar stocks this is a way of valuing stocks held at the end of the period by the organisation. By averaging out the purchase price of all similar stocks purchased during the period, it gives an average price for items held at the end of the period.

what if? analysis (p.38) provides a means of further investigation into a decision by changing the variables to examine the impact of such changes on the decision outcome. Often carried out using spreadsheet software.

window dressing (p.230) accounting practices designed to present financial information in a legally correct but misleading form.

work in progress (p.74) unfinished goods in the course of manufacture, or services supplied by the organisation, at a point in time. These form part of the asset called stock.

working capital (p.65) funds invested in current assets, mainly stock, debtors and cash, that enable a business to operate on a daily basis.

working capital management (p.107) the process of ensuring that the business has enough cash available at the right times.

Appendix: Present value table

This table gives the present value of one payment received n years in the future discounted at $x\%$ per year, e.g. with a discount rate of 5 per cent a single payment of £1 in 5 years' time has a present value of £0.7835.

Years	1%	2%	3%	4%	5%	6%	7%	8%	9%	10%
1	0.9901	0.9804	0.9709	0.9615	0.9524	0.9434	0.9346	0.9259	0.9174	0.9091
2	0.9803	0.9612	0.9426	0.9426	0.9070	0.8900	0.8734	0.8573	0.8417	0.8264
3	0.9706	0.9423	0.9151	0.8890	0.8638	0.8396	0.8163	0.7938	0.7722	0.7513
4	0.9610	0.9238	0.8885	0.8548	0.8227	0.7921	0.7629	0.7350	0.7084	0.6830
5	0.9515	0.9057	0.8626	0.8219	0.7835	0.7473	0.7130	0.6806	0.6499	0.6209
6	0.9420	0.8880	0.8375	0.7903	0.7462	0.7050	0.6663	0.6302	0.5963	0.5645
7	0.9327	0.8706	0.8131	0.7599	0.7107	0.6651	0.6227	0.5835	0.5470	0.5132
8	0.9235	0.8535	0.7894	0.7307	0.6768	0.6274	0.5820	0.5403	0.5019	0.4665
9	0.9143	0.8368	0.7664	0.7026	0.6446	0.5919	0.5439	0.5002	0.4604	0.4241
10	0.9053	0.8203	0.7441	0.6756	0.6139	0.5584	0.5083	0.4632	0.4224	0.3855
11	0.8963	0.8043	0.7224	0.6496	0.5847	0.5268	0.4751	0.4289	0.3875	0.3505
12	0.8874	0.7885	0.7014	0.6246	0.5568	0.4970	0.4440	0.3971	0.3555	0.3186
13	0.8787	0.7730	0.6810	0.6006	0.5303	0.4688	0.4150	0.3677	0.3262	0.2897
14	0.8700	0.7579	0.6611	0.5775	0.5051	0.4423	0.3878	0.3405	0.2992	0.2633
15	0.8613	0.7430	0.6419	0.5553	0.4810	0.4173	0.3624	0.3152	0.2745	0.2394
16	0.8528	0.7284	0.6232	0.5339	0.4581	0.3936	0.3387	0.2919	0.2519	0.2176
17	0.8444	0.7142	0.6050	0.5134	0.4363	0.3714	0.3166	0.2703	0.2311	0.1978
18	0.8360	0.7002	0.5874	0.4936	0.4155	0.3503	0.2959	0.2502	0.2120	0.1799
19	0.8277	0.6864	0.5703	0.4746	0.3957	0.3305	0.2765	0.2317	0.1945	0.1635
20	0.8195	0.6730	0.5537	0.4564	0.3769	0.3118	0.2584	0.2145	0.1784	0.1486
21	0.8114	0.6598	0.5375	0.4388	0.3589	0.2942	0.2415	0.1987	0.1637	0.1351
22	0.8034	0.6468	0.5219	0.4220	0.3418	0.2775	0.2257	0.1839	0.1502	0.1228
23	0.7954	0.6342	0.5067	0.4057	0.3256	0.2618	0.2109	0.1703	0.1378	0.1117
24	0.7876	0.6217	0.4919	0.3901	0.3101	0.2470	0.1971	0.1577	0.1264	0.1015
25	0.7798	0.6095	0.4776	0.3751	0.2953	0.2330	0.1842	0.1460	0.1160	0.0923
26	0.7720	0.5976	0.4637	0.3607	0.2812	0.2198	0.1722	0.1352	0.1064	0.0839
27	0.7644	0.5859	0.4502	0.3468	0.2678	0.2074	0.1609	0.1252	0.0976	0.0763
28	0.7568	0.5744	0.4371	0.3335	0.2551	0.1956	0.1504	0.1159	0.0895	0.0693
29	0.7493	0.5631	0.4243	0.3207	0.2429	0.1846	0.1406	0.1073	0.0822	0.0630
30	0.7419	0.5521	0.4120	0.3083	0.2314	0.1741	0.1314	0.0094	0.0754	0.0573
35	0.7059	0.5000	0.3554	0.2534	0.1813	0.1301	0.0937	0.0676	0.0490	0.0356
40	0.6717	0.4529	0.3066	0.2083	0.1420	0.0972	0.0668	0.0460	0.0318	0.0221
45	0.6391	0.4102	0.2644	0.1712	0.1113	0.0727	0.0476	0.0313	0.0207	0.0137
50	0.6080	0.3715	0.2281	0.1407	0.0872	0.0543	0.0339	0.0213	0.0134	0.0085

Years	11%	12%	13%	14%	15%	16%	17%	18%	19%	20%
1	0.9009	0.8929	0.8850	0.8772	0.8696	0.8621	0.8547	0.8475	0.8403	0.8333
2	0.8116	0.7972	0.7831	0.7695	0.7561	0.7432	0.7305	0.7182	0.7062	0.6944
3	0.7312	0.7118	0.6931	0.6750	0.6575	0.6407	0.6244	0.6086	0.5934	0.5787
4	0.6587	0.6355	0.6133	0.5921	0.5718	0.5523	0.5337	0.5158	0.4987	0.4823
5	0.5935	0.5674	0.5428	0.5194	0.4972	0.4761	0.4561	0.4371	0.4190	0.4019
6	0.5346	0.5066	0.4803	0.4556	0.4323	0.4104	0.3898	0.3704	0.3521	0.3349
7	0.4817	0.4523	0.4251	0.3996	0.3759	0.3538	0.3332	0.3139	0.2959	0.2791
8	0.4339	0.4039	0.3762	0.3506	0.3269	0.3050	0.2848	0.2660	0.2487	0.2326
9	0.3909	0.3606	0.3329	0.3075	0.2843	0.2630	0.2434	0.2255	0.2090	0.1938
10	0.3522	0.3220	0.2946	0.2697	0.2472	0.2267	0.2080	0.1911	0.1756	0.1615
11	0.3173	0.2875	0.2607	0.2366	0.2149	0.1954	0.1778	0.1619	0.1476	0.1346
12	0.2858	0.2567	0.2307	0.2076	0.1869	0.1685	0.1520	0.1372	0.1240	0.1122
13	0.2575	0.2292	0.2042	0.1821	0.1625	0.1452	0.1299	0.1163	0.1042	0.0935
14	0.2320	0.2046	0.1807	0.1597	0.1413	0.1252	0.1110	0.0985	0.0876	0.0779
15	0.2090	0.1827	0.1599	0.1401	0.1229	0.1079	0.0949	0.0835	0.0736	0.0649
16	0.1883	0.1631	0.1415	0.1229	0.1069	0.0930	0.0811	0.0708	0.0618	0.0541
17	0.1696	0.1456	0.1252	0.1078	0.0929	0.0802	0.0693	0.0600	0.0520	0.0451
18	0.1528	0.1300	0.1108	0.0946	0.0808	0.0691	0.0592	0.0508	0.0437	0.0376
19	0.1377	0.1161	0.0981	0.0829	0.0703	0.0596	0.0506	0.0431	0.0367	0.0313
20	0.1240	0.1037	0.0868	0.0728	0.0611	0.0514	0.0433	0.0365	0.0308	0.0261
21	0.1117	0.0926	0.0768	0.0638	0.0531	0.0443	0.0370	0.0309	0.0259	0.0217
22	0.1007	0.0826	0.0680	0.0560	0.0462	0.0382	0.0316	0.0262	0.0218	0.0181
23	0.0907	0.0738	0.0601	0.0491	0.0402	0.0329	0.0270	0.0222	0.0183	0.0151
24	0.0817	0.0659	0.0532	0.0431	0.0349	0.0284	0.0231	0.0188	0.0154	0.0126
25	0.0736	0.0588	0.0471	0.0378	0.0304	0.0245	0.0197	0.0160	0.0129	0.0105
26	0.0663	0.0525	0.0417	0.0331	0.0264	0.0211	0.0169	0.0135	0.0109	0.0087
27	0.0597	0.0469	0.0369	0.0291	0.0230	0.0182	0.0144	0.0115	0.0091	0.0073
28	0.0538	0.0419	0.0326	0.0255	0.0200	0.0157	0.0123	0.0097	0.0077	0.0061
29	0.0485	0.0374	0.0289	0.0224	0.0174	0.0135	0.0105	0.0082	0.0064	0.0051
30	0.0437	0.0334	0.0256	0.0196	0.0151	0.0116	0.0090	0.0070	0.0054	0.0042
35	0.0259	0.0189	0.0139	0.0102	0.0075	0.0055	0.0041	0.0030	0.0023	0.0017
40	0.0154	0.0107	0.0075	0.0053	0.0037	0.0026	0.0019	0.0013	0.0010	0.0007
45	0.0091	0.0061	0.0041	0.0027	0.0019	0.0013	0.0009	0.0006	0.0004	0.0003
50	0.0054	0.0035	0.0022	0.0014	0.0009	0.0006	0.0004	0.0003	0.0002	0.0001

Years	21%	22%	23%	24%	25%
1	0.8264	0.8197	0.8130	0.8065	0.8000
2	0.6830	0.6719	0.6610	0.6504	0.6400
3	0.5645	0.5507	0.5374	0.5245	0.5120
4	0.4665	0.4514	0.4369	0.4230	0.4096
5	0.3855	0.3700	0.3552	0.3411	0.3277
6	0.3186	0.3033	0.2888	0.2751	0.2621
7	0.2633	0.2486	0.2348	0.2218	0.2097
8	0.2176	0.2038	0.1909	0.1789	0.1678
9	0.1799	0.1670	0.1552	0.1443	0.1342
10	0.1486	0.1369	0.1262	0.1164	0.1074
11	0.1228	0.1122	0.1026	0.0938	0.0859
12	0.1015	0.0920	0.0834	0.0757	0.0687
13	0.0839	0.0754	0.0678	0.0610	0.0550
14	0.0693	0.0618	0.0551	0.0492	0.0440
15	0.0573	0.0507	0.0448	0.0397	0.0352
16	0.0474	0.0415	0.0364	0.0320	0.0281
17	0.0391	0.0340	0.0296	0.0258	0.0225
18	0.0323	0.0279	0.0241	0.0208	0.0180
19	0.0267	0.0229	0.0196	0.0168	0.0144
20	0.0221	0.0187	0.0159	0.0135	0.0115
21	0.0183	0.0154	0.0129	0.0109	0.0092
22	0.0151	0.0126	0.0105	0.0088	0.0074
23	0.0125	0.0103	0.0086	0.0071	0.0059
24	0.0103	0.0085	0.0070	0.0057	0.0047
25	0.0085	0.0069	0.0057	0.0046	0.0038
26	0.0070	0.0057	0.0046	0.0037	0.0030
27	0.0058	0.0047	0.0037	0.0030	0.0024
28	0.0048	0.0038	0.0030	0.0024	0.0019
29	0.0040	0.0031	0.0025	0.0020	0.0015
30	0.0033	0.0026	0.0020	0.0016	0.0012
35	0.0013	0.0009	0.0007	0.0005	0.0004
40	0.0005	0.0004	0.0003	0.0002	0.0001
45	0.0002	0.0001	0.0001	0.0001	
50	0.0001				

Index

accountants, defining 1–2
accounting
  criticisms 3
  defining 2
  scope 3
accounting bodies, UK and
    Ireland 95, 105
  see also Accounting Standards
    Board
Accounting Quadrant
  accounting reports/ reporting
    51–61
  double-entry bookkeeping 57
  duality concept 99
  insurance expense 78–9
  prepayments 78–9
  reflections 57–61
accounting reports/reporting
    46–67
  Accounting Quadrant 51–61
  Accounting Standards Board 92
  format 62–5
  interpreting accounting
    statements 123–54
  money measurement 47–9,
    70–1, 91
  objective 92
  recording financial transactions
    47
  reporting financial transactions
    47
  users 91–3, 96–100
  see also financial
    reports/reporting
accounting standards 95–6
  see also corporate governance;
    legal issues; regulations
Accounting Standards Board
    (ASB)
  accounting reports/reporting 92
  concepts, accounting 98
  regulations 105
accruals concept 98
  accruals-based profit 98
  cash-based profit 98
  expenses 77–9

matching expenses 72
airlines 215
ASB see Accounting Standards
    Board
asset turnover ratio 130
assets
  Accounting Quadrant 51–61
  budgets/budgeting 162–3
  current 64
  defining 52
  fixed 64, 72–3
  net 65
audit 3
audit committees
  corporate governance 230,
    236–7
  NEDs 236–7
auditors' report 95, 114–15

balance sheet gearing 136–7
balance sheets 69
  Accounting Quadrant 51–61
  depreciation 73, 84–5
  reflections 62
  revaluations 84–5
  worksheet: corporate reports
    103–4
benchmarking, budgets/budgeting
    172
best or worst analysis
  decisions/decision-
    making 38
  long-term decisions/decision-
    making 211
break-even 12, 15
budgets/budgeting 155–94
  assets 162–3
  benchmarking 172
  capital expenditure budgets
    166–7
  case study 187–94
  cash budgeting 169–70
  control 172
  coordination 172
  cost budgeting 167–8

decisions/decision-making
    172
  environment review 164
  financial predictions 157–62
  fixed costs 158–62, 189
  flexing the budget 175–7
  furniture 174
  getting right 171
  liabilities 162–3
  linearity 175–9
  market stall 174–5
  master budgets 170–1
  operating cost budgets 167–8
  opportunities review 165
  PBFs 165
  personal budgets 156–7
  planning 171
  printing/publishing 167–8
  problems review 165
  process 158, 163–71
  reasons 171–2
  sales budgets 165–6
  standard costing 175–81
  targets 172
  variable costs 158–62
budgets/budgeting cont.
  variance analysis 175–81
  variances 173–5
  working capital 189–91

Cadbury Report, corporate
    governance 229–31
capital, cost of see cost of capital
capital expenditure 2
  budgets 166–7
capital maintenance 70
  depreciation 80
capital, working see working
    capital
case studies
  Blackthorn 187–94
  budgets/budgeting 187–94
  Countryside Dairies 42–5
  decisions/decision-making
    42–5

hotels 222–6
long-term decisions/decision-
    making 222–6
tourism 222–6
Zorbis Hotels 222–6
cash
    costs 145
    profits 146
cash budgeting 109, 169–70
cash-flow statements (CFSs)
    109–13
cash flows 28, 106–22
    case study 193–4
    cycle 106–9
    defining 28
    discounted cash flows 203–5
    expansion 145–6
    long-term decisions/decision-
        making 198–9, 201
    NPV 203–5
    predicting 201
    working capital 106–9
CFSs see cash-flow statements
chairpersons, corporate
    governance 230, 231
chief executives, corporate
    governance 230, 231
COGS see cost of goods sold
Companies Act (1985) 94–5
concepts, accounting
    terminology 96
    users and 96–100
consolidated accounts 116–17
contribution 11–12
control
    budgets/budgeting 172
    internal control, corporate
        governance 230
    long-term decisions/decision-
        making 200–1
coordination, budgets/budgeting
    172
corporate governance 227–39
    audit committees 230, 236–7
    Cadbury Report 229–31
    chairpersons 230, 231
    chief executives 230, 231
    defining 229
    development 229–30
    directors 227–8, 231–6
    effects 237–8
    emergence 228
    internal control 230
    Marconi 232–3
    NEDs 230, 231–2
    Railtrack 233

remuneration 230, 232–6
shareholders 227–8, 229,
    232–3
Smith Review 237
stakeholders 229
see also legal issues; regulations
corporate reports worksheet
    102–4
corporation tax 61–2
cost behaviour 10–26
cost budgeting 167–8
    case study 189
cost concept 99
cost of capital
    discount rate 209–10
    long-term decisions/decision-
        making 209–10
    personal 209
cost of goods sold (COGS) 73–4
cost of sales 73–4
cost-volume-profit analysis (CVP
    analysis) 15–16
costs
    cash 145
    fixed 10–11, 13–14, 15, 36–7,
        158–62
    full cost 16–17
    marginal cost 16–17
    pricing 17–19
    profitability 17–19
    semi-variable costs 20–1
    stepped fixed costs 20
    sunk costs 30
    variable 10–11, 13–14, 15,
        20–1, 158–62
    see also product costs
courses, business
    long-term decisions/decision-
        making 216–17
    product costs 216–17
creditor turn(over) 133–5
current assets 64
current liabilities 64
current ratio 130–1
CVP analysis see cost-volume-
    profit analysis

debtor turn(over) 133
decisions/decision-making 27–45
    accounting 18–19
    best or worst analysis 38
    budgets/budgeting 172
    case study 42–5
    financial reports/reporting
        51–61

long-term see long-term
    decisions/decision-making
managers' 27–45
pricing 17–19
short-term 37, 196–8
uncertainty 38, 198
what if? analysis 38, 211
dependent variables, graphic
    analysis 13–15
depreciation 79–85
    balance sheets 73, 84–5
    capital maintenance 80
    legal requirement 80
    methods 80–4
    rationale 79–80
    reducing balance 82–4
    revaluations 84–5
    stock 73
    straight line 81–2
    see also valuations
directors
    corporate governance 227–8,
        231–6
    remuneration 228, 232–6
    and shareholders 227–8
    see also non-executive directors
directors' report 114
discounted cash flows 203–5
dividend per share 138–9
dividend yield 139
double-entry bookkeeping
    Accounting Quadrant 57
    duality concept 99
duality concept 57, 99

earnings per share (EPS) 138
economics 70
entity concept 98–9
environment review,
    budgets/budgeting 164
EPS see earnings per share
equity 65
evaluating choices 200
evaluating performance, methods
    124
expansion, cash flows 145–6
expenses
    Accounting Quadrant 51–61
    accruals 77–9
    defining 52
    matching 72
    prepayments 77–9
feedback, long-term decisions/
    decision-making 200–1
FIFO see First In First Out

financial accounting 9
financial information, and markets 91
financial interactions, accounting 3
financial predictions, budgets/budgeting 157–62
Financial Reporting Review Panel (FRRP) 105
Financial Reporting Standards (FRSs) 95–6, 98
financial reports/reporting
    decisions/decision-making 51–61
    framework 90–105
    groups of companies 116–17
    legal issues 94–6
    published accounts 69, 91
    published accounts, contents 94–100
    published accounts, drawbacks 117
    worksheet: corporate reports 102–4
    see also accounting reports
financial views of a business 50–1
finished goods, stock 74–5
First In First Out (FIFO), stock valuations 75–7
fixed assets 64, 72–3
fixed costs 10–11
    allocating 36–7
    budgets/budgeting 158–62, 189
    case study 189
    graphic analysis 13–14, 15
    stepped fixed costs 20
flexing the budget 175–7
FlyCheap 215
Footsie see FTSE 100 index
FRRP see Financial Reporting Review Panel
FRSs see Financial Reporting Standards
FTSE 100 index 48–9
full cost 16–17
future accounting see budgets/budgeting

Garnier, Jean Paul 233
gearing ratios 135–7
    balance sheet gearing 136–7
    interest cover 136
glossary 287–93
goals, long-term

decisions/decision-making 213–14
going concern concept 98
governance, corporate see corporate governance
graphic analysis
    dependent variables 13–15
    independent variables 13–15
    product costs 12–15
Greenbury Report, remuneration 234
gross profit 63
gross profit margin 11–12, 128–9
groups of companies, financial reports/reporting 116–17

Hampel Report, remuneration 234
holding companies, financial reports/reporting 116–17
hotels
    case study 222–6
    Jackson Hotel 34–6
    Zorbis Hotels 222–6
Hutchings, Greg 228

IFRSs see international financial reporting standards
implementation, long-term decisions/decision-making 200
independent variables, graphic analysis 13–15
Industrial Revolution 4
information, non-financial 116
information revolution 4
insolvency 145
interactions, accounting information 3
interest cover 136
internal control, corporate governance 230
internal information see management accounting
internal rate of return (IRR)
    long-term decisions/decision-making 207–8
    NPV 207–8
international financial reporting standards (IFRSs) 95–6
interpreting accounting statements 123–54
interpreting ratios 132
investment ratios 137–43
    dividend per share 138–9

dividend yield 139
EPS 138
P/E ratio 140
IRR see internal rate of return

Last In First Out (LIFO), stock valuations 76–7
legal issues
    Companies Act (1985) 94–5
    depreciation 80
    financial reports/reporting 94–6
    FRSs 95–6
    interactions, accounting 3
    SSAPs 95–6
    see also corporate governance; regulations
liabilities
    Accounting Quadrant 51–61
    budgets/budgeting 162–3
    current 64
    defining 52
LIFO see Last In First Out
limited liability 3
limiting factors 31–2
linearity, budgets/budgeting 175–9
liquidity, CFSs 109–13
liquidity ratios 130–5
    creditor turn(over) 133–5
    current ratio 130–1
    debtor turn(over) 133
    quick ratio 131–2
    stock turn(over) 132–3
long-term decisions/decision-making 37, 195–226
    best or worst analysis 211
    broader context 212–13
    case study 222–6
    cash flows 198–9, 201
    choices evaluation 200
    control 200–1
    cost of capital 209–10
    feedback 200–1
    goals 213–14
    implementation 200
    IRR 207–8
    key features 198–9
    monitoring 200–1
    opportunities review 200
    payback 206
    personal 196
    product costs 214–17
    railways 197–8
    real companies 211–12

reversing decisions 199
screening 200
shareholders 213–14
stages 199–201
strategic direction 198
time scale 198
TVoM 202–5
uncertainty 198, 211
wealth maximisation 213–14
what if? analysis 211

management accounting 9, 91
managers' decisions 27–45
Marconi, corporate governance 232–3
margin of safety 15–16
marginal cost 16–17
mark-up 11–12
markets, and financial information 91
Marks and Spencer Group plc, auditors' report 114–15
master budgets 170–1
  case study 191–2
matching expenses *see* accruals concept
materiality, information 97
Maw, G.L. 229
money measurement 47–9, 70–1, 99
  flow measurement 48
monitoring, long-term decisions/decision-making 200–1

NEDs *see* non-executive directors
net assets 65
Net Present Value (NPV)
  cash flows 203–5
  IRR 207–8
net profit after tax 63
net profit before tax 63
net profit to sales ratio 129–30
net realisable value (NRV), stock valuations 77
non-executive directors (NEDs)
  audit committees 236–7
  corporate governance 230, 231–2
  role 231–2
non-financial information 116
Notes to the Accounts 116
NPV *see* Net Present Value
NRV *see* net realisable value

objectivity concept 100
OECD *see* Overseas Economic Council for Development
operating cost budgets 167–8
opportunities review
  budgets/budgeting 165
  long-term decisions/decision-making 200
opportunity cost of money 202–5
opportunity costs 28–30
  defining 28
overheads
  allocating 36–7
  see also fixed costs
Overseas Economic Council for Development (OECD) 229

P/E ratio *see* price/earnings ratio
parent companies, financial reports/reporting 116–17
payback, long-term decisions/decision-making 206
PBFs *see* principle budget factors
performance
  evaluating methods 124
  remuneration 234
planning, budgets/budgeting 171
postulate, terminology 96
predicting cash flows 201
predictions, financial, budgets/budgeting 157–62
prepayments
  Accounting Quadrant 78–9
  expenses 77–9
present value table 294–6
price/earnings (P/E) ratio 140
pricing 17–19
  costs 17–19
  decisions/decision-making 17–19
  importance 17
  profitability 17–19
  theories 17–18
principle budget factors (PBFs), budgets/budgeting 165
principle, terminology 96
problems review, budgets/budgeting 165
product costs 10–11
  graphic analysis 12–15
  long-term decisions/decision-making 214–17
  see also costs
product viability 34–7

products and services, context 8–26
products, unique/multiple 9
profit and loss accounts 69
  Accounting Quadrant 51–61
  depreciation 73
  reflections 61–2
  worksheet: corporate reports 103
profit margin 11–12
profit retained 63
profitability 17–19
profitability ratios 125–30
  asset turnover ratio 130
  gross profit margin 11–12, 128–9
  net profit to sales ratio 129–30
  return on equity 125–7
  ROCE 127–8
profits 61–2, 69–71
  accruals-based profit 98
  cash 146
  cash-based profit 98
  CVP analysis 15–16
  defining 70
  differences 161–2
  gross profit 63
  gross profit margin 11–12, 128–9
  levels 63
  net profit after tax 63
  net profit before tax 63
  retained 63
published accounts *see* financial reports/reporting

quick ratio 131–2

Railtrack, corporate governance 233
railways, long-term decisions/decision-making 197–8
ratio analysis 124–54
  cautionary note 143
  gearing ratios 135–7
  interpreting ratios 132
  investment ratios 137–43
  liquidity ratios 130–5
  profitability ratios 125–30
  Sainsbury's 125–40
  Tesco 125–40
raw materials, stock 74–5
realisation concept 99–100
recognition, revenue 71–2

recording/reporting financial
    transactions 47
reducing balance depreciation
    82–4
regulations 98
    ASB 105
    Stock Exchange 96
    see also corporate governance;
        legal issues
relevance, information 97
relevant range 16
reliability, information 97
remuneration
    committees 230, 232–6
    corporate governance 228, 230,
        232–6, 233–4
    directors 228, 232–6
    disclosure 234–6
    examples 233–4
    Greenbury Report 234
    Hampel Report 234
    performance 234
reports/reporting
    auditors' report 95, 114–15
    directors' report 114
    worksheet: corporate reports
        102–4
    see also accounting
        reports/reporting; financial
        reports/reporting
retail therapy 212
retained profits 63
return on capital employed
    (ROCE) 127–8
revaluations, depreciation 84–5
revenue recognition 71–2
revenues 11, 15
    Accounting Quadrant 51–61
    defining 52
ROCE see return on capital
    employed

Sainsbury's, ratio analysis 125–40
sales budgets 165–6
screening, long-term
    decisions/decision-making 200
semi-variable costs 20–1
services and products, context
    8–26
share capital 65
share options 228, 232–3
shareholders
    corporate governance 227–8,
        229, 232–3
    and directors 227–8

long-term decisions/decision-
    making 213–14
short-term decisions/decision-
    making 37, 196–8
Smith, Adam 227
Smith Review, corporate
    governance 237
social interactions, accounting 3
SSAPs see statements of standard
    accounting practice
stakeholders, corporate
    governance 229
standard costing,
    budgets/budgeting 175–81
standards, accounting 95–6, 105
    see also legal issues
statement of historical cost profits
    and losses 113–14
statement of total recognised
    gains and losses 113
statements, cash-flow see cash-
    flow statements
statements of standard accounting
    practice (SSAPs) 95–6
stepped fixed costs 20
stock 72–7
    depreciation 73
    FIFO 75–7
    finished goods 74–5
    LIFO 75–7
    raw materials 74–5
    valuations 74–7
    WAC 77
    work in progress 74–5
Stock Exchange, regulations 96
Stock Market 69
stock turn(over) 132–3
straight line depreciation 81–2
strategic direction, long-term
    decisions/decision-making
    198
subsidiary companies, financial
    reports/reporting 116–17
sunk costs 30

targets, budgets/budgeting 172
tax
    corporation tax 61–2
    net profit after tax 63
    net profit before tax 63
Tesco, ratio analysis 125–40
time scale, long-term
    decisions/decision-making 198
time value of money (TVoM)
    202–5

tourism, case study 222–6
TVoM see time value of money

uncertainty
    decisions/decision-
        making 38
    long-term decisions/decision-
        making 198, 211
users
    accounting reports/reporting
        91–3, 96–100
    concepts, accounting 96–100

valuations
    revaluations 84–5
    stock 74–7
    see also depreciation
variable costs 10–11
    budgets/budgeting 158–62
    graphic analysis 13–14, 15
    semi-variable costs 20–1
variance analysis
    budgets/budgeting 175–81
    detailed 180
    linearity 175–9
    sales quantities 181
    variance notation 177–8
variances, budgets/budgeting
    173–5
vehicle costs, graphic analysis 13

WAC see weighted average cost
wealth maximisation 213–14
The Wealth of Nations 227
weighted average cost (WAC),
    stock valuations 77
what if? analysis
    decisions/decision-making 38,
        211
    long-term decisions/decision-
        making 211
work in progress, stock 74–5
working capital 65
    budgets/budgeting 189–91
    case study 189–91
    cash flows 106–9
    management 144–6
    worksheet: corporate reports
        102–4